INSIGHT
GUIDES

New Zealand

Directed and Designed by Hans Höfer
Edited by Gordon McLauchlan
Photography by Max Lawrence and others
Updated by Annette Seear

A P A
PUBLICATIONS

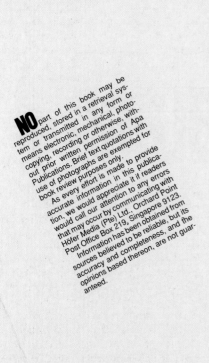
New Zealand

Third Edition (2nd Reprint)
© **1990 APA PUBLICATIONS (HK) LTD**
All Rights Reserved
Printed in Singapore by Höfer Press Pte. Ltd

ABOUT THIS BOOK

Rudyard Kipling found "the eighth wonder of the world" in New Zealand. James Michener called these islands "probably the most beautiful place on earth."

It was not easy to capture in words and photographic images a place that evokes such admiration. Few countries in the world encampass such contrasts in geography and culture as New Zealand. But this is the kind of challenge that APA Publications relishes.

Since 1970 when founder **Hans Höfer** published the prize-winning *Insight Guide: Bali*, APA has been producing one title after another in a library of new travel literature. The concept that Höfer formed calls for books that contain outstanding writing, fine photographs and clear, honest journalism.

Insight Guide: New Zealand was produced by a team of the best available local writers and photographers working under the leadership of a single project editor. The guide takes readers beyond the usual tourist book with an edition for the serious traveller. For this book, the team leader was **Gordon McLauchlan**, one of New Zealand's leading freelance journalists.

A fourth-generation New Zealander, McLauchlan was born in Dunedin and worked for several provincial newspapers before turning to freelance writing and broadcasting in 1973. He published the controversial and highly-acclaimed *The Passionless People*, an incisive 1976 critique of New Zealand society from within, and the one-volume *New Zealand Encyclopedia*.

The geologic history chapter was written by **Graeme Stevens**, chief palaeontologist for the New Zealand Geological Survey, and twice winner of New Zealand's premier book

award, the Wattie, for *Rugged Landscape* (1974) and *New Zealand Adrift* (1980).

Both Maori experts **Michael King** (pre-European history and the Maori today) and **Terrence Barrow** (Maori arts and Pacific dependencies) are widely published. King is the author of 12 books and numerous magazine articles. Barrow, a former ethnologist for the Dominion Museum in Wellington and the Bishop Museum in Honolulu, authored several books, including *An Illustrated Guide to Maori Art*.

Also knowledgeable about peoples of the Pacific is **Cluny Macpherson** (Pacific Island immigrants), a University of Auckland sociologist and former teacher in Samoa. Journalist **David McGill** (Kiwi Melting Pot and Wellington), a columnist for the *Evening Post* in Wellington, has looked at non-Pacific immigrants in his book, *The Other New Zealanders*. **Colin Taylor** (Auckland and Rotorua) is a freelance photojournalist who took an assignment in 1984 as publicity and promotions manager for the New Zealand Government Tourist Office in Los Angeles.

Jack Adlington (Northland) is the retired travel editor of the Auckland Star. **Joseph Frahm** (Coromandel and the Bay of Plenty) is senior journalist with the New Zealand Tourist and Publicity Department; formerly editor of the *Challenge Weekly* newspaper, he grew up on a Bay of Plenty dairy farm.

Janet Leggett (Waikato/Taranaki), a resident of the region of which she writes, was a reporter and editor for the *Waikato Times* in Hamilton before freelancing in 1982. **Geoff Conly** (Poverty and Hawkes Bays) was the editor of the *Napier Daily Telegraph*; and author of *The Shock of '31*, a book on the history of Napier's great earthquake.

John Harvey (Manawatu/Wanganui) is a

McLauchlan

Stevens

King

Adlington

Leggett

reporter for the *Manawatu Standard* in Palmerston North. **William Hobbs** (Nelson/Marlborough) is a freelancer from Nelson, where he was once Radio New Zealand's chief Nelson reporter. He had also worked for *The Dominion* newspaper in Wellington. **John Goulter** (Christchurch, the Chatham Islands and the sheep industry) is a journalist for *The Star* in Christchurch.

The travel writer team of **Anne Stark** and **Les Bloxham** tackled three lengthy pieces of text – Canterbury, Westland and Central Otago, the latter by Anne alone. Les has a regular travel column in nine New Zealand newspapers, and is travel and aviation editor for *The Press* in Christchurch.

Robin Charteris (Dunedin) is a deputy editor for the *Otago Daily Times*, after a period as London correspondent. **Clive Lind** (Southland/Fiordland and Stewart Island), chief reporter for *The Southland Times* of Invercargill since 1975, had written four books on Southland history.

Katherine Findlay (modern New Zealand arts) has been a reporter and director of *Kaleidoscope*, the TV New Zealand arts programme since 1981. **Phil Gifford** (spectator sports) has been a sports journalist for all his adult life. He is a columnist for *The NZ Listener* and a commentator for Radio Hauraki in Auckland.

John Costello (The Winning Breed), a racing writer and editor with the *New Zealand Herald* and *Auckland Star*, has written books on horse-racing in New Zealand. **Digby Law** (food, Travel Tips section) was the nation's best known cookery consultant, and the author of three cookbooks. **Jim Wilson** (outdoor sports) leads a double life as a mountain climber and a University of Canterbury senior lecturer in philosophy and

(Hindu) religion. He is a longtime adventure companion of Sir Edmund Hillary.

Peter Hutton, a New Zealander who authored *Insight Guide: Java*, edited and strengthened this book's history section. **Wendy Canning**, Auckland-based photo researcher, gathered historical and art materials from sources throughout New Zealand.

New Zealander **Max Lawrence** was commissioned as chief photographer for the book. He spent several months and travelled thousands of miles criss-crossing the North and South islands with his camera. The late New Zealand photographer **Brian Brake** reviewed a large portion of Lawrence's work and offered constructive criticism.

Others who contributed were **Ray Joyce** of Lansdowne Press, Sydney; **Allen Seidon** of Honolulu; **Dawn Kendall** of Auckland; **G.R. Roberts** from Nelson; **Dr David Skinner** from Auckland; **David Lowe** of Lodestone Press in Auckland; **Photobank (NZ) Limited** whose stock improved the photo selection; and **Terence Barrow** who supplied pictures on Maoris and their arts.

Other contributors who helped to make *Insight Guide: New Zealand* possible were **Bruce Crossan**, **Gavin Ellis**, **Jan** and **Ted Hart**, **Gordon McBride**, **Dawn McLauchlan** and **Linda Carlock**. **Christine Young**, **Jill Nicholas**, **Sue Weston** and **Christine Negus** assisted **Annette Seear** in the updating of this edition.

Max Lawrence offers his thanks to: **Mount Cook Line**; **Kodak New Zealand**; **Mourie and Dingle Adventures**; **Tourist Hotel Corporation**; **Paul Green and Fiordland National Parl**; **Elliott Lawrence**; **Fiordland Travel Limited**; **Wildlife Service**; **Royal Akarana Yacht Club**; **Air New Zealand** and **Documentary Photographs**.

Charteris

Lind

Findlay

Wilson

Lawrence

CONTENTS

HISTORY AND PEOPLE

PLACES

FEATURES

MAPS

TRAVEL TIPS

GENESIS

This is New Zealand. *Haere mai*. Welcome.

This is a land of majestic snow-capped peaks and unexplored rain forests, of pristine lakes swarming with trout and turquoise ocean bays speckled with wooded isles, of glaciers and fiords, geysers and volcanoes. It is a land of *kauri* forests and kiwifruit plantations, of modern cosmopolitan cities and backcountry sheep stations, of the flightless *kiwi*, the prehistoric *tuatara*, Phar Lap, Split Enz and Sir Edmund Hillary. Perhaps most important of all, it is the land of the Maori, the indigenous Polynesian inhabitants who have made these islands their home for at least 12 centuries.

Pacific anthropologists say the Maori came to these islands by outrigger canoe about the A.D. 8th century. Maori legend tells a much different story, about the birth of all life in the stillness of a long dark night, Te Po, from the primordial parents – Rangi, the sky father, and Papa, the earth mother.

Tane, the god of the forests and their eldest son, pulled himself free of his parents in the darkness and with great effort, over a long time period, pushed them apart. He decorated Rangi with the sun, moon and stars, and Papa with plant and animal life, thereby flooding this new universe with light and colour. But Rangi's sorrow at the parting from his mate caused tears to flood from his eyes, filling her surface with oceans and lakes.

Today, it is not hard to understand why New Zealanders have such a strong attachment to their native land. The waters of Rangi's tears have contributed to a recreational wonderland perhaps unrivalled on Mother Earth. The unique flora and fauna are only part of a staggering variety of attractions. Enter these pages and discover them.

A GEOLOGIC HISTORY

New Zealand is surrounded on all sides by a vast undersea panorama of submerged ridges and troughs, rises, swells and plateaus together providing dramatic evidence of the way the earth's crust in this part of the world has been crumpled into huge folds, rather like a gigantic rumpled tablecloth. These features are in turn often cleft by deep submarine trenches and peppered by submarine volcanoes, all providing a measure of the stresses and strains accompanying such movements. Although much of this great system of folds is submerged, a small part of it has been shaped into a group of mountainous islands known as New Zealand.

Movements similar to those that have shaped the sea floor have also affected the New Zealand land mass. The evidence for these upheavals is recorded in the rocks exposed in mountains, rivers and streams and in sea cliffs around the coasts. The intense folding and cracking often seen in these rocks suggests that New Zealand has long been part of one of the earth's "mobile belts" – zones of weakness in the earth's crust along which breaking occurs.

The rocks are cut by innumerable great fractures called faults, along which up, down and sideways movements have occurred. Many of the faults have broken the present land surface, showing that they have been moving during the past few thousand years. Some faults have moved in the last century (producing major earthquakes) and these movements, together with almost continuous smaller-scale earthquake and volcanic activity, indicate that New Zealand is very much "on the move" today.

Earth movements in the region have tended to be concentrated into "bursts," of which the recent activity is an example, but geological record indicates that change has nevertheless been continuous for at least the past 500 million years. The change has involved geographic position (latitude and longitude) as well as size, shape and degree of insularity. New Zealand has not always been a sea-girt island country and up to some 130 million years ago shared a common coastline with

New Caledonia, eastern Australia, Tasmania and Antarctica. The modern shape of the country is largely a product of the last 10,000 years.

Great Gondwana

New Zealand's long voyage through time commenced in the Cambrian period of geological history, 570 to 500 million years ago, when it was part of a super-continent called Gondwana, made up of the land masses now comprising Australia, New Guinea, New Caledonia, New Zealand, Antarctica, South America, Africa, Arabia, Malagasy and India. New Zealand lay on the eastern edge of the super-continent, wedged between Australia, Tasmania and Antarctica, and facing an ancestral ocean called the Tethys, separating Gondwana from another super-continent called Laurasia which was then a number of separate lands that were later to coalesce. The Laurasian lands included North America, Kazakhstan, southern and central Europe, Baltica (Scandinavia and European Russia), Mongolia, Siberia, China and Southeast Asia.

In the early part of New Zealand's history, during the Cambrian and succeeding Ordovician and Silurian periods (500 to 410 million years ago), the edge of Gondwana occupied by New Zealand, New Caledonia and Australia projected northwards into the Northern Hemisphere, lying in latitudes 45 degrees north in the Cambrian, and 20 degrees north in the Ordovician and the Silurian. The northward orientation of Gondwana brought New Zealand and Australia into contact with China, Southeast Asia and Kazakhstan so that New Zealand and Australia shared with these countries a number of coastal marine animals and their close relatives.

Such coastal links gradually faded, however, as Gondwana began to swing to the south, bringing Australia and New Zealand into the Southern Hemisphere. Southeast Asia, China and Kazakhstan moved in a northwards direction towards their present geographic position. Thus by the Devonian period, 410 to 350 million years ago, New Zealand, while still retaining strong coastal links with Australia, also developed marine links to southern South America, via Antarctica – reflecting the gradual southward shift of this part of Gondwana.

Southerly drift continued throughout the

succeeding Carboniferous and Permian periods (350 to 235 million years ago) and many areas of Gondwana, including Australia and New Zealand, were carried into close proximity to the South Pole and felt the effects of glaciation.

About this time most of the area that now forms parts of New Zealand and New Caledonia became part of a huge slowly sinking broad depression in the sea floor, called a geosyncline. Mud, sand and gravel eroded from the surrounding areas of Gondwana accumulated in this depression. Erupting volcanoes on both land and sea also contributed deposits of lava and ash. The geosyncline extended northwards to New Caledonia, eastwards to beyond the Chatham Islands, westwards to the Lord

tive native forest trees came at this time – including the New Zealand kauri (*Agathis australis*), some of the distinctive New Zealand native pines, called podocarps (rimu, totara, kahikatea) and many ferns.

Rotation of Gondwana away from the South Pole continued into the succeeding period of geological time, the Jurassic (192 to 135 million years ago). The rotating movements were such that by middle and late Jurassic times southern South America, southern Africa, Antarctica, New Zealand, New Caledonia and Australia were all situated in middle and low latitudes and had tropical, subtropical and warm temperate climates. The equable nature of the climate, together with the close grouping of the continents – so that a variety of

Howe Rise and southwards to beyond Auckland and Campbell Islands.

In the Triassic (235 to 192 million years ago), continuing rotation of Gondwana moved much of the continental areas away from the South Pole, leading to retreat and eventual disappearance of the ice sheets. Nonetheless rivers and the sea continued to erode the land, thus maintaining the flow of sediments into the geosyncline. By middle and late Triassic times, however, earth movements within the geosyncline had compressed and squeezed up areas of old sediment to form small archipelagos of land. Much of this land had links to the adjacent continental areas and it is likely that the ancestors of some New Zealand's distinc-

routes were available across land and around shorelines – provided numerous opportunities for both terrestrial and marine organisms to spread across Gondwana.

It is highly probable, therefore, that during this period New Zealand received the ancestors of many of its native plants and animals. Probable Middle Jurassic migrants include the ancestors of animals such as the tuatara (*Sphenodon*) and native frog (*Leiopelma*). Other animal groups that reached New Zealand at this time included the ancestors of the native earthworms, native snails, and slugs, some insects (notably wetas and some spiders), freshwater crayfish, freshwater mussels and some freshwater fish. More native pines and varieties of ferns probably also arrived at this time. These animals and plants are today often called "living fossils."

The reptiles gave rise to the first birds in the late Jurassic. Early birds, with their superior means of dispersal, soon spread to many parts of the world. It is thought that one group of distinctive primitive birds, called the ratites, appeared in South America about this time and, using Antarctica as a stepping stone, gained access to New Zealand, Australia, New Guinea, Malagasy and southern Africa – to develop into the moas and kiwis in New Zealand, emus (Australia), cassowaries (New Guinea, Australia), elephant birds (Malagasy), ostriches (southern Africa) and rheas (South America).

Birth of the Tasman Sea

The first substantial land mass to exist in the present New Zealand region extended southward to the edge of the Campbell Plateau, eastward to beyond Chatham Island and westward to the Lord Howe Rise. Long fingers of newly created land also stretched northward towards New Caledonia, Lord Howe Island and Norfolk Island. Almost as soon as it was created this "Greater New Zealand" was eaten into by rivers and streams while the sea

Left, the tuatara is a prehistoric relic – a living fossil. Above, New Zealand's geology produces features such as this bubbling hot pool of mud.

nibbled away at its edges. By the end of early Cretaceous time (110 million years ago) some areas, especially those around the edges of the land mass, had been worn down to such an extent that the sea was beginning to flood in across the eroded remains of the folded and contorted rocks.

About this time the first cracks and splits in the earth's crust appeared along the site of the modern Tasman Sea and also in the area lying between the edge of the Campbell Plateau and the coast of Antarctica's Marie Byrd Land. These huge rifts, into which the sea soon flooded, heralded the opening of the oceans now separating New Zealand from Australia and Antarctica. Marine incursions along the rift valleys soon began to disrupt the overland migration routes to the north and west of New Zealand. Southern land routes remained, however, and New Zealand continued to be linked with western Antarctica.

The splitting movements along the embryonic Tasman Sea and Southern Ocean were accompanied by similar movements signalling the start of the opening of the South Atlantic and Indian Oceans. The days of the old super-continent Gondwana were drawing to a close. Such splitting movements on a global scale had the effect of swinging the eastern edge of Gondwana – comprising New Zealand, New Caledonia, Australia, Antarctica and southern South America – closer to the South Pole, so that in early Cretaceous times New Zealand was at 70 to 80 degrees South Latitude, and in the middle Cretaceous it was within a few degrees of the South Pole.

Although land links to the north and west of New Zealand had been lost early in the Cretaceous, southern links were still evident, allowing ancestors of the Protea family to enter New Zealand in the early Cretaceous and southern beech (*Nothofagus*) in the middle Cretaceous – both using Antarctica as a stepping stone. However, 80 million years ago a new sea floor began to form both in the Tasman Sea and in that part of the Southern Ocean lying between New Zealand and Antarctica. New Zealand became surrounded by continuous coastlines and seas of oceanic depths. At about this time the first marsupials (kangaroos, koalas, etc.) appeared in South America and probably migrated into Australia via Antarctica, their way into New Zealand was barred by stretches of open ocean.

The Tasman Sea opened up to its full width over the period between 80 and 60 million years ago. However it is likely that at some time before attaining its full width the Tasman was crossed by ancestral bats, using their powers of flight (and perhaps with some assistance from westerly winds) to cross the new ocean before it became too wide and too stormy. The bats that came to New Zealand at this time gave rise to a distinctive New Zealand Bat of a primitive type – the only mammals in the country's original fauna. The early Polynesians later introduced dogs and rats.

It is also likely that the ancestors of some of New Zealand's distinctive native birds such as the wattlebirds (huia, saddleback and kokako), native thrushes (piopio) and native wrens (rifleman, bush wren and rock wren) also arrived at the same time after winging their way across the infant Tasman.

Although creation of new sea floor waned

linked with that already forming between New Zealand and Antarctica, so that Australia and New Zealand together began their long journey northwards into warmer seas, and Antarctica its journey southwards.

As Antarctica had moved into higher latitudes it lost its role as a stepping stone for southern migrants. Initially in Paleocene, Eocene and Oligocene times (65 to 24 million years ago), many parts of Antarctica, especially the coastal areas of western Antarctica, were covered by beech forests similar to those in New Zealand and southern South America today. However, as Antarctica moved southwards, and as cold marine currents began to flow around the now-ocean-encircled continent, ice fields formed on the mountaintops

and then ceased altogether in the Tasman 60 millions years ago, opening of the Southern Ocean continued inexorably, progressively weakening New Zealand's marine connections to South America via Antarctica. Thus although many "southern" coastal marine animals were still shared by New Zealand, western Antarctica and southern South America in Paleocene and early Eocene times (65 to 49 million years ago), such forms had been drastically reduced by late Eocene times and disappeared completely at the end of the Eocene (37 million years ago).

Meantime, about 55 million years ago, sea began to open up between Australia and Antarctica. The new area of sea floor thus created

and glaciers began to reach down the valleys towards the sea.

At the same time as ice was building up on Antarctica, the oceanic gaps between this southernmost continent and its neighbours were widening. This allowed free oceanic circulation; combined with the onset of cyclonic conditions developed around the Antarctic ice cap, it set the scene for development of the circum-Antarctica system of winds and ocean currents that today dominates Southern Hemisphere meteorology and oceanology.

The Circum-Antarctic Current, the world's largest ocean current, circulates clockwise around the entire Antarctic continent, and is associated with systems of prevailing westerly winds that encircle the globe at latitudes between 40 and 60 degrees south, giving rise to the "Roaring Forties," "Furious Fifties" and "Screaming Sixties." These winds are so powerful and constant that floating material can be readily transported between the southern continents. The transporting efficiency of such a wind and current system is so high that once initiated, many animals and plants started to use it as a means of crossing the southern ocean after Antarctica ceased to be available as a stepping stone.

While all these changes were going on around New Zealand, the huge ancestral land mass formed of late Jurassic and early Cretaceous times had been slowly shrinking in size and shape. The originally rugged mountainous

Tropical Immigrants

The steady northwards drift of New Zealand and Australia gradually brought them into the mid-latitude regions of the Southern Hemisphere. At the same time, southward movement of the Southeast Asia-Indonesia region, resulting from opening and expansion of the South China Sea, progressively closed the gap between the Indonesian islands and Papua New Guinea. Thus an increasing number of oceanic currents of tropical origin were able to reach the Australian and New Zealand coasts, bringing with them a great variety of warm-water organisms (but only those capable of crossing open ocean, either as eggs, larvae or adults).

terrain had been progressively lowered by eroding rivers and streams. The open Pacific to the east and the newly created oceans to north, west and south established eroding coastlines around the entire perimeter of the land mass. The scene was set therefore for gradual wearing-away of "Greater New Zealand" and its progressive submergence by the sea. By 37 to 24 million years ago, the remnants of land consisted of an elongated, narrow-gutted archipelago and a few scattered islands.

Left, New Zealand's molden interior is not yet at rest as attested to by smouldering White Island in the Bay of Plenty. Above, geothermal power at Wairakei near Rotorua.

Although migrants from tropical sources first appeared in New Zealand waters in late Eocene times, their numbers declined in the uppermost Eocene and lowermost Oligocene as the sea cooled in response to the build up of ice fields on Antarctica. Climate improved, however, in the early and middle Miocene (24 to 12 million years ago). At this time tropical seas lapped around New Zealand and reef-building corals lived around the northern and central parts of the North Island. Temperatures of these seas were 7 to 10 degrees (Centigrade) warmer than today. On the land, palms were particularly abundant and widespread at this time and coconut groves existed in parts of the northern North Island.

Meantime, continued expansion of the South China Sea rotated Malaysia, Indonesia and the Philippines closer to Papua New Guinea. The intervening oceanic gap was progressively closed until in the Miocene it had been narrowed to such an extent, and had probably been at least partially bridged by volcanic archipelagos, that land snakes were able to move into Papua New Guinea and eventually into Australia.

By this time, however, the Tasman Sea had opened up its full width and ancestral New Zealand and New Caledonia had lost their land links to the remainder of eastern Gondwana. Snakes therefore were unable to reach either New Zealand or New Caledonia – and they became two of the few snake-free countries in

the world, much to the relief of the present inhabitants!

Throughout this entire period the ancestral New Zealand land mass was essentially stable; this stability allowed it to be gradually worn away and to be eventually submerged by the sea. The comparative tranquillity ended, however, in the Miocene, and from this time onwards the New Zealand islands were the scene of restless activity. Patterns of folds, welts and troughs developed under the influence of deep-seated earth movements. Changes in geography occurred frequently as troughs sank rapidly and welts rose in complementary fashion. Segments of land moved up and down under the influence of interfingering

and branching folds. Large areas of New Zealand had the form of an ever-changing archipelago.

One of the most obvious consequences of the establishment of the westerly pattern of winds and oceanic currents was substantial strengthening of trans-Tasman migration. Although New Zealand has always received animals and plants from Australia and Tasmania, the sheer numbers involved increased dramatically from Miocene times onwards. Many of the sea creatures that populate New Zealand's shores today came originally from the west, having been transported by the west wind drift – either from Australia and Tasmania, or from even farther westwards around the globe, as far as South Africa or South America.

Birds are also notable riders of the west wind and from Miocene times onwards New Zealand gained a number of groups of land birds of Australian origin. Some bird groups have been in New Zealand longer than others and therefore have had sufficient time to diverge genetically from the parent Australian stock. The takahe, for example, represents an older migration; whereas the pukeko is from a younger migration and is indistinguishable from Australian forms.

Trans-Tasman migration of Australian land birds continues today: colonists in the past century include the spur-wing plover, black-fronted dotterel, white-faced heron, Australian coot, royal spoonbill, grey teal, welcome swallow and wax eye. Other would-be colonists have lingered but not survived – the avocet, little bittern and white-eyed duck. Many Australian insects also arrive in the aftermath of westerly gales, but few survive to colonize, although the monarch butterfly is a notable survivor.

The Ice Age Cometh

Although steady deterioration of climate in the late Miocene and Pliocene times had progressively thinned out many of the warmth-loving immigrants New Zealand had received in earlier times, the *coup de grace* was delivered by the severe climates of the Pleistocene glacial occurring between 2 million and 10,000 years ago. During a number of these glacials, temperate organisms were restricted to northernmost New Zealand and to a few coastal refuges where the influence of the sea moderated the glacial climate. As there was no escape northwards beyond 35 degrees South Latitude, many of the warmth-loving organisms disappeared completely, never to return.

The northern retreat of warm and temperate organisms was matched by advance of those with cold-temperate requirements. Thus fur seals and subantarctic shellfish and crabs moved northwards into the central part of the North Island in the early Pleistocene. During the last glacial phase, extending from about 65,000 to 10,000 years ago, native pine (podocarp) forests were pushed into the area north of Hamilton.

Then, as the climate warmed 10,000 years ago, some of the gaps in the New Zealand flora and fauna resulting from Pleistocene extinctions were filled by temperate organisms riding the west wind drift. Forest gradually became re-established throughout New Zealand but its recovery from the repeated disruptions

people about 1,000 years ago initiated a long train of biological events that continued even more rapidly after the visits of Tasman and Cook and the arrival of European settlers. The early Polynesians (the "Moa Hunters") used the easily hunted birds as protein sources, and so deprived the New Zealand fauna of many of its older distinctive elements – including moas, and native New Zealand geese, swans, eagles and crows. The fire brought by humans, and used by them in hunting and agriculture, destroyed large areas of forest in coastal and central North Island and eastern South Island and reactivated many areas of hitherto stable sandy country so that sand dunes invaded fertile land in many coastal regions.

The Polynesian rat and dog added to the

during the successive glacials was a long and slow process; it is believed that even within the span of man's occupation of New Zealand, vegetation changes have occurred which are related to this long-term recovery process. Coupled with this, however, has been the effect of climatic changes – notably the Climatic Optimum (a warm period 7,000 to 4,000 years ago) and the Little Ice Age (a cold period between A.D. 1550 and 1800).

Without a doubt, the arrival of Polynesian

Left, a landslip at Abbotsford, Dunedin. Above left and right, New Zealand's distinctive flora include the pohutukawa blossom and the kowhai blossom.

effects of hunting and use of the fire. European settlers introduced, by accident or design, a wide variety of animals and plants from other parts of the world that competed, often successfully, with native species. In particular, New Zealand's formerly abundant bird life was decimated. Many birds disappeared altogether, while others became restricted to Fiordland and various islands off the New Zealand coast.

Thus the arrival of the human race, with fire, rats and dogs, coming on top of the effects of the Ice Age, sounded the death-knell for many of New Zealand's unique primeval organisms, some dating as far back as tens of millions of years ago.

London, Published by Alex. Hogg at the Kings Arms No.16 Paternoster Row.

A curiously ARCHED ROCK on the Coast of New Zealand.

A New Zealand Chief whose head is ingeniously TATAWED and a Subaltern Warrior of the same Country.

28

Apart from Antarctica, New Zealand was the last major land mass to be reached and explored by people. These earliest Pacific navigators preceded those from Europe by some 800 years. They were, in the words of one of their descendants, "Vikings of the sunrise." They were people whose descendants came to be called Maori.

Few subjects have been the source of more controversy than the origins of the Maori. Nineteenth century scholars devised bizarre theories. Some asserted Maori were wandering Aryans, others believed that they were originally Hindu, and still others that they were indisputably a lost tribe of Israel. Interpretations of evidence in the 20th century have been more cautious. The current consensus among scholars is that Maori were descendants of Austronesian people who originated in Southeast Asia. A few authorities dispute this. Minority opinions have suggested they came from Egypt, from Mesopotamia and from South America.

Linguistic and archaeological evidence establishes, however, that New Zealand Maori are Polynesian people; and that the ancestors of the Polynesians sailed into the South China Sea from the Asian mainland some 2,000 to 3,000 years ago. Some went southwest, ultimately to Madagascar; others southeast along the Malaysian, Indonesian and Philippine chains of islands.

What appears to have inspired these vast journeys was the introduction of the sail to Southeast Asia and the invention of the outrigger to stabilise craft on ocean voyaging. Among the Austronesian languages shared by the people of the Pacific and the Southeast Asian archipelagos, the words for sail, mast, outrigger float and outrigger boom are among the most widespread and therefore among the oldest.

The Pacific Austronesians who made their way along the Melanesian chain of islands, reaching Fiji by about 1300 B.C. and Tonga before 1100 B.C., left behind fragments of pottery with distinctive decorations. It has been called Lapita, and the same name has been given by archaeologists to the people who made it. With their pottery they also

Preceding pages and **left**, images of the Maori by an artist on one of Cook's expeditions. **Right**, a tattooed chief wearing a feather headdress.

carried pigs, dogs, rats, fowls and cultivated plants. All of these originated on the mainland of Southeast Asia, with the exception of the *kumara*, which is a sweet potato from South America.

Polynesian culture as recognised today evolved among the Lapita people in Tonga and Samoa. It was from this East Polynesian region that a migration was eventually launched to New Zealand. The East Polynesian characteristics of early Maori remains, the earliest carbon dates and the rate of growth and spread of the Maori population, all indicate that a

landfall was made in New Zealand around A.D. 800.

The First New Zealanders

The land that the earliest settlers reached about 1,200 years ago was unlike anything that Polynesians had encountered elsewhere in the Pacific. It was far larger – more than 1,500 km (over 800 miles) from north to south – and more varied than islands they had colonised previously. It was temperate rather than tropical and sufficiently cold in much of the South Island to prevent the growing of crops. Other than bats, there were no mammals ashore until the ancestors of the Maori released the rats (*kiore*) and dogs (*kuri*) they had brought with them. It is probable that they also brought pigs and fowls, but these did not survive.

The lack of meat was compensated for by a proliferation of seafood: fish, shellfish, crayfish, crab, seaweed, sea-egg and the sea mammals, whales, dolphins and seals. The land provided fern root that offered a staple food (though it had to be heavily pounded), and there were nearly 200 species of bird, many of them edible. Inland waterways contained additional resources: waterfowl, eel, fish and more shellfish.

To all these the immigrants added the cultivated vegetables they had carried with them, *taro, kumara*, yam, gourds and the paper mulberry. For meat, in addition to birds, fish

Polynesians developed one of the world's most sophisticated neolithic cultures.

Perhaps the most spectacular of the new country's resources was the huge flightless bird, the moa. There were originally some 24 species of this bird, ranging from the turkey-sized *anomalopteryx* to the gigantic *dinornis maximus*. They offered a food supply on a scale never before encountered in Polynesia (drumsticks the size of bullocks' legs), other than when whales were cast ashore. Some early groups of Maori based their economy around moas in areas where the birds were relatively plentiful, until extensive exploitation led to their extinction.

The history of the first colonists from the time of their arrival until the advent of Europe-

Representation of A WAR CANOE of NEW ZEALAND, with a View of Gable End Foreland.

and sea mammals, there were limited supplies of dog and rat.

The New Zealand forests offered larger trees than Polynesians had seen previously. With these they built bigger dugout canoes and evolved a complex tradition of carving. Later, they used wooden beams in the construction of dwellings. Materials such as *raupo* and *nikau* made excellent house walls and roofs. Flax plaited well into cords and baskets and provided fine fibre for garments. There was an ample sufficiency of suitable stone materials for adzes, chisels and drill points, varieties of bone for fish-hooks, spear-heads and ornaments, and obsidian for flake knives. Through these artefacts and crafts the New Zealand

ans is a history of their adaptation to the environment just described – the matching of their skills and cultural resources to it, and the evolution of new features in their culture in response to the conditions that the environment imposed.

Competitive Tribalism

Ethnologists now recognise two distinguishable but related phases in that culture. The first is New Zealand East Polynesian, or Archaic Maori, displayed by the archaeological remains of the earliest settlers and their immediate descendants. The second is Classic Maori, the culture encountered and recorded by the earliest European navigators to reach the country. The process by which the first phase evolved into the second is complex, and one on which scholars have not yet reached agreement.

What can be said with confidence, however, is that by the time James Cook and his men observed New Zealand in 1769, New Zealand Polynesians had settled the land from the far north to Foveaux Strait in the south. The language these inhabitants shared was similar enough for a speaker to be understood anywhere in the country, although dialectal differences were pronounced, particularly between the North and South Islands. While regional variations were apparent in the details and traditions of the culture, the most important related to every other. Art, religion, war, food gathering, love-making, death – all were an integrated pattern on a single fabric. And the universal acceptance of concepts such as *tapu* (sacredness), *mana* (spiritual authority), *mauri* (life force), *utu* (satisfaction) and a belief in *mekutu* (sorcery) regulated all these aspects of life.

Maori Hierarchy

Maori society was stratified. People were born into *rangatira* or chiefly families, or they were *tutua* (commoners). They became slaves if they were captured as a consequence of warfare. Immediate authority was exercised by *kaumatua*, the elders who were family

features of it were practised nationally.

Competitive tribalism, for example, was the basis of Maori life. The family and *hapu* (subtribe) were the unit of society that determined who married whom, where people lived, where and when they fought other people and why. Tribal ancestors were venerated, as were gods representing the natural elements (the earth, the sky, the wind, the sea, and so on). The whole of life was bound up in a unified vision in which every aspect of living was

Left and above, the Maori war canoe and the Maori fortification (*pa*) are two vivid reminders that the Maori were potentially fierce and courageous warriors.

heads. Whole communities, sharing as they did descent from a common ancestor, were under the jurisdiction of the *rangatira* families whose authority was in part hereditary and in part based on past achievement. Occasionally federations of *hapu* and tribes would come together and join forces under an *ariki* (paramount chief) for joint ventures such as waging war against foreign elements, trading or foraging for resources. The most common relationship among *hapu*, however, even closely related *hapu*, was fierce competition.

Communities ranging from a handful of households to more than 500 lived in *kainga* or villages. These were usually based on membership of a single *hapu*. The *kainga* would be close to water, food sources and cultivations. Sometimes the settlements were fortified (in which case they were called *pa*), although fortifications were by no means universal. More often the *kainga* were adjacent to hilltop *pa*, to which communities could retreat when they were under threat.

Maori *pa* were elaborately constructed with an interior stronghold, ditches, banks and palisades. Some proved impregnable; others were taken and lost several times in the course of a lifetime. Such defences were one of the features of Polynesian life that evolved in a more extensive and more complex manner in New Zealand than elsewhere in the Pacific. Some scholars speculate that the need for hilltop *pa* originated out of the need to protect *kumara*

(stone for tool-making, for example); sometimes to avenge insults, either real or imagined; sometimes to obtain satisfaction from *hapu* whose members had allegedly transgressed the social code; and sometimes as a result of serious disagreements over control or authority.

Such reasons were often flimsy and could be nurtured from generation to generation. The more important factor, perhaps, was that war or rumours of war kept successful communities and individuals alert, strong and resilient. It also brought about the annihilation of some *hapu* who did not display these qualities. For the most part, however, warfare was not totally destructive prior to the introduction of the musket. It often involved only individuals or

tubers from marauders.

Communal patterns of life in Maori settlements were organised around food gathering, food growing and (in areas where fighting was common) warfare. Cultivation and foraging were carried out by large parties of workers, seasonally. When items of food became scarce, they had a *rahui* or prohibition laid on them to conserve supplies.

The Spoils of War

Warfare evolved as an important competitive feature of Maori life in most parts of the country. It was sometimes conducted to obtain territory with food or other natural resources

small raiding parties, and ambush or sporadic attacks of short duration. Even when larger groups met in head-on confrontation or siege, the dead rarely amounted to more than a few score. Most battles occurred in summer months only and, except when a migration was under way, fighting was rarely carried on far from a tribe's home territory.

For individual males as for tribes, the concept of *mana* was paramount. It was intensified and enlarged by the status of victor, and diminished by that of vanquished. Courage and proficiency in combat were also essential ingredients in initiation, and in acceptance by male peers, especially in the case of chiefs, who had to establish their authority over others. The weapons most favoured in this combat were *taiaha* (long wooden-bladed swords) and short clubs known as *patu* and *mere*.

Artistic Refinement

Non-combatants were able to achieve high standing in the arts, or in the exercise of esoteric powers as *tohunga* (priests or experts). An ability to carve was prized highly and the working of wood, bone and stone reached heights of intricacy and delicacy in New Zealand seldom seen elsewhere. The best of the woodcarving was seen on door lintels, house gables and canoe prows; and in stone and bone in personal ornaments such as *tikis*, pendants and necklace units. New Zealand jade or

greenstone was especially valued for this latter purpose. Like the other Polynesians, the Maori had no access to metals.

Personal decoration in the form of *moko* or tattooing was also a feature of Maori art. Men were marked primarily on the face or buttocks, women largely on the face and breasts. Only in the Marquesas Islands did such decoration achieve comparable intricacy, with patterns apparent both positively and negatively. The Maori practice of the art usually involved a straight rather than a serrated blade. This

Left, these early Maori are performing the traditional greeting of pressing noses (*hongi*). **Above**, a Maori chief in dogskin cloak.

served not only to inject pigment under the skin; it left a grooved scar which was more like carving in appearance than tattooing.

In spite of competition, warfare and regional and tribal demarcations among Maori, trading was also extensive. South Islanders exported greenstone to other parts of the country for use in *patu*, adzes, chisels and ornaments. Bay of Plenty settlers distributed high quality obsidian from Mayor Island. Nelson and D'Urville Island inhabitants quarried and distributed argillite. Food that was readily available in some districts but not in others, such as mutton birds, was also preserved and bartered. People were prepared to travel long distances for materials and food delicacies. Although ocean-going vessels appeared to have disappeared from New Zealand by the 18th century, canoes were still used extensively for river, lake and coastal transport in the course of trade or war.

A Short, British Life

The gauze of romance that early fictional and ethnological accounts threw over pre-European Maori life was misleading. In many of its aspects, that life was brutish and short. There was always the danger of being tortured or killed as a result of warfare. There was ritual cannibalism. There was the possibility of disinheritance and enslavement in defeat.

Further, medical examination of pre-European remains reveals that the span of life was unlikely to exceed 30 years. From their late twenties, most people would have been suffering considerably as a consequence of arthritis, and from infected gums and loss of teeth brought about by the staple fern-root diet. Many of the healthy-looking "elderly" men, on whose condition James Cook commented favourably in 1770, may have been, at the most, around 40 years of age.

Such were the contours of Maori life that Cook and other European navigators encountered towards the end of the 18th century. The population was probably some 100,000 to 120,000. The Maori people had no concept of nationhood or race, having been so long separated from other races and cultures. They were tribal beings who were fiercely assertive of the identity that they took from their ancestry and from their *hapu* membership. Most of them felt as far removed from Maori to whom they were not related as they did from the Europeans who were soon to invade their country, which they called Aotearoa – "the land of the long white cloud."

The southern Pacific was the last habitable part of the world to be reached by Europeans. It was then inaccessible by sea except at the end of long-haul routes down the coast of South America on one side and Africa on the other. And once inside the rim of the world's largest ocean, seafarers faced vast areas to be crossed, always hundreds or thousands of miles away from any familiar territory.

So it required not only steady, enduring courage to venture into this unknown region but a high degree of navigational skill and experience.

The countries of the South Pacific – tucked down near the bottom of the globe away from any of the obvious routes across the world – were left to the Polynesians undisturbed for nearly 150 years after the Europeans first burst into the Western Pacific. And then New Zealand was left alone for another 130 years after the Dutchman Abel Janszoon Tasman first sighted the coast and paid these shores a brief visit.

It was the Englishman James Cook who rediscovered it and put all the Pacific in the context of the world.

A famous New Zealand historian and biographer of Cook, Dr. J.C. Beaglehole, wrote of the three great Cook voyages of discovery: "... his career is one of which the justification lies not so much in the underlining of its detail as in the comparison of the map of the Pacific before his first voyage with that at the end of the century. For his was a life consistent and integrated; to a passion for scientific precision he added the inexhaustible effort of the dedicated discoverer; and his own devotion was matched, as nearly as any leader could hope, by the allegiance which was rendered him by his men."

The Dutch Traders

European knowledge of the Pacific Ocean had gradually expanded during the 16th and 17th centuries following the first view of it by Vasco Nuñez de Balboa from the Isthmus of Panama in 1513. Intrepid Spanish and Portu-

guese seafarers such as Magellan, Mendana and Quiros, and England's Francis Drake, made their epic expeditions. The Spanish were motivated by their evangelising for the Catholic Church and the search for rare and precious metals and spices to satisfy their more temporal aspirations.

But towards the end of the 16th century, the Dutch emerged as the great seafaring and trading nation of the central and western Pacific, setting up a major administrative and trading centre at Batavia (now Jakarta) in Java early in the 17th century, an operation dominated by the Dutch East India Company. For 200 years the Dutch were a power in the region. For most of that period, voyages of exploration were incidental to the activities of trade. The Dutch sailors seemed by temperament and training to be concerned almost exclusively with the business of sailing their ships along proven routes safely and methodically in the interests of commerce. On the few occasions when they did divert, it was generally in response to rumours of other lands with commodities of potential value for trade.

The Dutch ships eventually found that by staying south after rounding the Cape of Good Hope and catching the consistent westerlies almost as far as the western coast of Australia, they could make the journey to Java more quickly than by adopting the traditional route – sailing north close to the east coast of Africa and then catching seasonal winds for the journey eastwards. And so islands off the west coast of Australia and stretches of the coast itself began to be noted on charts but were not recognised at the time as the western side of a huge continent.

Then an ambitious and highly competent governor of Batavia, Anthony van Dieman, showed a more imaginative interest in discovering new lands for trade than most of his predecessors, during the second quarter of the 17th century. Tasman, then in his thirties, was the captain of one of two ships in an expedition dispatched by van Dieman to explore Japan and the northern Pacific.

Tasman's Visit

Left, a wax figure of Captain Cook. Having established an early reputation as a marine surveyor, Cook produced a chart of New Zealand relied upon for 150 years.

Tasman was next chosen to lead a new expedition, to be accompanied by a highly competent specialist navigator, Frans Visscher. This was in 1642. The proposed voyage had been planned in detail, mainly by Visscher, and would take them first to Mauritius, then southwest to between 50 and 55 degrees south in search of the great southern continent, Terra Australis Incognita. The expedition, aboard the vessels *Heemskerck* and *Zeehaen*, was then to come eastwards if no land had been found to impede their progress and to sail across to investigate a shorter route to Chile, a rich trading area at that time and monopoly of the Spanish. The expedition went only as far as 49 degrees south before turning eastwards, whereupon it made two great South Pacific discoveries – Tasmania (or van Dieman's Land, as he named it) and New Zealand (or Staten Landt).

On December 13, 1642, they saw what was

He did not land again anywhere in New Zealand and had much better luck with the Polynesians on Tongatapu, which he put on European maps on the way home. He also sailed through the Fiji group.

Tasman's voyage was not regarded as a major success immediately but ultimately he was given his due for a gallant and well-recorded journey of exploration. Later he charted a large segment of the northern and western coast of Australia and retired, a wealthy man, in Batavia.

Cook's Oyster

Within a year or two, other navigators had discovered that New Zealand could not be

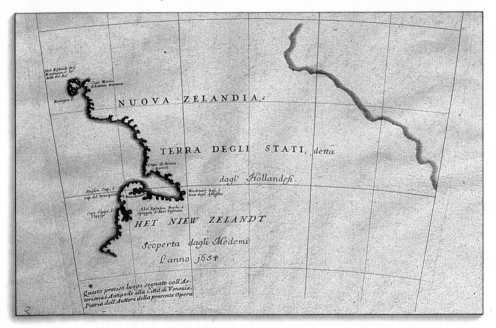

described as "land uplifted high," the Southern Alps of the South Island, and in strong winds and heavy seas sailed northwards up the coast of Westland, rounded Cape Farewell into what is now called Golden Bay.

Tasman's first and only encounter with the Maori was disastrous. When a canoe rammed a small boat travelling from the *Zeehaen* to the *Heemskerck*, fighting broke out and there was loss of life on both sides. Tasman called the place Murderers' Bay and headed north again, not realising that he was inside the western entrance to Cook Strait. A voyage eastwards of only a few miles would have shown him that he was not on the edge of a continent but in the centre of two islands.

attached to a huge continent which ran across to South America. The name was therefore changed from Staten Landt (the Dutch name for South America) to New Zealand.

James Cook opened the South Pacific up like a huge oyster and revealed its contents. The son of a Yorkshire labourer, Cook was born in 1728. He served as an apprentice seaman on a collier, and then volunteered as an able seaman with the Royal Navy during the Seven Years' War. He helped survey Canada's St. Lawrence River, an essential preliminary to the capture of Quebec by General James Wolfe, and he enhanced an already growing reputation as a marine surveyor by charting in detail the St. Lawrence and parts of the Newfoundland and Nova Scotian coasts. In 1766, he observed an eclipse of the sun and the Royal Society and the Admiralty were both impressed with his report.

It was primarily to observe the transit of the planet Venus over the disc of the sun in June 1769 that he was dispatched in 1768 to the South Seas in the 368-ton *Endeavour*, a bark built in Whitby, similar to the colliers he had sailed in as a young seaman. He was instructed to sail to Otaheite (Tahiti) for the transit and then to sail southwards as far as 50 degrees South Latitude on another search for the great southern continent, fixing on the map the positions of any islands he may incidentally discover.

Cook rounded Cape Horn and entered the

Pacific Ocean for the first time on January 27, 1769. After observing the transit of Venus and investigating other islands in the group which he named the Society Islands, he sailed south and then westwards. On October 6, a ship's boy, Nicholas Young, sighted the east coast of the North Island where it is today called Young Nick's Head.

Two days after this first sighting of what he knew to be the east coast of New Zealand, the

Left, based on Dutch explorations, a sheet by cartographer Vincenzo Coronelli, published in Venice in 1690, shows Cape Maria van Dieman of North Island. **Above**, Tasman.

land reported by Tasman, the *Endeavour* sailed into a bay where smoke made it obvious there were inhabitants. As New Zealand historian Keith Sinclair has pointed out, the arrival of the Englishmen must have been to the Maori what a Martian invasion would be to the modern New Zealander. Their first visit ashore ended with violence when a band of Maori attacked four boys left guarding the ship's boat and one of the attackers was shot dead.

It was discovered that a Tahitian chief on board the *Endeavour*, Tupaea, could converse with the Maori in his own tongue. He was taken back ashore with Cook the next morning. But the Maori were in a threatening mood and Cook was forced to order one of them shot to make them retreat. That afternoon, the firing of a musket over a canoe (to attract the attention of its occupants) brought an attack on the ship's boat from which the shot had been fired; to repel the canoe, three or more Maori were shot. Cook was saddened by the violence but he had learnt quickly that the inhabitants of this country were powerful, aggressive and brave. He called the place Poverty Bay because he could not find the supplies he wanted.

The *Endeavour* sailed south into Hawke's Bay, and then north again around the top of East Cape. It spent 10 days in what is now called Mercury Bay because an observation of the transit of the planet Mercury was made there. In Mercury Bay, for the first time, the explorers made friends with the local Maori and traded trinkets for supplies of fish, birds and clean water. They were shown over the Maori settlement and inspected a nearby fortified *pa* which greatly impressed Cook.

The expedition circumnavigated New Zealand and with brilliant accuracy made a chart of the coastline which proved basically reliable for more than 150 years. Cook's two celebrated errors were attaching Stewart Island to the mainland as a peninsular, and mapping Banks Peninsula as an island.

Cook and his crew spent weeks in Ship Cove, in a long inlet which he called Queen Charlotte's Sound, on the northern coast of the South Island, refurbishing the ship and gathering wood, water and supplies. The stay gave the two botanists aboard, Joseph Banks and Daniel Solander, a wonderful opportunity to study closely the flora and fauna of the area, and while the ship was being cleaned, the boats did detailed survey work.

The *Endeavour* left for home at the end of March 1770, sailing up the east coast of Australia, through the Dutch East Indies and then rounding the Cape of Good Hope to complete a circumnavigation of the world. The expedition was an extraordinary feat of seamanship putting New Zealand firmly on the map and gathering a huge amount of data for publication in England.

Antarctic R & R

Cook twice again led expeditions into the Pacific – from 1772 to 1775 and from 1776 to 1780. During the second of these, this prince of navigators twice took his ship south into the Antarctic Circle where no vessel was known to have gone before; he was unlucky not to become the first person ever to see the Antarctic continent.

Hawke's Bay before he again sailed for Ship Cove to a rendezvous with another vessel of the expedition, *Adventure*.

On his third voyage, Cook sailed into the Arctic Circle through the Bering Strait in search of a northwest passage from the Atlantic into the Pacific. He again came to New Zealand, especially to his home away from home at Ship Cove. By now he had a friendship with some of the local Maori that had lasted nearly 10 years. And he was impressed with them despite his anathema for the cannibalism. In his journals, he referred to the Maori as "manly and mild" in their dealings with him, less given to stealing than other Polynesians in the Pacific and "they have some arts among them which they execute with great judgement and

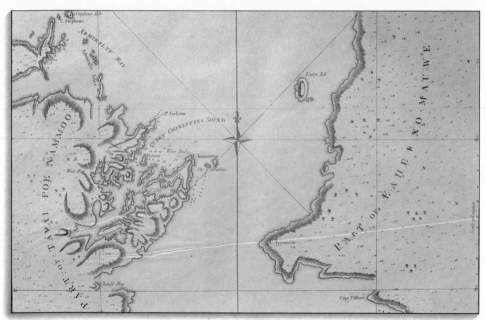

It was to Dusky Sound in New Zealand that he repaired for rest and recovery after the extreme hardships faced by crew in the southern ocean. During the 7 weeks his expedition was there, the crews set up a workshop, an observatory, and restored their health with spruce beer (to defeat scurvy) and the plenitude of fish and birds. They made contact with a single family of Maori in an area which has never been thickly populated, then or now. They planted seeds on the shore of the sound, and then sailed for their favourite anchorage in Ship Cove at the other end of the South Island.

On his later return to New Zealand during his second voyage, on his way home, he gave pigs, fowls and vegetable seeds to Maori near

unwearied patience."

Cook seemed to personify the Great Discoverer as defined by his biographer, Beaglehole: "In every great discoverer there is a dual passion – the passion to see, the passion to report; and in the greatest this duality is fused into one – a passion to see and to report truly." Cook's first voyage was one of the most expert and detailed expeditions of exploration in all history.

In January 1778, Cook and his men became the first Europeans ever to set eyes on Hawaii. And then after his drive up into the Bering Sea, he returned to where the people seemed awed by the Europeans to the point almost of worship and whose hospitality and gifts of food were lavish – so lavish, in fact, that it began to cut deeply into the Hawaiians' reserves. He died later at the hands of the natives of Hawaii.

After their departure, the ship suffered damage in a storm and although Cook felt he might have outworn his welcome, he was virtually forced to return to the same community in Kealakekua Bay. After a series of thefts from the expedition, a ship's cutter was stolen and Cook went ashore to seize a hostage in order to have the boat returned. It was during the confused outcome of this stratagem that Cook was struck, pushed into the water and stabbed to death.

Cook had done such a thorough job of charting the coasts of New Zealand that there was little else for explorers to discover without

established as a British convict settlement. Traders were soon based there ready to extract what valuable goods they could find in the region.

First there came the sealers, with the first gang put ashore on the southwest coast of the South Island in 1792. There was a brief boom in the early years of the 19th century but it wasn't long before the seals became in short supply and the ships had to go farther south to the sub-Antarctic Islands.

Next came the whalers at the turn of the century, some of them driven from the Pacific coast of South America because of the dangers there brought about by the war between Spain and Britain. These ships from Britain, Australia and the United States sought the sperm

going inland. But a number of navigators followed during the remaining years of the 18th century – Frenchmen de Surville (only two months after Cook arrived the first time), due Fresne and D'Entrecasteux; an Italian, Malaspina, who commanded a Spanish expedition; and George Vancouver.

In 10 years, within the decade of the 1770s, Cook and his contemporaries had opened up the Pacific entirely and in 1788, Sydney was

Left, a map of Cook Strait taken from Cook's expeditions. **Above**, a somewhat irreverent depiction of a group of Maori entertaining on board a European vessel.

whale in this region and visits brought their crew into frequent contact with the Maori of Northland at Kororareka (later, Russell).

At first, relations between Europeans and Maori were peaceful and friendly. But visits were infrequent for a few years after the burning of a vessel called the *Boyd* in 1809, and the massacre of its crew as a reprisal against previous punishment of high-born Maori seamen by Pakeha skippers.

The inland exploration of New Zealand took place mostly during the second quarter of the 19th century, mainly in those parts which were fairly accessible from the coast. But vast areas of the interior of the South Island were not fully explored until this century.

HARRIETT
HEKIS WIFE   HEKI   KAWITI

THE WARRIOR CHIEFTAINS
of
NEW ZEALAND

Drawn by Jos.ᴾ J. Merrett   Drawn on Stone by W Nicholas

Published by M.ʳ W.ᵐ Ford.
George S.ᵗ Sydney

SETTLEMENT AND COLONISATION

The bleak experiences of Abel Tasman along New Zealand's West Coast and the much more successful endeavours of James Cook 127 years later had no immediate impact on the future of the two main islands. The Dutch were preoccupied with getting all they could out of the Indonesian archipaelago; the British (in the form of the Honourable East India Company) were concerned with consolidating and expanding their trading territories in India.

New Zealand, it seemed, had little to offer a colonial power. "Botany Bay," not so far across the Tasman Sea, was established as a penal settlement in 1788 as a direct result of American victory in the War of Independence (and as a by-product of Cook's voyages), but the Land of the Long White Cloud remained ignored – or almost so.

As the 19th century opened, Europe was engulfed in war. Although international trade suffered through a series of blockades and battles, demand increased for so-called "essential" commodities, and such commodities included sealskins and whale oil. Seals and whales were plentiful in New Zealand waters, and enterprising skippers from Port Jackson (Sydney's harbour, and not the Botany Bay so loved by ballad-mongers of the time) and the newer settlement of Hobart, in Van Dieman's Land, Tasmania, were soon complying with the economic law of supply and demand.

Many of them found a convenient watering-hole at Kororareka (now Russell) in the Bay of Islands. The anchorage there was calm and well-protected; there was a ready supply of *kauri* wood for spars and masts; and they were not too worried by occasional visits by French ships. The Napoleonic wars were reaching their crescendo, and Anglo-French rivalry – back home in Europe – was at its peak. Who cared? Most of the sealers and whalers were renegades of one sort or another, escaped convicts or remittance men who had broken a bond; their captains weren't much better; and the French hadn't been in touch with France for a year or more.

Kororareka, with its new European arrivals, rapidly became a lusty, brawling town. What-

ever its size in the early 1800s, the missionaries who followed swiftly on the heels of the Pakeha intruders were equally swift in damning it as the "hell-hole of the Southwest Pacific." This was hardly surprising: the newcomers, few of whom ever settled ashore or established permanent ties with the Bay of Islands, managed to introduce a destructive influence which in time completely eradicated some of the Maori tribes and *hapu*, and seriously affected others. The influence arrived in the form of muskets, hard liquor or "grog," prostitution, and a host of infectious diseases – many of which could prove fatal – to which the Maori had never previously been exposed.

Nevertheless, relations between Maori and Pakeha were relatively tranquil in the early decades of the 19th century. Isolated hostilities, such as the burning of the brig *Boyd* and the killing and eating of its crew in Whangaroa Harbour in 1809, certainly occurred, and "the *Boyd* incident" discouraged Europeans from attempting to settle in the Whangaroa area for another 10 years.

"The *Boyd* massacre," as it was also known, was bitterly revenged some months later by whaling crews in the Bay of Islands. Some 60 Maori were killed, among them a chieftain whom the Pakehas wrongly believed to have been responsible for the *Boyd* tragedy.

That tragedy, and its savage aftermath, could have been avoided: unfortunately, it was a classic example of "culture shock." A Whangaroa chief, sailing as a crew-member on the *Boyd* from the North Island to Sydney, had been flogged for some misdemeanour on the return voyage. The flogging insulted his *mana*, and tribal loyalty demanded *utu* (or vengeance) for the insult. The crew of the *Boyd*, and their fellow-whalers and shipmates in Kororareka, had no understanding of either *mana* or *utu*; equally, the Maori themselves would not have understood the discipline demanded by the commander of a 600-ton brig in 1809.

Despite such ugly episodes, contacts between Maori and Pakeha remained essentially peaceful. A barter trade flourished, the Maori trading vegetables and flax for a variety of European trinkets and tools and weapons (including, of course, the musket, which they employed in their inter-tribal forays). The Maori helped cut down giant *kauri* trees and drag the trunks from bush to beach; they

Preceding pages, Forest Rangers engage the Maori. Left, Honi Heke flanked by his wife, Harriet, on his right and Chief Kawiti on his left.

crewed on European sealing and whaling vessels; they were physically strong and vigorous; and they were also proud – a fact regrettably overlooked by most Europeans.

"Marsden's Missionaries"

The Reverend Samuel Marsden is still reviled in Australia as the "flogging parson," a result of his tenure as a magistrate at Port Jackson. Kiwis see him in a different light, as the man who introduced Christianity to New Zealand.

James Cook had claimed New Zealand for the British Crown in 1769. The Dutch had done much the same thing more than a century previously, and the French were playing with the same idea towards the end of the 18th century. Curiously enough, nobody really seemed to want the place, and Cook's claim on behalf of Great Britain was never disputed.

Nor, in the 1780s, did anyone in Britain suggest that New Zealand be developed as a repository for convicted felons – that dubious honour being granted to what is now Sydney, the capital of New South Wales, to which many Maori sailed in the early 1800s.

The sealers and whalers who penetrated the Bay of Islands and areas farther south in the early years were, in a sense, accidents: they were not part of any grand British plan to colonise the islands, and they themselves certainly did not see their role as that of colonists.

British colonisation of Australia had begun in 1788. Even though the first 30 years of New South Wales' existence had been full of problems there was some semblance of law and order. In 1817 the legislation of the Colony of New South Wales was extended to include New Zealand; six years later, in 1823, the local juridical implementation of such legislation was introduced.

Amid this turbulence, Samuel Marsden arrived from New South Wales in 1814. His decision to go to New Zealand in a missionary role had been influenced by the Maori he had met in Sydney, including Ruatara, a nephew of the renowned fighting chief Hongi Hika. Marsden had been planning to establish a Christian mission in New Zealand as early as 1808, a plan frustrated by the reverberations of the *Boyd* incident in 1809.

Whatever his shortcomings as a magistrate, Marsden was a dedicated evangelist. He sincerely believed that missionary tradesmen, "imported" from England under the auspices of the Church Missionary Society would not only encourage the conversion of Maori to Christianity but also develop their expertise in carpentry, farming and the use of European technology. The Maori had been an agricultural people, with their staple crop being the sweet potato (or *kumara*), but with no experience in animal husbandry or grain-growing. (It is said that when Maori first grew wheat, they pulled the ripening crop from the ground and looked for food at the roots – the edible tubers that had been their principal source of nourishment for generations.)

Marsden also introduced the country's first horses and cattle, gifts from governor Lachlan Macquarie in New South Wales. The excitement of the Maori on seeing these animals for the first time, according to one account, "was soon turned into alarm and confusion, for one

of the cows, impatient of restraint and unmanageable, rushed in among them and caused a serious panic. They thought the animal was some preternatural monster which had been let loose to destroy them and took to their heels in fright. Later when Marsden mounted a horse and rode up and down the beach he was at once given a status of more than mortal."

Six years later, in 1820, the first plough was demonstrated by John Butler, another Bay of Islands missionary. Butler wrote: "On the morning of Wednesday the 3rd of May, 1820, the agricultural plough was for the first time put into the land of New Zealand at Kiddie Kiddie (now Kerikeri) and I felt much pleasure in holding it after a team of six bullocks brought down by the 'Dromedary' I trust that this auspicious day will be remembered with gratitude and its anniversary kept by ages yet unborn." Such pomposity was typical of Butler. He was also an irascible man, and quite soon left the country following bitter arguments with fellow missionaries.

The missionary-tradesmen-teachers in whom Marsden had placed his faith were in fact an ill-assorted bunch, most of whom fairly quickly fell before the onslaught of temptations in a heathen land. They bickered quite violently among themselves, and could hardly be regarded as a civilising, evangelising force by the people they had come to convert when so many of them became involved in gunrunning, adultery, drunkenness, and even sor-

1820 accompanied two famous chiefs, Hongi and Waikato, to Britain. Then there was William Colenso, who arrived at Paihia in 1834 and set up a printing press that played a major role in the development of Maori literacy.

By 1830, Maori were involved in export trading. In that year 28 ships (averaging 110 tonnes) made 56 cross-Tasman voyages, and carried substantial cargos of Maori-grown potatoes on their return from Sydney. In 1835, the famous naturalist Charles Darwin visited the mission station at Waimate North and wrote: "On an adjoining slope fine crops of barley and wheat were standing in full ear; and in another fields of potatoes and clover.... There were large gardens with every fruit and vegetable which England produces."

Kororarika Bay of Islands N.Z. 1836

ties into pagan rites. It is not surprising that 10 years passed before the first Maori baptism, and another 10 before the second. Not until the third decade of the century did the Maori begin to find Christianity an attractive proposition.

Despite the missionaries' shortcomings, some achievements were registered. Thomas Kendall, who succumbed to the Maori's different attitude towards sex, was nonetheless instrumental in compiling the first grammar and dictionary of the Maori language, and in

Left, Samuel Marsden, the "flogging parson." **Above**, early settlement in the Bay of Islands begins to take shape on the shoreline.

The inclusion of New Zealand within the framework of the laws of New South Wales in 1817 and 1823 had not made New Zealand a British colony. The extension of legislation across the Tasman Sea from Sydney had been prompted by the desire of the early governors of New South Wales to control the lawlessness prevailing in the Bay of Islands. The sentiment was admirable enough. The main problem was that the legislation was directed principally against the crews of British ships, and the governors had no way of proving charges nor of enforcing their authority while a ship was in New Zealand waters; and they had no authority whatsoever over American vessels and their crews.

Additionally, the missionaries who found their way to New Zealand in the two or three decades after 1814 were, for once, united in a common aim: they did not want to see New Zealand colonised. This was a view shared by virtually all British Christian humanitarians and evangelists of the period, who felt that New Zealand should be left to the missionaries who (it was hoped) would spread what they saw as the benefits of Christian civilisation among the Maori, leaving the latter uncorrupted by depravity introduced to earlier colonies by European settlers and adventurers.

But, inevitably, there was dissension "back home". The powerful Church Missionary Society ideally wanted British protection for New Zealand, and perhaps even some formal some of New Zealand's early missionaries.

On a less idealistic level, there was also pressure among Britons for new colonies with land for settlement, and it was becoming known that the New Zealand climate was just about perfect for Europeans. It was also becoming obvious (or so it seemed at the time) that if Britain did not take sovereignty over New Zealand and populate it with European immigrants, some other colonial power – most probably France – would do so. In retrospect, it seems doubtful that the French in the opening decades of the 19th century had any specific designs upon New Zealand, but their explorers and seamen had been to New Zealand waters since the time of James Cook.

Predictably, the "home government" re-

inclusion of the country within the British Empire, with an orderly government administration but without the previously common consequences of colonisation and extensive settlement.

On the other hand, there was a substantial body of opinion which believed that settlement arranged in an organised and responsible manner by "good men" would be able to avoid the disasters inflicted by Europeans upon indigenous peoples of other countries. The leading proselytiser of this view in Britain was Edward Gibbon Wakefield whose theories on colonisation strongly influenced the settlement of New Zealand, South Australia and parts of Canada; his view was also shared by mained steadfastly irresolute, and the issue of colonisation was allowed to drift. By the 1830s, the scramble for land was in full swing – a scramble that was to produce tragic results within 20 years.

"Man-of-War Without Guns"

The Maori had no concept of permanent, private ownership of land. Their land was held by tribes traditionally inheriting it. A chief's authority was generally strong enough to have a sale accepted by most members of the tribe – but even this could be complicated by conflicting claims of ownership among tribes or subtribes, and such claims could involve very large areas. Many deals in land transfer between Pakeha and Maori led to conflicts in the 1860s; some of them are still being legally contested today.

There was also the problem of what was being bought. The settlers, and the rapacious speculators in Britain, thought they were buying outright freehold land; in many cases, the Maori believed they were merely leasing their lands for a fee.

The missionaries (with the possible exception of Marsden, whose idea of justice was to strip the flesh off a man's back with the cat-o'-nine-tails) were not skilled in matters of British law, and certainly not in the area of land conveyancing. Nor were they renowned as administrators of their professed anti-settle-

ment beliefs. The time had finally come for government intervention, however reluctant.

That came, in 1833, with the arrival in the Bay of Islands of James Busby as British Resident.

The notion of "resident" was vague in 1833 and became no clearer in the next century of British colonial rule in many parts of the world. A resident, in most cases, had the full backing of Her or His Majesty's Government

as a diplomat representing British interests in a territory that had not yet been annexed by the Crown. He could advise local chieftains, he could cajole, he could woo – but he had no real power, either legal or military.

Poor Busby! Lacking any means of enforcing his authority, such as it was, he became known among the Maori as "the man-of-war without guns."

Busby did what he could. He attempted to create some unity and overall sovereignty among the disparate Maori by formally establishing a confederation of Maori chiefs, and in 1835 he proposed that Britain and the United Tribes of New Zealand should agree to an arrangement under which the confederation would represent the Maori people and gradually expand their influence as a government while the British government, in the meantime, administered the country in trust.

Despite his nickname, Busby won personal respect from the Maori. Even so, he keenly felt his own impotence and knew he could never achieve law and order without the backing of some adequate force.

The missionaries, divided as they were, could not prevent the annexation and eventual large-scale colonisation of New Zealand, and in 1840 their anti-settlement policy was rebuffed with the signing of Treaty of Waitangi.

Men Who Came to Stay

While most of the British and American whalers and sealers were not the type of men to settle down on *terra firma* in a remote corner of the globe, there were from the early 19th century, a number of men of European stock who were willing to put down roots in the new land and to face the risks and hardships involved. By the 1830s a few thousand Pakehas had settled, almost all of them in the Bay of Islands.

The Weller brothers – Edward, George and Joseph – were among the pioneer settlers in Otago. As whalers, they became so well established that in 1833 they sent a trial export shipment of merchandise to London. Unhappily for them, what could have proved a bonanza was thwarted by British Customs: New Zealand was a "foreign country," and the Wellers faced duties of £26 per ton on whale oil. They abandoned the enterprise and, later, Otago.

· John Jones, another whaler, established a base a few miles north of Dunedin, and in the late 1830s had a chain of seven whaling stations operating in the south of the South Island

Left, Nelson Haven in Tasman Bay – from a painting by Charles Heaphy 1841. **Above**, Edward Gibbon Wakefield, a theorist of colonisation, founded the Colonisation Society.

and employed 280 people. Born in Sydney, and believed to have been the son of a transported convict, he later operated a shipping line and owned large land-holdings at Waikouaiti on the coast north of Dunedin.

Richard Barrett, widely known as "Dickie," arrived in New Zealand as an adventurer in 1828. He married Rawinia Waikaiua of the Taranaki Ngati-te-Whiti tribe and fought for his wife's people in tribal wars. He later became a whaler in the Cook Strait region, and a notable translator and mediator in land-sale deals around Wellington; he also took part in negotiations for the Wellington land purchase by the New Zealand Company for the initial settlement there in 1840.

Others of the original settlers also threw in their lot with the Maori. Philip Tapsel was a Dane who served with the British merchant marine and first arrived in New Zealand in 1803. In the late 1820s he set up a trading post on behalf of a Sydney merchant at Maketu in the Bay of Plenty. He married three Maori women, had a number of children, and his name is now a common one among the Arawa people of the area – including that of a Member of Parliament.

Frederick Maning emigrated to Tasmania with his father and brothers in 1824, and decided to settle in Hokianga, North Auckland, in 1833. He married Moengaroa, the sister of a powerful Maori chief, Hauraki, and they had four children before she died in 1847. Maning took part in inter-tribal warfare, supporting his wife's people, and was later appointed a judge of the Native Land Court. Maning wrote two books about his experiences, both under the pseudonym "A Pakeha-Maori." They were *War in the North* and the more famous *Old New Zealand*, both of which give vivid accounts of Maori tribal life and practices (although he was inclined to some exaggeration).

"Pakeha-Maori" was a common term used to describe those Europeans who joined the tribal life. It is important to remember that while the violence, drunkenness and debauchery of the Bay of Islands' Pakehas was causing concern in Sydney and London before New Zealand was annexed, there were a number of men treating the Maori with respect and actually adopting their way of life.

There were also farcical interludes. A character calling himself Baron Charles Philip Hippolytus de Thierry, Sovereign Chief of New Zealand, King of Nukuheva, decided to establish himself at Hokianga. He had arranged the purchase of a large estate from Hongi Hika through the agency of Thomas

Kendall when they visited Britain. De Thierry arrived in New Zealand in 1837, was quickly deserted by most of his followers, soon ran out of money, and fairly quickly faded into a bizarre chapter of history. His life was the basis for a New Zealand novel, *Check to Your King*, by Robin Hyde.

De Thierry's background was mostly English, but there was one other genuine if half-hearted French interest in the country. A colonising organisation, the Nanto-Bordelaise Company, established a settlement at Akaroa on Banks Peninsula, with some support from the French government, on the eve of the British decision to annexe New Zealand. The French operation, however, was a small one, and any influence it might have had on the

TOMIKA TE MUTU
Chief MOTUHOA Is^d 29.12.1865

British move to colonise New Zealand has been overstated in the past.

The Wakefield Scheme

In the course of the 1830s it had become obvious in New South Wales, which provided what little British administrative control there was over New Zealand, that land buying was going to cause serious trouble. Speculators were gambling on Britain taking over and settling the country; while Busby, the British Resident, was powerless to prevent such "deals" from taking place.

Colonisation, in fact, was developing a kind of inevitability. In 1836, Edward Gibbon

Wakefield told a committee of the House of Commons that Britain was colonising New Zealand already, but "in a most slovenly and scrambling and disgraceful manner."

In 1837, at the behest of the government of New South Wales, Captain William Hobson, commanding HMS *Rattlesnake*, sailed from Sydney to the Bay of Islands to report on the situation in New Zealand and to recommend possible action. Hobson suggested a treaty with the Maori chiefs (which Busby thought he had already achieved) and the placing of all British subjects in New Zealand under British rule. Hobson's report provoked a response, but without Wakefield's influence there might not have been such an outcome.

Wakefield was born in London in 1796, the

fired. He was apprehended, tried, and sentenced to three years in prison for abduction.

While in prison Wakefield wrote two books. One, *A Letter from Sydney*, outlined his philosophy of colonisation and attracted the attention of some influential people. Following his release, he founded the Colonisation Society to spread his theories.

Disliking what he perceived as the bad results of colonisation in the United States, Canada, New South Wales and Tasmania, he believed that if land was sold at what he called "a sufficient price" to "capitalist" settlers, labourers among the immigrants would not disperse thinly through the new country but would stay in the new communities working for landowners – at least for a few years until

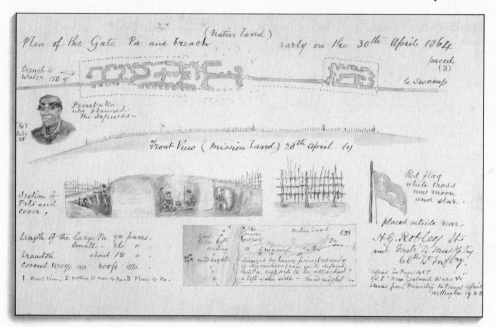

eldest of a large family. He was educated at Westminster School for a year and then at Edinburgh High School. In 1816 he persuaded a wealthy young woman, Eliza Susan Pattle, to elope with him. She died soon afterwards, but had borne a son. Edward Jerningham Wakefield, who was to become a significant figure in New Zealand's history.

Ten years later, in 1826, Wakefield made a second runaway marriage with a schoolgirl heiress, Ellen Turner. This time his plan mis-

Left, Tomika Te Mutu, chief of Motuhoa Island. **Above**, a plan of the Gate *Pa* The New Zealand Wars were often indecisive though bloody.

they could save enough to buy land for themselves at the "sufficient price" and employ more recently arrived immigrant labour.

Land prices were crucial to Wakefield's system. Unfortunately for the system, he underestimated the aspirations of immigrant labourers who were prepared to suffer extreme isolation in order to farm their own land; and he did not foresee the readiness with which "capitalists" would move out of the centralised settlements to areas they considered more profitable.

During the late 1830s and early 1840s Wakefield was ostensibly involved in Canadian colonisation matters, but much of his time and energy were in fact absorbed by the organisation of the New Zealand Company. The Company, originally formed as the New Zealand Association in 1837, was revamped in the following year as a joint stock company at the behest of the British Secretary of State for the Colonies, who (not unreasonably) wanted to ensure that the people involved would bear the costs of establishing the settlements they planned.

The Treaty of Waitangi

At the same time as Wakefield's hopeful "capitalists" and "labourers" were starting to pack their sea-trunks, the British Government was at last responding to the anti-colonial feelings of the missionary groups. Britain

decided that the Maori should be consulted on their own future, and that their consent should be given to the annexation of their country. The result was the Treaty of Waitangi, signed at the Bay of Islands on February 6, 1840, by Lieutenant-Governor William Hobson on behalf of the British government, and by a number of Maori leaders. The treaty was later taken to other parts of the country for signing by most of the Maori chiefs.

Ironically, the treaty was never ratified. Within a decade the Chief Justice, Sir William Martin, ruled that it had no legal validity because it was not incorporated in New Zealand's statutory law. The second irony is that the date of the original signing of the treaty

is now said to be the "founding day" of New Zealand as a British colony, the reverse of what the missionaries had hoped to achieve.

The treaty itself remains a bone of contention. The text of the document was written in English, apparently amended by Hobson after it was first explained to the assembled Maori leaders, with a rather loosely translated version in Maori (that version being the one signed by most of the Maori leaders). The Maori had put much faith in advice from the missionaries, being told that they were signing a solemn pact between two races, under which New Zealand sovereignty was being vested in the British Crown in return for guarantees of certain Maori rights. Many Europeans (and Maori) genuinely believed this, and for some years the British Government upheld the agreement.

It is almost impossible now to regard the treaty objectively. In the context of its time it was an example of enlightened and humane respect for the rights of an indigenous population. But because it was never ratified, and never truly honoured by the white settlers (hungry for land and impatient with Maori culture and traditions), it is easily construed these days as an expedient fraud.

Organised Immigration

The formal British annexation of New Zealand implicit in the 1840 Treaty of Waitangi was quickly followed by the arrival of the first ships carrying immigrants organised by Wakefield's New Zealand Company. *Tory*, despatched from English before the treaty had been signed and arriving early in 1840, long before the treaty could have been received in London, carried Colonel William Wakefield (who had earlier assisted his brother Edward in the abduction of Ellen Turner, and had been gaoled for his pains) and a batch of immigrants who were to settle in Wellington.

The Wanganui district received its first settlers shortly afterwards, and in 1841 a subsidiary of the Company, based in Plymouth, England, and drawing emigrants from Devon and Cornwall, established New Plymouth.

The South Island was not ignored. Captain Arthur Wakefield, another of Edward's many brothers, arrived at Nelson in 1841 and was followed by 3,000 settlers in 1842.

Despite (or perhaps because of) the Treaty of Waitangi, land claims soon became a matter of dispute between Maori and Pakeha. Arthur Wakefield, in 1843, led a party of 21 other Nelson settlers into the fertile Wairau Valley, near Nelson, which he contended had been bought by the Company. The local chief Te Rauparaha and his nephew Rangihaeata thought otherwise: they assembled their warriors and killed all 22 of the Pakehas.

Nor was the Wellington settlement in the bloom of health. The first site in the Hutt Valley had been flooded; there had been serious clashes with the local tribes; potentially arable land was scarce, and even when available such land was proving difficult and expensive to develop.

Way up north, in the Bay of Islands, the events in the south were having their repercussions. Hone Heke, a signatory to the Treaty of Waitangi, had become more than disenchanted with the treaty's implications. Al-

fractious. He and his warriors demolished the flagpole (symbol of royal authority) on three occasions, and once sacked the entire town as Pakehas scampered off into the woods or took to boats.

George Grey, who arrived as Governor in 1845, called in the army to suppress Hone Heke. With the help of Maori dissidents who refused to support Heke, Grey won the day.

Pragmatic Pastoralism

Open conflict between Pakehas and Maori did not encourage enthusiasm for emigration to New Zealand. The New Zealand Company, Wakefield's idealistic dream, went into a decline. It eventually became almost bankrupt in

though Kororareka (Russell) had been the *de facto* "capital" of New Zealand before the signing of the treaty, Lieutenant-Governor Hobson – in his wisdom – decided that Auckland should be the site of the new country's capital. The protective sweep of Auckland's harbour quickly proved his point, but left a lot of noses out of joint in Russell. Well-established Yankee skippers felt badly done by, the town's trade declined, and Hone Heke got

Left, the reverse side of the New Zealand Cross medal awarded for gallantry during the New Zealand Wars. <u>Above</u>, a stagecoach fords a North Island stream.

the late 1840s, surrendered its charter, and handed over to the government of some 400,000 hectares (about 1 million acres) of land for which about $500,000 were due; it was dissolved in 1858.

Even with the writing on the wall in its last decade of operation, the New Zealand Company remained active, lending its organisational support to members of the Scottish Free Church who established Dunedin in 1848, and to the Anglicans who founded Christchurch in 1850 and quickly opened up the excellent pasturelands of the Canterbury Plains. Although Governor Grey was less than enthusiastic about pastoralism – indeed, he does not seem to have understood what it was all about

– more and more new settlers imported sheep, mostly merinos, from Australia. What became New Zealand's principal economic asset was soon under way: sheep-farming on a large scale, at first purely for wool, later for lamb and mutton.

Edward Wakefield, architect-in-absence of planned settlement, eventually arrived in New Zealand for the first time in 1852, the year in which the colony was granted self-government by Britain. He was elected to the Wellington Provincial Council and the House of Representatives in 1853, but retired shortly afterwards because of ill health.

Wakefield achieved much. At the same time, he lived long enough (he died in 1862) to see that his ideal of cohesive but expanding communities, complete with "capitalists" and "labourers," was not viable. The immigrants didn't necessarily make the choice for "town life," and many left the infant settlements to establish – or, at least, attempt to establish – agricultural or pastoral properties well beyond the confines of the towns. But thanks largely to his efforts, the settlement and colonisation of New Zealand were achieved in a more orderly manner than had been the case, several decades earlier, in Canada and Australia.

The new settlers were not the only people interested in taking advantage of the fertile land. The Maori themselves had quickly learned the agricultural lessons taught by the early missionaries (even if they had responded less quickly to the lure of Christianity), and by the end of the 1850s huge areas of Maori land in Waikato and the Bay of Plenty were under cultivation or carrying livestock. One commentator reported that a Maori population of about 8,000 in the Taupo-Rotorua region "had upwards of 3,000 acres of land in wheat, 3,000 acres in potatoes, nearly 2,000 acres in maize and upwards of 1,000 acres planted with kumara." On the surface, the new colony appeared peaceful.

The New Zealand Wars: 1860-1881

In fact, the new colony was anything but peaceful. There had been a great deal of speculation in land sales, and many Maori were beginning to realise this: land was being sold for as much as 20 times what they had been paid for it.

A direct result of this injustice was the election in 1858 of a Maori "king" by tribes in the centre of the North Island. There had never been such a title among the Maori, who owed their allegiance to a tribe or sub-tribe, but it was hoped that the *mana* of a king, uniting many tribes, would help protect their land against purchase by the Pakehas. It didn't work out that way.

To the west of the king's domain, the Taranaki, another group of tribes rose up against the government in June 1860 following a blatantly fraudulent land purchase by the colonial administration, the Waitara Land Deal. British regular troops, hastily assembled to meet the insurrection, were virtually annihilated south of Waitara.

For the next few days, the North Island was ablaze with clashes between Maori and Pakeha. The "Second Maori War," as military historians term it (remembering the outbreaks in 1840), was marked by extraordinary courage on both sides. The conflicts were frequently indecisive, but they were bloody when they occurred. On the Pakeha side, the brunt of the early fighting, until 1865, was borne by British regular troops, 14 of whom received Britain's highest battle honour, the Victoria Cross.

Between 1865 and 1872 (which was the "official" end of the war, though there was sporadic fighting until the formal surrender of the Maori king in 1881), locally raised militia and constabulary forces played an important role – assisted, perhaps surprisingly, by a large number of Maori tribes that had decided not to join the king's confederation.

A little-known sidelight of the New Zealand Wars was the institution of the New Zealand Cross, a unique and extremely rare medal awarded for gallantry. A fifteenth Victoria Cross had been awarded to a member of the Auckland Militia who took part in an action at Waikato in 1864, but because the VC could be won only by a man serving with the Imperial Forces, or under imperial command, the NZC was created as an honour for outstanding gallantry shown by a member of a locally raised non-imperial unit. Only 23 medals were ever awarded – three of them going to Maori.

Despite war, the prospects of the country continued to improve. The discovery of gold in the South Island led to a fresh influx of migrants in the early 1860s; the capital was moved from Auckland to Wellington in 1865; and the pursuit of pasture was opening up vast tracts of the country. Wakefield might not have liked it, but the individualistic "cowcockie" was on his way!

Right, gold was the magnet that drew a large number of settlers in the 19th century.

Progress towards New Zealand's full independence from Britain began almost as soon as the Maori-Pakeha land wars began to settle down.

An economic boom in the 1870s was sparked by Sir Julius Vogel, who as colonial treasurer borrowed heavily overseas for public works construction, notably railways. A flood of immigrants, mainly from Britain but also from Scandinavia and Germany, followed. But Vogel – an ebullient, imaginative and impatient man who remained in the forefront of New Zealand politics from 1873 to 1887,

and was twice premier during that time – miscalculated the negative impact of his borrow-to-boom credo.

By the end of the 1870s, British banks had begun to contract their credit. In 1880, New Zealand only narrowly averted bankruptcy. Within a few years, the prices of first wool, then grain, dropped so hard that depression set in and unemployment spread rapidly. In 1888, more than 9,000 hungry settlers left the colony, most of them for Australia, which had remained relatively prosperous.

These years of hardship may have had something to do with the emergence of New Zealand as one of the most socially progressive communities in the world. Free, compul-

sory and secular public-school education was created by law in 1877, and another piece of legislation two years later gave every adult man – Maori as well as Pakeha – the right to vote.

In the 1880s, Sir Harry Atkinson, a cautious man who had reacted against Vogel's borrowing and "profligacy," advocated a national social security scheme to protect New Zealanders against illness and pauperism. Although he was elected premier five times between 1876 and 1891, Atkinson's scheme was ridiculed by his Parliamentary colleagues. "It's unChristian," they told him. Unrepentant in defeat, Atkinson responded: "Our successors in office will take up and pass every one of these measures."

He was right. In the waning years of the 19th century, a barrage of social reforms was fired by a new Liberal Party government headed by John Ballance. Sweeping land reforms were introduced, breaking down the large inland estates and providing first mortgage money to put people on the land. Industrial legislation provided improved conditions for workers, as well as a compulsory system of industrial arbitration, the first of its kind in the world. The aged poor were awarded a pension. And for the first time anywhere (with the exceptions of tiny Pitcairn Island and the American state of Wyoming) women were granted the right to vote on an equal basis with men, to the delight of the women's suffrage movement throughout the world.

The principal minds behind these great social reforms were William Pember Reeves, a New Zealand-born socialist, the political theorist of the Liberal Party and a man determined to test the intellectually exciting new Fabian ideas then in vogue in Britain; and Richard John Seddon, who succeeded to the office of Prime Minister when Ballance died in 1893. Perhaps the most admired leader in New Zealand history, Seddon's legendary toughness and political judgement gave him enormous power within the party and, as a result, in the country. He remained in office until his death in 1906.

Sheep and "Cow-cockies"

Even in the depths of the depression of the 1880s, a new industry was being created. In 1882, the refrigerated vessel *Dunedin* was loaded with sheep's carcasses at Port Chalmers, the deepwater port for the South Island city of Dunedin. It sailed on February 13 and arrived in England 3½ months later, on May 24. The voyage was an anxious one: sparks from the refrigeration machinery several times set fire to the sails, and the captain was nearly frozen to death as he attended to a malfunction in the main air duct of the freezing chamber. Nevertheless the meat arrived safely and, despite the transport costs, profits in England were much higher than they would have been for the same meat back in New Zealand. This was a blessing from the gods for the isolated Pacific colony.

The timing was perfect for Britain, too. Population was increasing with urbanisation,

Canterbury run and led them across vast distances of open land. He was arrested and brought to trial, but was subsequently pardoned. Today the vast Mackenzie Country west of Christchurch bears his (misspelled) name.

The new and burgeoning frozen meat industry and the expansion of dairy exports during the early years of the 20th century saw the rise of the small farmer in both the North and South Island – especially the "cow-cockie," as the dairy farmer came to be known. While Seddon became more conservative in the latter years of his Liberal administration, the farmers' affluence and influence grew, until in 1911 – a few years after New Zealand had politely refused an invitation to become a part of the new

and people had more money to spend on food. As farmers began breeding sheep for their meat as well as wool, the frozen meat industry became an economic staple.

Wealth wrought by sheep-breeding naturally attracted a handful of men who sought to get rich quick, most notably New Zealand's best known scalawag, one James MacKenzie. Assisted only by a remarkable sheepdog named Friday who took its orders in Gaelic, he is said to have stolen 1,000 sheep from a

Commonwealth of Australia, and was subsequently upgraded in status by the British Empire from "colony" to "dominion" – the new Reform Party squeezed into power. New Prime Minister William Massey was himself a dairy farmer, and while his government had the backing of conservative businessmen, his election helped to strongly consolidate New Zealand's position as an offshore farm for Britain.

World War I

The advent of World War I brought a new sense of nationalism to New Zealand while at the same time reinforcing the country's ties to

Left, Richard John Seddon, Prime Minister from 1893 to his death in 1906. **Above**, Labour Day Procession in Auckland's Queen Street, 1899.

England. Under Seddon in 1899, 6,500 Kiwis had volunteered for service in the Boer War in South Africa; now, between 1914 and 1918, 100,000 joined the Australia-New Zealand Army Corps (ANZAC) forces and sailed for North Africa and Europe.

By the time the war had ended, almost 17,000 New Zealanders had lost their lives, and many thousands more returned home with crippling wounds. Indeed, the casualties were out of all proportion to the country's population, then about a million. The futility was underscored by the debacle on Turkey's Gallipoli Peninsula, from April 25, 1915 (a day now marked in memoriam as "Anzac Day") until British naval evacuation some eight months later; the affair cost dearly the lives of

8,587 Anzacs, and there were another 25,000 casualties. Somehow this heroic tragedy gave New Zealand a new identity within the British Empire.

The Great Depression of the 1930s gripped hard on New Zealand, dependent as it was on overseas prices. Curtailed British demand for meat, wool and dairy products led to severe unemployment and several bloody riots, notably on Queen Street, Auckland, in April 1932. The new Labour Party swept into power in 1935 to take advantage of the resurgent world economy and quickly pull New Zealand out of the doldrums. Under Prime Minister Michael Savage, the nation again moved to the forefront of world social change, establishing a full social security system and comprehensive health-care plan.

Savage died soon after the outbreak of World War II, into which he threw his country with vigour on September 2, 1939, only 1½ hours after Britain declared war on Hitler's Germany. He was succeeded as Prime Minister by Peter Fraser, whose administration financed the war effort almost entirely from taxation and internal borrowing. This time, nearly 200,000 Kiwis were called to battle, many of them under General Douglas MacArthur in the nearby Pacific campaign, others in North Africa, Italy and Crete. More than 10,000 died.

Enhanced Self-Respect

Back home, a successful economic stabilisation policy and full employment made the 1940s a decade of relative prosperity. The country emerged from the war with enhanced self-respect and a developed sense of nationhood. It was an appropriate time, in 1947, for the government to adopt the Statute of Westminster and formally achieve full independence from Britain. (In fact, the statute had been approved by commonwealth legislatures before it was passed by British Parliament in 1931, granting complete independence to self-governing member countries. But it did not, however, apply automatically to New Zealand or Australia, both of which had to adopt it by legislation.)

The Labour Party had lost its vigour. The young men who had steered it to victory in the mid-1930s, and who had transformed the nation into a modern welfare state, could not meet the challenge of the new era. They were dilatory in decontrolling the economy after the war and were in effect suppressing the desire of the community to enjoy a freer economic environment.

They were defeated in 1949 by the National Party, a political movement which had first fought a general election in 1938 and been soundly beaten by Labour. National had in the meantime attracted many young businessmen who wanted a greater private-enterprise influence in the management of the economy. National's victory ended an era and paved the way for the shaping of modern New Zealand.

Left, two New Zealand faces from the 1920s – "thoroughly modern" girls. Right, the tallest and the shortest members of the New Zealand regiment sent to aid Britain in the Boer War.

The years following World War II can be fairly accurately divided into two phases – before and after British entry into the European Economic Community (Common Market) in 1973.

Before this event New Zealanders were living, as they used to say, "high on the sheep's back." But after the nation's chief dairy-product market committed itself to purchasing butter, milk and cheese from other EEC members, Kiwis were forced to tighten their belts and look long and hard at tough measures to derail rising unemployment and inflation.

Politics have been dominated throughout the period by the National Party, which has let power slip from its hands for only three brief spells since 1949. These have been years of growing industrialisation, social innovations and increasing activism and environmental awareness.

Power In One House

The 1950s began with a political tremor as the National Party government abolished the Legislative Council, the often-ineffectual upper house of the national Parliament. This appointive body had been modelled upon the British House of Lords to give New Zealand a bicameral Parliament. When it was done away with in 1950, the government promised to replace it with an elective body. This has never occurred; ever since, New Zealand has been one of few democratic nations on earth with a unicameral legislature. Critics maintain that with no written constitution and no upper house, the New Zealand parliamentary system gives almost untrammelled power to the prime minister, who comes to power as the leader of the party with an elected majority in the House of Representatives.

One of the first actions taken by the unicameral House was the ratification of the Anzus (Australia-New Zealand-United States) mutual security pact in 1951. In World War II, the United States had played the major role in protecting both South Pacific nations from the Japanese advance (ironically, the ANZAC

forces were in Europe at the time); and the signing of this Anzus pact was a clear indication on the part of New Zealand and Australia that they had to look away from Great Britain to meet their defence requirements.

Except for a three-year period (1957-1960) during which the Labour Party briefly regained the upper hand in Parliament, the National Party remained in power and controlled the country's destiny for 23 years, from 1949 to 1972 – principally under just two prime ministers, Sir Sidney Holland (1949-1957) and Sir Keith Holyoake (1957 and 1960-

1972). With Holyoake at the helm, New Zealand reverted to its socially progressive past in becoming the first nation outside of Scandinavia to create within the government the appointive position of "ombudsman."

In effect a parliamentary commissioner, the ombudsman's role is to investigate and expedite the claims of private citizens against bureaucracy and officialdom. Where the claims are justified, the ombudsman assures that action is taken – restoring lost pensions, moving boundary markers, and the like. Where the claims are not justified, he explains the government's position to the complainant. This idea has proven to be tremendously successful since it was first enacted in 1962.

Left, Queen Elizabeth II chats with New Zealanders during a visit to Auckland. **Right**, Sir Keith Holyoake was Prime Minister between 1960 and 1972 and later became Governor General.

Environmentalists also began to speak their piece in the 1960s. The biggest issue initially was a government plan to raise the water level of beautiful Lake Manapouri in Fiordland National Park, to produce cheap hydro-electric power for the Australia-owned aluminium smelter at Tiwai Point near Bluff. The conservationists forced a compromise on the issue, the lake's waters being used for hydro-electricity but the water level being maintained.

Numerous other issues have raised the choler of environmentalists in recent years, often involving the damming of previously untouched steams for hydro-power. Another major concern is the use of chemical defoliants to clear the bush for farming. But of even more far-reaching consequence to many New Zeal-

pending. Prime Minister Norman Kirk earned immediate kudos among many New Zealanders by withdrawing Kiwi troops from Vietnam, where they had been serving since 1965 in support of United States forces under the Anzus agreement. But in an effort to reduce the burden for New Zealand citizens, Kirk placed restrictions on the previously uncontrolled immigration to New Zealand of British nationals and all other Commonwealth citizens of European blood.

A British Farm

In order to understand the effect of Britain's EEC membership on the New Zealand economy, one must realize the importance of over-

SHOULD AULD ACQUAINTANCE BE FORGOT?

anders is the nuclear issue.

Again in the 1960s, as France began stepping up a campaign of nuclear testing in its Polynesian possessions, New Zealand scientists began to monitor radioactivity in the region. Protest ships travelled to French Polynesia to intentionally block tests; back home, there were several mass demonstrations. Meanwhile, there was an increasing outcry against nuclear-armed or nuclear-powered United States naval vessels being permitted in New Zealand ports, as part of the Anzus pact. But the issue didn't really reach a head until the 1984 elections.

A Labour government was returned to power in 1972 with the economic crisis im-

seas trade on an economy almost entirely dependent upon primary production.

New Zealand lives on grass. Its temperate climate, with rainfall spread evenly through the year, grows grass better than just about anywhere else. Grass feeds sheep and cattle, which in turn feed New Zealanders. When Britain joined the Common Market, New Zealand's No. 1 market virtually disappeared; and pastoral products are hard to sell elsewhere in the world at prices to which New Zealanders had become accustomed.

Through the 1950s, New Zealand was virtually an offshore British farm. In a country whose export trade, as a proportion of gross national product is among the highest in the world, New Zealand depended almost entirely upon its sales to England. About three-quarters of all exports went in bulk to Britain, peaking at close to 90 percent at the beginning of World War II. These exports were almost completely animal products. In return, nearly half of New Zealand's imports came from Britain, with most of the rest from Australia or the United States.

At the beginning of the 1960s, the whole scenario began to change. It became apparent that Britain was beginning to look to Europe, and the long-standing familiar relationship with New Zealand would have to change. Because production had so long been so closely tied to British tastes, this meant New Zealanders would have to diversify their pro-

oil prices, sent the cost of industrial goods sky high. So New Zealand on the one hand was producing goods whose prices dawdled behind, held back by artificially underpriced competition from subsidised, over-protected production in the EEC and the United States; and on the other hand was paying more and more for industrial goods because it had to import most of them.

Most Western countries have political barriers against the import of pastoral products. New Zealand, with 3.3 million people, had neither the industrial market size nor the political muscle to fight back. It had no choice but to borrow against trade deficits and for capital development, an option which left it with an increasing national overseas debt.

duction to gain diversification of markets.

It was a matter of marketing. But marketing was something New Zealanders had never needed to do. They had lived well, high on the sheep's back, for so long, by the relatively simple process of farming well, that the British jump into the EEC in 1973 left them in confusion and bewilderment.

The trade barriers imposed on Britain by EEC membership, combined with rocketing

Left, Britain's entry into the European Common Market was a serious blow to the new Zealand economy. Above, Robert Muldoon was Prime Minister between 1975 and 1984.

With the economic crises, New Zealand's public mood favoured the dismantling of much of the welfare legislation of prior years – more commercial freedom with less government intervention and more dominance by the marketplace. But Kirk introduced a landmark accident compensation scheme in the early 1970s. This scheme covers medical costs and gives income protection for anyone injured in an accident, irrespective of who was directly to blame or indirectly responsible for the accident. He also maintained a national superannuation scheme which gives indexed pensions to everyone, regardless of personal wealth, from age 60.

Kirk died in office in August 1974, and was

succeeded to the post by prime minister by Wallace (Bill) Rowling. Within a year, the Labour government had devalued the dollar twice, placed numerous import restrictions, and borrowed heavily abroad. Nevertheless, inflation reached above 17 percent. The public reacted by returning the National Party to office in November 1975.

Tight Measures

Led by Sir Robert Muldoon – who had served as finance minister in the Holyoake ministry – National doubled the tight measures imposed by Labour on immigration, imports and the dollar. Muldoon, pugnacious and controversial but never dull, provoked the

Japan and the United States taking 12 percent and the rest of the world 42 percent.

Internal inflation raged so strongly at the end of the 1970s and the beginning of the 1980s (up to 17 percent) that farm costs skyrocketed and the Muldoon ministry humiliatingly had to subsidise New Zealand's own farmers through supplementary minimum prices (SMPs). A wages-price freeze from 1982 cut inflation to around 4 percent, but all the regulation and readjustment caused an agony of doubt about the short-term future of the economy. By 1984, unemployment had reached 130,000 and the national overseas debt stood at NZ$14.3 billion.

The economic woes and Muldoon's own gritty personality wore away his Parliamen-

anger of trade unionists throughout the country by imposing a wage freeze, but held his line in the face of numerous retaliatory strikes and demonstrations. The Muldoon government also had to deal with some racial problems, and with a brain drain of young New Zealanders to Australia and other foreign countries. In the 1980s, more than 30,000 Kiwis were leaving annually to seek better opportunities elsewhere. Muldoon shrugged – the average intelligence quotient of departing New Zealanders, he said, compared to the average IQ of Australians, meant the migration was "raising the collective IQ of both countries".

By 1975, Britain was taking only 22 percent of New Zealand's exports, with Australia,

tary majority until in mid-1984, with the defection of a National Party member, the prime minister called a snap election – and was soundly defeated by a restructured Labour Party. Labour captured 56 seats in the House of Representatives to National's 37 (with two going to the fledgling Social Credit party).

Led by David Lange, a former lawyer for the poor who at 41 became New Zealand's youngest Prime Minister of the 20th century. Labour pledged to set up a 320-km (200-mile) nuclear-free zone around the shores of New Zealand, and to re-negotiate the 33-year old Anzus security pact to force the United States to keep nuclear armaments out of New Zealand ports. David Lange resigned in 1989 and his deputy,

Geoffrey Palmer, took over as Prime Minister. Palmer resigned in early September 1990, almost two months before the national elections, and was succeeded by Foreign Minister Mike Moore.

New Zealand today sees its economic future as closely tied to Australia. A New-Zealand-Australia Free Trade Agreement (NAFTA) was signed in August 1965, came into effect in January the following year, ran for a 10-year period and was extended for another 10 years. It did not survive the second term. The aim of NAFTA was to set aside impediments to the expansion of mutually beneficial trade across the Tasman Sea. But the progressive reduction of duties on goods listed in an appendix to the agreement was subject to heavy pressure from

industrial interests in each country.

As a response to this pressure from industry, and as an inexorable move toward freer trade between Australia and New Zealand, a new agreement came into force on January 1, 1983. Called Closer Economic Relations (CER), it provides for a gradual but inevitable phasing out of import-export controls for trade between the two nations. Detailed in its approach, it provides for the phased removal of duties as well as the progressive liberalisation of all remaining quantitative restrictions and their total elimination by 1995.

While New Zealand will almost certainly remain in its economic crisis in the near future, economic union with Australia now seems inevitable. New Zealand delegates also took part in discussions on political union last century when Australia became a federation of states; right through to the turn of the 20th century, there was a body of opinion in New Zealand that favoured Australian state-hood. Now it is extremely unlikely.

There is some good news on the economic front. A kiwifruit-led resurgence of horticulture has begun to make a dramatic contribution to overseas earnings. A large natural-gas field off the west coast of Taranaki, the Maui field, is the basis of a petrochemical industry and a large energy source for the growing productivity of light industry. A number of small but economically viable oil fields have been located onshore in Taranaki and there is some confidence among geologists that large deposits will be found. In fact, the country has huge energy resources. Abundant hydro-electric sources are still being tapped and there are known recoverable reserves of nearly 3œ million tonnes of coal, most of it low in ash and sulphur and highly reactive.

If the diversification of markets for exports has developed well, the diversification of production has lagged. Animal products from the pastoral industry still represent more than 52 percent of the value of exports (though manufacture of woollen fabrics, carpets and yarns is increasing), and other agricultural products such as fruit, flowers, vegetables and grass seed, as well as timber products (including paper and wood pulp), mean this country is still largely dependent for its livelihood on primary production.

New Zealand remains one of the world's largest exporters of butter and cheese, wool and meat. More than half the butter and lamb exports go to Europe (with the Middle East the major new market for lamb); more than half the cheese is shipped to Japan and the United States; and three-quarters of the mutton to the Soviet Union. Wool remains an international commodity with few artificial trade barriers.

Tourism has become a valuable gatherer of foreign exchange. New Zealand is far from the high-density tourism routes of the world and is relatively expensive to reach. But as the value of the New Zealand dollar declined during the early 1980s, it became a low-cost destination.

Left, anti-nuclear sentiment, expressed here at the arrival of the US *Texas* in 1983, was certainly a factor in the election of the Labour Government in July 1984. **Above**, David Lange was Prime Minister between 1984 and 1989.

PEOPLE

The idea persists that the archetypal Kiwi is a country person – a farmer: dogs at heel, sandpaper hand holding a stick, face burnished by the nor'wester, eyes creased against the hard light of the afternoon as he peers into the hills for sheep to muster. Perhaps it is New Zealand's continuing dependence on the state of the international market for meat, wool, dairy and horticultural products that gives an outsider little reason to think otherwise. In reality, the New Zealander is an urbanite. More than 2 million of the 3.3 million New Zealanders live in or on the perimeter of major cities; there are nearly as many people in the Auckland urban area as in the South Island. Eight-five percent of New Zealanders live in towns of more than 1,000 people; in some rural areas hundreds of families living on their farms may be less than a half-hour away from a city of 50,000.

The majority of the Europeans (given the name *pakehas* by the Maori) who began to populate New Zealand, less than 200 years ago, were of British origin. Today they comprise about 90 percent of the population. That figure is misleading; Auckland is the largest Polynesian city in the world, with well over 100,000 Maori and other Pacific Islanders making their homes there. All over New Zealand a wide cross-section of other nationalities represents an indispensable ingredient in the Kiwi melting pot. Beginning with the Chinese in the last century and followed by Scandinavians, Germans, Dalmatians, Greeks, Italians, Lebanese, refugees from Nazi-occupied Europe and from more recent tragedies in Indochina, there has been a steady flow of immigrants into New Zealand.

Together, Maori, Pacific Islanders and *pakehas* are evolving in New Zealand a culture that is neither wholly Polynesian nor wholly Western, but an exciting amalgam of both – something that is distinctively New Zealand in character.

Many New Zealanders are undergoing an abrupt transmutation – culturally from Briton to American, and temperamentally from laid-back, do-it-yourself weekender to round-the-clock urbanite.

The causes, many and subtle, include economic and social adversity, the jet-age breakdown of isolation and remoteness, and the pervasive influence of TV.

New Zealand has had one of the least diverse population mixes of any country colonised during the great expansion of European colonialism in the 18th and 19th centuries. Settlement was predominantly organised and achieved by English and Scots, with some Irish sneaking in through the West Coast, mostly from Australia during the gold rush period, and through Auckland which has always been the most commercial and cosmopolitan of the cities.

There have been other pockets of immigrants, usually originating from Europe, but which have been completely absorbed within a generation. The exception is the large influx of Pacific Islanders during the past two decades who actually managed to beat the system of finding work, for a while during the affluent good times, that Pakehas didn't want to do. The Pacific Islanders have given colour and character to life in Auckland making it more a part of Polynesia.

The British Connection

While the population mix is predominantly Maori, English, Scottish and Pacific Island, since the middle of last century the ambience has been unremittingly British. Historian Keith Sinclair wrote:

"Ever since the late 19th century New Zealand has commonly been considered the most dutiful of Britain's daughters. It is a reputation which many New Zealanders, especially prime ministers intent on making an impression in London, or on securing commercial concessions, have fostered on every oratorical opportunity. Few Canadi-

ans, Australians or South Africans have cared to contest the claim ...."

Journalist and novelist David Ballantyne wrote a few years ago:

"New Zealand immigration policies through the years have been pretty shrewdly geared to ensuring that the country keeps its low-key image. God's Own country has no need of stirrers. The preference has always been for folk of British stock, meaning working-class and middle-class types from the Old Country – dependable, more likely to fit in than Italians and such like flighty

foreigners. Next preference has been for the Dutch, maybe because it was a Dutchman Abel Tasman, who first sighted New Zealand (in 1642), more likely because the phlegmatic Dutch don't play up. . . ."

In the lazy summer of New Zealand culture (about the middle of the century when the country moved without the slightest lurch into adulthood with the adoption of the Statute of Westminster 1947, which ended its status as a Dominion of Britain) there was more than a touch of xenophobia about Kiwis, who had formulated a set of aspirations and a fair measure of contempt for those of other peoples. One of of the most perceptive essays written about the country and its people, at

Preceding pages, Haka's group; paying tribute to New Zealand's landscape; the fair-haired girl is from the Slav community. **Left**, axemanship is put to the test. **Above**, memorable pin-up: she would have passed for a British festival queen.

about that time, came from James A. Michener in the preface of his New Zealand story in the *Return to Paradise* collection. The story, later made into a major Hollywood feature film, was "*Until They Sail,*" but the essay transfixed the New Zealand of the time with unerring skill and accuracy:

"The typical New Zealander wears grey flannel trousers, an expensive sleeveless sweater, and a trim sports coat. When he dresses up it's in a stiff, high-breasted dark suit with vest, which he never discards, even on sweltering days. He is quiet, modest, eager to defend his honour, and addicted to dreadful jokes…Along with the Spaniard, he is probably the most conservative white man still living…He is most unsentimental,

jawed chap" whose "behaviour under fire seems incredible," the only fighting man ever to win the Victoria Cross twice, Charles Upham.

The beginning of the jet-age was the first of many changes to affect New Zealand. At Mangere in 1965 the new Auckland International Airport was opened and the national carrier, TEAL (Tasman Empire Airways) changed its name to Air New Zealand and bought DC8 jets. With Auckland 1,900 km (1,180 miles) from Sydney and five times as far from any major Western city, New Zealanders previously had to embark on weeks-long ocean journeys in order to trace their cultural roots in Europe or the United States. Travel outside New Zealand, and Britain was invari-

which probably explains why there has been no first-rate art of any kind produced in New Zealand to date. Yet he can become maudlin if you mention the gallant All Blacks, (their) famous Rugby team (all-black jerseys with silver badges)…Few Americans appreciate the tremendous sacrifices made by New Zealand in the last two wars. Among the Allies she had the highest percentage of men in arms – much higher than the United States – the greatest percentage overseas, and the largest percentage killed…"

Michener said it could be claimed that the bravest soldier in each of the world wars was a New Zealander – Bernard Freyberg in the first, and in the second "a stumpy square-

ably the destination, involved such large distances that there had to be a friend or relative at the end of the journey. Just about the only ones to leave New Zealand in the two generations before World War II were those who went to the Middle East or France to fight in World War I.

In the 1950s a number of young people began to travel to Britain by sea in search of "OE" (overseas experience). Travelling back on the very ships which brought immigrants out, they stayed for maybe a year. The 1960s saw New Zealanders embarking on the mass overseas travel that has so deeply changed their attitudes and lifestyles. Going first to Australia or Fiji, Norfolk Island, New Caledonia and other nearby destinations, they now go in ever-increasing numbers to the United States and all over the world.

Until the end of the 1970s, New Zealanders going overseas were usually "ethnic" travellers; they were people going back to the homeland of their forebears – Britain. More New Zealanders go to the United States now than they do to Europe; the 100 percent increase in the number of Americans coming to New Zealand as either tourists or on business is one indication of this new relationship.

All this has led to an explosion of modernity. Whereas, in the 1960s, it was difficult to find a restaurant outside a hotel (and only hotel restaurants served wine then), there are now hundreds of ethnic restaurants in Auckland,

the range of goods those corner stores could sell was severely prescribed by legislation. Now shops are allowed to be open through Saturday and some are seeking Sunday licences as well.

Social Attitudes

Cosmopolitan influences, and the economic infrastructure which has broadened business opportunities, have dramatically re-oriented New Zealanders' social attitudes. Whereas for 150 years there was a national sense of egalitarianism, a levelling out of income and opportunity in a bid to gain widespread security, there has been a new belief spreading – that to hold its place in the world the country and its

Wellington, Christchurch and some of the smaller provincial cities. Wine, once regarded as "plonk" and never drunk regularly with meals, is today a thriving industry. In fact, New Zealand white wines now rank with the world's best and the quality of the reds is improving too.

Until the beginning of the 1980s, all shops, except some corner stores, were closed from Friday evening until Monday morning. And

Left, prized stock on parade at the 9th World Hereford Conference. **Above left,** something for the ladies, perhaps? **Above right,** a voice in the wilderness.

people must work harder and compete more fiercely, both on the domestic market and overseas, in a bid to achieve greater economic efficiency. This has changed the society from one in which everyone was considered entitled to a job and a share of the national cake into one in which unemployment is high and in which there is a growing division between the rich and the poor.

With more Maori unemployed, proportionately speaking, than Pakehas, social unrest, which sometimes assumes racial overtones, is greater than at any time since the land wars between the two races in the third quarter of the last century. This, in turn has brought a new volatility to national politics. The old and narrow division between the two political groupings, neither far from the centre, doesn't seem wide enough to contain the national aspirations anymore. New parties, however, blooming briefly in the discontent with the two main parties (National and Labour), give way when it seems they cannot articulate the confused aspirations of the dissidents.

Pacific Partners

The unrest and confusion began when Britain joined the European Economic Community and New Zealand was no longer an ancillary producer of the British economy, growing food and fibre from pastoral animals on the other side of the world. Exposed to the erratic

commodities markets of the world, Kiwis found they had never developed real trading expertise, and that they needed to do so quickly. This new sense of marketing and the new urge to compete have spread through a domestic market which had long slumbered in a kindly cost-plus world.

The cutting of the umbilical cord to Britain and the subsequent need to sell in other markets has led to cultural changes. Trade with New Zealand's traditional partner, Australia, has grown and business with North America has expanded year by year until it is now more important in many ways than trading with Europe. Major trading partners now are Japan, Singapore, Hong Kong and countries of the

Middle East. As a result, New Zealand seems to sit more comfortably in the Pacific these days, acknowledging its presence among the Polynesian islands, the peoples of Southeast Asia and those with the same roots in European culture, Australia and the United States. Both New Zealanders and Australians are becoming perceptibly more like Americans than people of the old Western world in dress, manner and in a full range of social mores.

If the indications are fulfilled, New Zealanders should make a strong contribution to this region, now that its orientation is to the Pacific and away from Europe. Since before the end of last century, when New Zealand-born Ernest Rutherford, a great scientist in the field of nuclear physics, left for Britain, a consistent trickle of people from this small country has gone to Europe and done gifted work for science, medicine and in many other forms of endeavour. Already New Zealand entertainers and film-makers are beginning to attract considerable attention around the Pacific rim, and in Australia expatriate Kiwis have been steadily emerging as leaders in the media and in business.

Change is always relative and there is much about New Zealand life at home that is still enviable. The weekend is not inviolate anymore but it is still a pleasant time for families, especially throughout the summer; and the long and leisurely Christmas break of about three weeks is a kind of relaxed southern outdoors fiesta. Although some people now choose to live in apartments in the inner cities – almost unheard of 25 years ago – most Kiwis still prefer a house, garden and a lawn to hold barbecue parties on.

As New Zealand faces the 1990s, Wally Hirsch – race relations conciliator (1986-1989) – believes the challenge for this country now is to realise we are moving away from a monocultural society to one of diverse cultures. "We should welcome the Maori renaissance and try to understand the Treaty of Waitangi and the recommendations made by the Waitangi Tribunal – and understanding will come only through education," he said, "Fear, anxiety, blame and guilt must be substituted; they have no place in improving race relations."

Reminders of links to what used to be called the "mother" country: horn player in the New Zealand Air Force Band (left), and a participant in Scottish tartan at the Stratford Centenary celebration (right).

Thirty years ago visitors could have mistaken New Zealand for a European country with native reservations. The cities and towns were overwhelmingly Pakeha in appearance and orientation. The Maori population was confined largely to remote rural settlements and the only contact tourists were likely to have with the indigenous people was in the resort centre Rotorua, where Maori culture could be seen.

By the 1980s all that had changed; Maori had surged into urban areas. Maori faces were as likely to be seen on busy city streets and in the work place as Pakeha ones. Maori were going into business and the professions in small but increasing numbers. Meeting houses were springing up where previously there had been only European dwellings and community facilities.

The features of 20th century Maori culture that can now be seen throughout New Zealand are a fusion of both Polynesian and Western ingredients. Maori wear European clothes, the vast majority speak English and many are active members of Christian churches. But those who identify with their Maori background do all these things in a distinctively Maori way. A Maori wedding, twenty-first birthday party, christening or funeral is quite different in character from that of the Pakeha counterpart. They will include speeches in Maori, Maori songs, Maori proverbs, and an openness about expressing feelings – joy, sorrow, anger – that one does not see to the same extent among New Zealanders of Anglo-Saxon origin.

Maori values, too, pulsate beneath the cloak of Western appearances. Concepts such as *tapu* (sacredness), its opposite, *noa, wairua* (things of the spirit) and *mana* (authority), all persist in modern Maori life. The fact that the country's two major races now live shoulder to shoulder means that non-Maori are having to show more respect than they displayed previously for Maori ritual, and for places that are *tapu* (sites of sacred objects, historic events or burials) according to Maori beliefs. Maori ceremonials – especially the *hui* (gathering), the *tangi* (mourning), and *karakia* (prayer) –

are increasingly honoured by Pakehas. Governments no longer try to impose Western values and institutions on them. Maori are no longer punished in schools for speaking their own languages.

The *hui* offers the most revealing and most moving glimpse of the Maori being Maori. It will usually be held on a *marae* (a courtyard in front of a meeting house) under the supervision of the *tangata whenua* or host tribe. Visitors are called on to the *marae* with a *karanga* – a long, wailing call that beckons the living and commemorates the dead. This is per-

formed by women only. Answering the call, the visitors enter the *marae* led by their own women, who are usually dressed in black. Then follows a pause and a *tangi* (ritual weeping) for the dead of both sides. This is succeeded by the *mihi* (speeches) of welcome and reply, which will be made by male elders. At the end of each speech the orator's companions get to their feet and join him for a *waiata* (song), usually a lament. These formalities over, the visitors come forward and *hongi* (press noses) with the locals and are absorbed into the ranks of *tangata whenua* for the remainder of the function.

The *hui* will then be taken up with public and private discussion of matters of local, tribal

Left, the late Sir James Henare, a noted Maori leader. **Right**, warm welcome smile from a young Maori.

and national Maori interest, especially land issues (many earlier instances of European seizure of Maori land are currently under official investigation). It will also include community eating, singing and religious services. The participants sleep together in the large meeting house or hall, where further discussion is likely to go on until the early hours of the morning.

Even the food served on such occasions is likely to be different from that which Europeans would serve: meat and vegetables are steamed and cooked in a *hangi* or earth oven. There will be a preponderance of seafood, with delicacies such as shellfish, *kina* (sea egg), eel and dried shark. Fermented corn is a speciality, as is *titi* (mutton bird). The bread offered is

The extent and variety of his contributions to Maoridom make him a figure of enormous significance. By the late 1920s, knighted and made Minister of Native Affairs, Ngata had devised legislation to develop Maori land, established a caring school at Rotorua and initiated a work programme for the building of meeting houses and other Maori community facilities.

Working closely with Ngata to implement national policy at a local level was a group of community leaders such as Princess Te Puea Herangi of Waikato (1883-1952). Te Puea was for 40 years the effective force behind the Maori King Movement, which had grown out of the Maori-Pakeha wars of the 1860s. She raised the morale of her people, revived their

likely to be *rewena* (a scone-like loaf) or another variety similar to fried doughnuts. Far more than in Pakeha society, eating together is a ritual means of sharing common concerns and communicating goodwill. Acceptance of such hospitality is as important as being prepared to offer it.

A Maori Knight and A Maori Princess

If there has been one person more responsible than any other for the survival of Maori culture into modern times, it was the great parliamentarian from the East Coast of the North Island, Sir Apirana Ngata (1874-1950).

cultural activities, built a model village at Ngaruawahia which became the nerve centre of the King Movement, and established thousands of Waikato Maori back on farm land. She also won a wide degree of Maori and Pakeha acceptance for the institution of the Maori kingship, which had previously been regarded with suspicion outside Waikato. Turangawaewae Marae at Ngaruawahia became and remains a focal point for national Maori gatherings. Today Te Puea's greatniece, Queen Te Atairangikaahu, keeps the movement alive and commands the direct allegiance of about 30,000 Maori and the respect of the remaining 270,000.

Further consolidation for the Maori people

came with the election of a Labour Government towards the end of the Great Depression in the 1930s. Labour's welfare programme did more to lift Maori standards of living and health than any previous measures and ensured the physical survival of the Maori race. The Maori electorate acknowledged this fact by returning only Labour Members of Parliament from that time.

Maori-Pakeha Relations

Following World War II, however, there was a major shift in the balance of Maori-Pakeha relations. Previously the majority of Pakehas did not know any Maori personally and had never seen them in indigenous environments. The decline in rural employment coinciding with a rapid expansion of secondary industry in urban areas brought Maori into the cities in increasing numbers. In 1945, for example, more than 80 percent of Maori still lived in rural settlements. By the 1980s the figure was less than 10 percent. For the first time, Maori and Pakeha New Zealanders had to live alongside one another.

This new relationship brought difficulties. There was a degree of anti-Maori discrimination in some areas of employment and accommodation. Most migrants to the city had had no preparation for the life and many initially floundered. Some youngsters born in the new environment, feeling neither truly Maori nor Pakeha, reacted in a strongly anti-social manner and the Maori crime rate increased.

Over a generation, however, these problems have been dealt with patiently by members of both races. Citizens' advice bureaux and social workers have helped adults with matters such as budgeting and legal difficulties. Legal aid and translation facilities are now available through the courts. The education system has made a concerted effort to promote Maori language and aspects of Maori culture while a Race Relations Office has been set up under

the Justice Department to monitor and correct instances of racial discrimination.

Slowly, as a result of these measures, Maori and Pakeha have been learning to live alongside one another as amicably as they once did when racial harmony was the result of geographical separation. Many Pakehas are learning to speak Maori and to participate in functions on *maraes* in town and country. Maori writers such as Witi Ihimaera and Patricia Grace are skilfully communicating Maori experience to non-Maori audiences. Maori singers and musicians of the calibre of Dame Kiri Te Kanawa are heard nationally and internationally and Maori athletes dominate several sports.

Maori traditions and culture are alive and well in New Zealand. Left, a formal Maori greeting. Above, bravado on the Maori war canoe.

Two Polynesian migrations, more than 1,000 years apart, have had a marked influence on the culture of Aotearoa. The first saw the arrival of the ancestors of the Maori in sailing canoes, after epic voyages from a homeland in Polynesia known as Hawaiki. The arrival of Polynesians from various homelands scattered through the Pacific from Tonga in the west to the Cook Islands in the east represents the second wave of migrants.

The second Polynesian migration actually began in the mid-1800s when Pacific islanders were brought to New Zealand for training by

Niue, the Tokelaus and Tonga. The migration has had profound social, economic and political consequences for the islands which the migrants have left behind. More Niueans live abroad than in Niue itself and it is questionable whether the country can remain a viable national entity if migration continues at the same rate. Remittances from Samoan migrants living abroad have contributed to a deterioration of the Western Samoan economy. People have chosen to set aside the risky and often unprofitable business of tropical agriculture and wait instead for money from New Zealand, or bet-

missionaries. The pace increased after World War II as labour shortages beset New Zealand's planned industrial expansion. New Zealand governments looked to their territories and former territories in the Pacific and located a source of readily available and enthusiastic labour.

The first migrants were often people who had worked with New Zealanders in the various islands during the colonial period or who had served with New Zealanders in World War II. When these people were settled so they brought others of their families and forged the first links in a chain which continues to the present day and extends into virtually every village of the Cook Islands, Western Samoa,

ter still, the chance to go to New Zealand to work.

Migration is also having a serious impact on the islands to which they have come. Over the years the various groups have grown steadily; there was a stable population in the late 1980s of about 97,500 Pacific Islanders in New Zealand, mainly Western Samoans and Cook Islanders.

A Major Transition

Most of the migrants settle in urban centres in the hope of finding employment. This has meant a major transition from life in the largely rural village setting in which they had lived in the islands. Auckland, with its large-scale industry, has been the main centre for settlement, while Wellington has attracted smaller numbers to its industrial areas. A small proportion of migrants have gone to Kawerau, Rotorua and Tokoroa in the central North Island to work in the timber-processing industry.

Concentrations of Pacific Islanders in particular residential and occupational areas have developed and have highlighted the presence of these people. The most conspicuous signs are the growth of large numbers of new churches. Just as important, however, is the growth of a retail industry supplying such things as salted meat and coconut cream, fabrics and fish nets. Also, a small but important

industries and have influenced the shape and style of some sectors of industry.

Early migrants established reputations as keen and reliable employees. As vacancies occurred they sought permission to have close relatives considered and the concentration began. The possibility of securing positions for more relatives leads to a high level of internal discipline as all try to ensure opportunities for kinsmen. As Pacific Islanders are promoted they become the centre of a network which screens and places recommended kin and are able to use this position to recognise and encourage high standards among fellow workers.

Pacific Islanders are becoming increasingly interested in moving into entrepreneurial ac-

group of Pacific Island professionals has grown up whose practices are primarily geared to serving Pacific Island clients. The racks of cassette tapes of Pacific Island music blended with the sounds of reggae and rock, are another reminder of the presence of this ethnic group and represent the tip of a growing musical industry.

Successive chains of migration have also concentrated the new arrivals in particular

Left, couple from Cook Islands who are New Zealand citizens and British subjects. **Above**, Cook Islanders commemorate the fighting in World War II with an Anzac Day parade in Avarua.

tivity with the result that small businesses are springing up in areas as diverse as cane furniture manufacturing, engineering, fishing and tax consultancy. It is likely that this trend will continue apace as the economy picks up. Pacific Islanders, studies have shown, regard education highly and many migrants are taking advantage of training opportunities and hope to be promoted or to move into their own business.

Adults with unskilled and semi-skilled work are more ambitious for their young children; those who have succeeded are cited as models of what can be achieved by Pacific Islanders.

Other New Zealanders, in an attempt to

label the migrants, have assumed that they are a homogeneous group and have lumped them together as "islanders". In fact, the various groups have evolved traditions and customs over many generations, and regard themselves as distinct from each other, have resisted this tendency to be so conveniently labelled.

Accommodating the Realities of Life

The cultures and languages of the various groups have been transformed to accommodate the realities of life in a society dominated by wage labour and a cash nexus. Weddings, birthday parties and other ceremonies, which in the islands were leisurely events which gave people both the opportunity to get together and

small communities as facts of life must now be taught to children brought up in large cities in which that culture and language appears to be of peripheral importance. Not all parents lament the loss of ethnic awareness in their children and some have decided that their children's interests are best served by the language and culture of their hosts. Still others have encouraged their children to become familiar with both cultures.

Several factors seem certain to shape the future of the diverse Pacific Island communities. As the generation already born and raised in New Zealand comes to participate in community leadership and organisation, it is hoped they will draw on their twin heritage and forge new versions of old cultures. High levels of

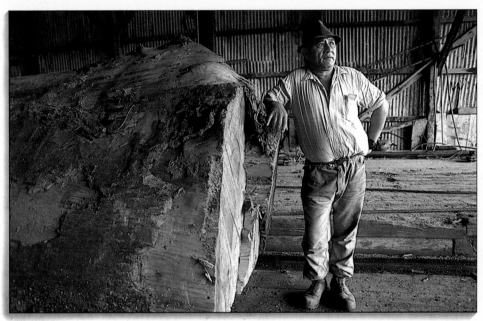

to renew old ties, have been condensed. Speeches, centrepieces of island-based events, have been shortened and as a result have been stripped of much of their esoteric knowledge and allusion. Home visits and shared meals have also had to be shortened or even dispensed with in favour of a telephone conversation.

While all of the groups have had to accommodate in these, and other, ways to a mainland lifestyle, significant differences remain between the cultures and lifestyles of the Pacific Island communities. Parents, in striving to foster an awareness of their culture in their children, face a difficult struggle; the culture and language which the parents learned in

intermarriage between Pacific Islanders and New Zealanders may hasten this process. The culture of the Pacific Islands will not die. The young, with growing confidence born of citizenship and with more vigour than their parents, will demand from New Zealand society a recognition of their right to nurture their own traditions. In the process they will contribute to a richer and more individual New Zealand culture.

Above, taking a break from heavy timber work. Right, three boys of Rarotonga island stand at the starting point of one of the early Polynesian migrations.

82

The sign reads:

NGATANGIIA PASSAGE

FROM THIS POINT
IN ABOUT THE YEAR 1350
THE GREAT POLYNESIAN
CANOE VOYAGE TO NEW ZEALAND
(AOTEAROA) SET FORTH

A few years ago in the suburb of Newtown in the capital city, Wellington, a multiracial class of nine-year-olds was showing how much they had learnt about the local Maori culture. Assimo, Irene, Maya, Sealli, Sharmily ... everybody had a try at talking about Maori foods such as *kumara, puha* and *pipis*. Maori action songs were performed, a Samoan boy was elected class chief and an Indian boy gave the best rendition of an ancient Maori. Then two newly arrived Russian girls, knowing nothing about things Maori, told Russian fairy stories instead.

In the same suburb, a generation ago, Elizabeth Raizis grew up speaking Greek. She ate Greek too. While the other kids had sandwiches spread with marmite and slices of cheese or sultanas, Elizabeth would go to school with her bag stuffed with olives and feta cheese and Greek pastries dripping with nuts and honey. The other kids held their noses and called her "garlic breath" and ran off laughing. Her only friend was a similarly ostracised Russian girl and the two practised their new language, English, on each other. Today, xenophobia, that evocative Greek word, is less in evidence.

Inner-city suburbs like Newtown and Grey Lynn are cheap and handy places where immigrants first congregate and give shape to the society to come. It would be impossible to find a school in the whole country with a more international roll call than the one in Newtown: Samoans, Niueans, Cook Islanders, Maori, Greeks, Indians, Chinese, Russians, Chileans, Hungarians, Italians, Rumanians, Tongans, Dutch, Turks, Lithuanians, Lebanese, Pitcairn Islanders, Zambians, Danish, Malays as well as the descendants of the British referred to by the Maori as *pakeha*.

Gold Rush

New Zealand society last century was made up of white Anglo-Saxon Protestants; its "W.A.S.P." sting was sharpened and then blunted first from conflict and then by cooperation with the Catholic French clergy and the Catholic Irish labourers. French is still one of the most popular foreign language options in New Zealand schools, one effect perhaps of the part played by French nuns and priests in the education of the Irish Catholic labourers who flooded into Auckland and, during the gold-rushes, to the West Coast and the southern part of South Island. Gold was a powerful magnet but the British were not happy about the arrival of the rebellious Irish. The Irish became concentrated on the West Coast and accounted for 25 percent of the population. Their pubs and their rough, brawling but hospitable image is still in evidence today.

Feeling between Irish Protestants and Irish Catholics, at first, ran high. The trial of a Catholic priest and an Irish editor, accused of treason for stirring up Fenian feelings of rebellion among the West-Coast miners, resulted in each being sentenced to a month in jail and was the culmination of a number of nasty encounters between these two religious factions.

The Irish, having been absorbed this century into the *pakeha* mainstream, were successful in pubs and politics right from the beginning. None had more of the gift of the gab than West-Coast orator Richard John Seddon who went on to become the country's most pugnacious and populist prime minister – thought Robert David Muldoon, of Irish-Liverpudlian extrac-

Left, traditional dances and ethnic costumes survive in the Kiwi melting pot. **Right**, Thai vendor of rattanware takes stock.

tion, challenged this position before his defeat in July 1984.

Seddon launched his career by attacking the Chinese miners. "From a race point of view," ran his maiden speech, "they are undesirable." Seddon's legislation restricted their entry into New Zealand and denied them old-age pensions. Those Chinese who did not strike it rich enough to pay their way out of this hostile land settled unobtrusively in inner cities where they moved slowly from laundry shops and Chinese restaurants (which the Irish police raided for gambling and opium) into the professions and into successful businesses. Today most of the 15,000 Chinese are in Auckland and Wellington, the latter community having built a Chinese Anglican community centre near the

In contrast to this were the Scandinavians, numbering more than 10,000, who cut down the forests of the central North Island and settled in places they called Dannevirke and Norsewood. They slipped quietly into the monoculture, as did the 1,000 Swiss dairy farmers on the other side of the island.

Last century a community of 5,000 or so Germans were the most popular of the non-British immigrants and the South Island in particular became dotted with little white Lutheran churches. Two world wars encouraged some to change their names, although this did not always save them from incarceration as prisoners of war on Somes Island in the middle of Wellington's harbour.

The Dalmatians, who, also at the end of the

Embassy of the People's Republic of China.

The Jews encountered no official discrimination and Jewish traders were among the leading citizens in the main centres. Two early and two recent mayors of Auckland were Jewish. In the 1870s Jewish prime minister Julius Vogel borrowed money from his London friends, the Rothschilds, to finance the country's great leap forward, bringing in 100,000 immigrants from Europe to create road and rail links through New Zealand's rugged terrain.

There were some failures however. The Italians entered the country only to find themselves dumped in marshes to be criticised later by government officials for being lazy.

last century, came to avoid conscription into the hated Austro-Hungarian army and to dig *kauri* gum in the north of North Island, were the only other ethnic minority to find themselves the victims of legislation. Again it was Seddon's work who, likening the Dalmatians to locusts ravaging the British settlers lands, reserved the best gumfields for the British.

Despite this treatment, the Dalmatians proved better gumdiggers than the British. When the gum was exhausted they moved to Auckland and established the country's wine industry, perhaps the single most significant ethnic contribution. Victimisation continued though they survived in the face of accusations of seducing British girls on the "vile, degrading and demoralising concoction" that came from the vineyards, and of being taken for the enemy in World War I.

One of New Zealand's best-known vineyards comes from a Lebanese family, the Corbans. The nation's 5,000 Lebanese are prominent in civic affairs and top business and professions.

Greeks and Italians enjoy much higher profiles perhaps as a result of their restaurants, which, after the cheap chop-suey houses of the past, have probably made the biggest impact on New Zealand palates. The Greeks, arriving during the gold-rush era in chain family migrations, settled first in windy Wellington. Considerations of community outweighed those of climate; the city's magnificent Greek Ortho-

from Gujurat province also had an impact on the nation's palate but, unlike the Chinese, they vociferously complained about prejudice and shamed the authorities out of thumb-printing proposals. Another strand to the Indian presence is indicated by a Sikh temple outside Hamilton. In Auckland, several thousand Muslims have established themselves and are building an Islamic Centre.

Indochinese refugees, numbering more than 3,000 and temporarily quartered in outer Auckland, are not the first refugees to come to New Zealand. In 1944 Prime Minister Peter Fraser's wife, Janet, sponsored 733 Polish children from Nazi-occupied Europe. They were followed by Jews, Czechs, Ukranians, Russians, Latvians, Lithuanians, Estonians

dox church is one result of the several thousand Greeks who followed and one reason, perhaps, why many Greeks come back to Wellington to retire.

The 3,000 Italians also settled mainly in Wellington as fishermen. Their fishing boats at anchor in the suburb of Island Bay, with evocative names like *Michelangelo* and *San Antonio,* have won for the area the nickname of "Little Italy." Not surprising, the 10,000 Indians who came to New Zealand in the 1920s

Left and **above**, a visitor to New Zealand can play an interesting ethnic guessing game at just about any street corner.

and Hungarians fleeing Soviet forces in later years.

The single largest influx after the British was the arrival, after World War II, of 30,000 Dutch. Despite initial objections that they worked too hard and spoke a foreign "lingo" they have fitted effortlessly into the society, giving Kiwis overnight a taste for coffee and pastries.

Wine bars, pizza parlours, delicatessens and ethnic restaurants are popping up all over a country that only two decades ago was dedicated to roast leg of lamb and strawberry pavlova with, for the men, all the beer they could down, and for the ladies, one (and *never* more than one) sherry each.

People aside – albeit friendly people worth knowing – it's places in New Zealand that nudge your sense of wonder, that make you take a quick breath with a sense that "Here and only here can I experience this." Milford Track with the Sound at its end, the pristine silver dazzle of the Southern Lakes, the bush-wrapped solitude of Lake Waikaremoana, the boiling surprises of the thermal regions ... they all have pulled superlatives from the mouths of even the most-travelled visitors.

Authors Rudyard Kipling, Anthony Trollope and Robert Louis Stevenson paid tribute to the loveliness of the landscape. James A. Michener wrote in *Return to Paradise* in 1951 that "New Zealand is probably the most beautiful place on earth" with "natural beauty difficult to believe." Thirty years later, in a magazine article entitled "The Memoirs of a Pacific Traveller," he listed Milford Sound as "The Most Stirring Sight."

It has been like that from the beginning, this sense of place. The Maori story of the creation reveals that land and human being are one, flesh and clay from the same source material. Maori emotional attachment to place is profound.

The first Europeans, 20,000 km from the tailored communities of Europe they still called home, tried at first to remake the face of the countryside into a Britain look-alike. They cut and burned the forest and sowed grass. But when they had the leisure to look around, they realised that packed into their small new country was a whole world of diverse and dramatic scenery.

The first place to attract world attention was Lake Rotomahana, with what were known as the Pink and White Terraces along her shore. The terraces were formed from silica deposits as water from boiling pools washed down the steep shore of the lake. Tourists could bathe in the cooler pools near the bottom of the Pink Terraces: "It is a spot," wrote Trollope, "for intense sensual enjoyment." The terraces were all brutally destroyed one night in 1886 when nearby Mount Tawawera exploded.

The spas and hot pools of the North Island earned an early reputation for their curative powers. In 1901, the government hired an official balneologist and formed a tourist department, the first government-sponsored tourism promotion organisation in the world.

The thermal regions today still draw enormous attention from travellers. But nowadays – in a world packed with ever-increasing numbers of people in dense and clogged cities – it is mainly the unsullied, uncluttered landscape, the sense of space and timelessness, that makes a visit to New Zealand's outposts of scenic beauty a sort of purification rite.

Preceding pages: stopover on icy ground; keeping watch over a sea of sheep; a lone ship cruises through calm waters, amidst the natural splendour of New Zealand.

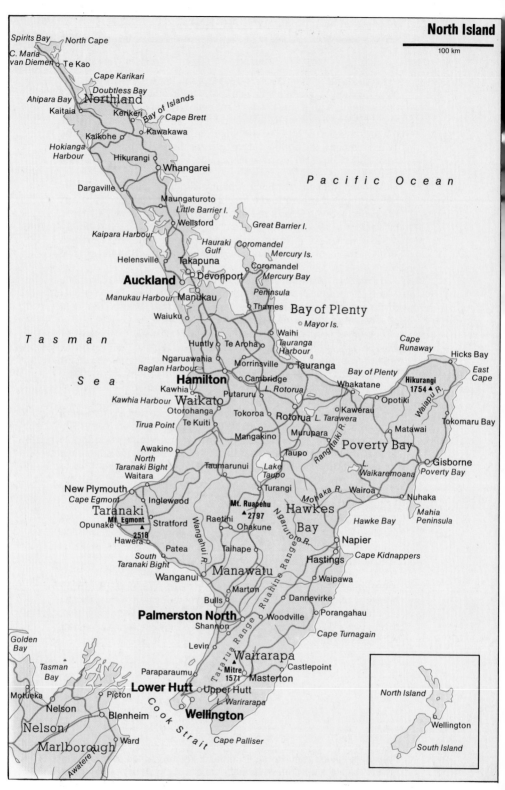

Spirits Bay
North Cape
C. Maria
van Diemen
Te Kao
Cape Karikari
Doubtless Bay
Ahipara Bay
Northland
Kaitaia
Kerikeri
Bay of Islands
Cape Brett
Kaikohe
Kawakawa
Hokianga
Harbour
Hikurangi
Dargaville
Whangarei

Pacific Ocean

Maungaturoto
Little Barrier I.
Wellsford
Great Barrier I.
Kaipara Harbour
Helensville
Hauraki
Gulf
Coromandel
Mercury Is.
Takapuna
Coromandel
Auckland
Devonport
Mercury Bay
Manukau Harbour
Manukau
Peninsula
Waiuku
Thames
Bay of **Plenty**
Mayor Is.
Waihi
Huntly
Te Aroha
Tauranga
Harbour
Cape
Runaway
Hicks Bay
Ngaruawahia
Morrinsville
Tauranga
Bay of Plenty
Whakatane
Hikurangi
East
Cape
Raglan Harbour
Hamilton
Cambridge
1754 ▲
Waiapu R.
Kawhia
Waikato
Putaruru
L. Rotorua
Kawerau
Opotiki
Kawhia Harbour
Otorohanga
Tokoroa
Rotorua
L. Tarawera
Tokomaru Bay
Tirua Point
Te Kuiti
Matawai
Mangakino
Murupara
Poverty Bay
Awakino
Taumarunui
Taupo
Rangitaiki R.
North
Taranaki Bight
Waitara
Taumarunui
Lake
Taupo
L.
Waikaremoana
Gisborne
Poverty Bay
New Plymouth
Turangi
Wairoa
Nuhaka
Cape Egmont
Inglewood
Mt. Ruapehu
Mohaka R.
Mahia
Peninsula
Taranaki
Mt. Egmont
Raetihi
▲ 2797
Hawkes
Opunake
▲
Stratford
Ohakune
Bay
Hawke Bay
Napier
2518
Wanganui R.
Ngaruroro R.
Hawera
Taihape
Patea
South
Taranaki Bight
Wanganui
Manawatu
Napier
Hastings
Cape Kidnappers
Marton
Waipawa
Bulls
Dannevirke
Ruahine Range
Palmerston North
Woodville
Porangahau
Shannon
Cape Turnagain
Golden
Bay
Levin
Wairarapa
Tasman
Bay
Paraparaumu
Mitre
Castlepoint
1571
Masterton
Tararua Range
Motueka
Lower Hutt
Upper Hutt
Nelson
Picton
L. Wairarapa
Blenheim
Wellington
Nelson
Cook Strait
Marlborough
Ward
Cape Palliser
Awatere

North Island

Wellington

South Island

Tasman

Sea

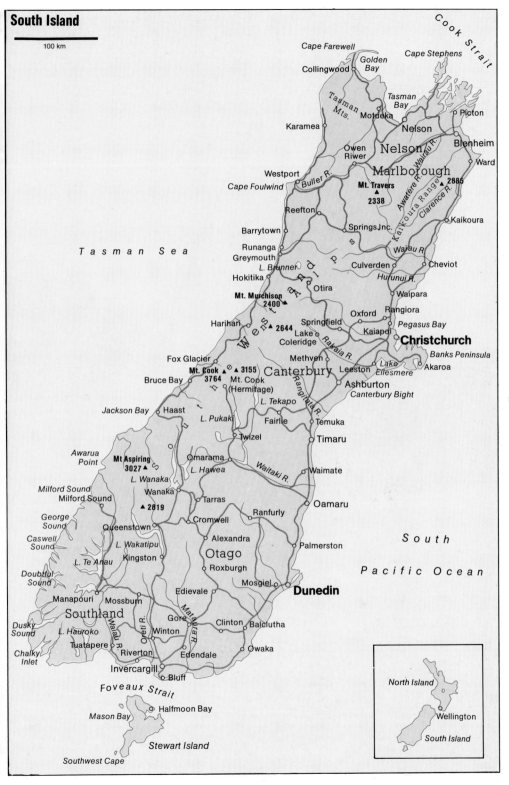

South Island

100 km

Cook Strait

Cape Farewell
Collingwood
Golden Bay
Cape Stephens

Tasman Mts.
Tasman Bay
Motdeka
Picton
Karamea
Nelson
Owen Riwer
Nelson
Blenheim
Westport
Marlborough
Ward
Cape Foulwind
Buller R.
Mt. Travers
2338
Awatere R.
Wairau R.
Kaikoura Range
Clarence R.
2885
Reefton
Springs Jnc.
Kaikoura
Barrytown
Waiau R.
Tasman Sea
Runanga
Greymouth
L. Brunner
Culverden
Cheviot
Hokitika
Otira
Hurunui R.
Waipara
Mt. Murchison
2400
Springfield
Oxford
Rangiora
Harihari
2644
Lake Coleridge
Kaiapoi
Pegasus Bay
Christchurch
Fox Glacier
Methven
Leeston
Lake Ellesmere
Banks Peninsula
Akaroa
Bruce Bay
Mt. Cook
3764
3155
Mt. Cook (Hermitage)
Canterbury
Ashburton
Canterbury Bight
Jackson Bay
Haast
L. Tekapo
Rangitata R.
L. Pukaki
Fairlie
Temuka
Twizel
Timaru
Mt Aspiring
3027
Omarama
Waitaki R.
Waimate
Awarua Point
L. Hawea
L. Wanaka
Wanaka
2819
Tarras
Oamaru
Milford Sound
Milford Sound
Cromwell
Ranfurly
George Sound
Queenstown
Alexandra
Palmerston
South
Caswell Sound
L. Wakatipu
Kingston
Otago
Roxburgh
Pacific Ocean
L. Te Anau
Mosgiel
Dunedin
Doubtful Sound
Manapouri
Mossburn
Edievale
Dusky Sound
Southland
Oreti R.
Gore
Clinton
Balclutha
L. Hauroko
Winton
Mataura R.
Tuatapere
Waiau R.
Riverton
Edendale
Owaka
Chalky Inlet
Invercargill
Bluff
Foveaux Strait
Mason Bay
Halfmoon Bay
Stewart Island
Southwest Cape

North Island
Wellington
South Island

97

AUCKLAND: CITY OF SAILS

To Aucklanders it is the "City of Sails" or the "Queen City," the biggest and brightest metropolis in New Zealand.

Some immodest residents may claim "New Zealand ends at the Bombay Hills," about 40 km (25 miles) south of the city. While this statement is made tongue-in-cheek, it effectively summarises the sentiments of many of the 922,000 inhabitants – that everything they need can be found within the boundaries of the Auckland region. For such smug souls, the rest of the country does not exist.

To underprivileged Kiwis living in New Zealand's *wop-wops* (provincial backcountry), and especially those in the capital city of Wellington, Auckland is "The Big Smoke" and "Sin City," where people are preoccupied with the three b's: beaches, boats and barbecues. The allegation contains more than an element of truth, but who can blame Aucklanders? They happen to be blessed with two beautiful harbours, scores of safe swimming beaches, a coastline dotted with secluded offshore islands, sophisticated city living and a summer climate that insists on outdoor life.

Is it any wonder Aucklanders desert their homes in droves at every available opportunity to head for the nearest beach or boat harbour, armed with battered barbecue sets and polystyrene "chilly bins" packed full with ice-cold beer?

Water, Water Everywhere

This agreeable, aquatic lifestyle has largely been decreed by the city's geographical situation within the North Island's Hauraki Gulf. Apart from slender necks of land to the west and south, Auckland is surrounded by water and the natives love it. They paddle in it, swim in it, surf on it, sail on it, ski on it, dive in it and fish in it.

The city is bounded by the Waitemata Harbour in the north and east, by the Manukau Harbour to the south and west. Just outside Waitemata Harbour, Hauraki Gulf is one of the most favoured small-boat sailing playgrounds anywhere.

Within one hour's drive of the city centre there are 102 mainland beaches and, while these beaches may appear to be sparsely populated to most overseas visitors, Auckland's "boat people" can seek total solitude in the hundreds of sandy bays nestled in 23 offshore islands in the Gulf. To celebrate this natural, marine playground, Auckland employs the greatest number of pleasure boats per capita of any coastal city in the world. A conservative estimate puts the total number of yachts, launches and powerboats at between 60,000 and 70,000; one for every four homes in the Greater Auckland area.

Fittingly, the sporting highlight of the year is the Auckland Anniversary Day Regatta, held annually towards the end of January, in which up to 1,000 sail-boats ranging from two-metre yachts to 30-metre keelers compete on the Waitemata Harbour.

Equally spectacular is "The Round-the-Bays Run" held annually in March in which up to 80,000 joggers (one in 12 Aucklanders) "run for fun" over a 10.5-km (6.5-mile) course from Victoria Park along the waterfront to Saint Heliers Bay.

Preceding pages, Coruba Cup Series yacht race in Auckland Harbour. **Left,** aerial view of downtown Auckland. **Right,** Round-the-Bays Run.

The Guinness Book of Records lists the race as having more participants than any other single athletic event in the world.

The regatta and the run symbolise much of what Auckland offers – thousand of sails and outdoor runners all competing under a clear, blue sky against a backdrop of sparkling water, sandy beaches and green rolling hills.

The Auckland isthmus itself was formed dynamically through the geologically recent eruption of 60 volcanoes, the oldest 50,000 years ago and the youngest – the bush-clad offshore island of Rangitoto – blasted from the sea only 750 years ago. Just two centuries ago, Rangitoto's last blast buried a Maori settlement on the adjoining island of Motutapu. Some speculate that the island, only 8 km (5 miles) from downtown Auckland, is only slumbering and will one day again burst into life. But experts believe Auckland's volcanoes were gentle members of their breed; if Rangitoto did erupt it would probably make a nice tourist attraction rather than a fiery holocaust.

Human habitation of Auckland has a no less turbulent history. Ancestors of the

Maori are believed to have arrived around A.D. 800 and settled on the offshore islands of the Hauraki Gulf after journeying from eastern Polynesia. Traditions of the Maori tribes tell the visitor of incessant warfare and bloodshed as the population expanded.

Auckland's waterways assumed tremendous strategic importance as "canoe highways." At one time or another, every volcanic cone in Auckland was the site of a fortified *pa* or Maori village. Some vantage points like One Tree Hill and Mount Eden still bear the evidence of a system of terraces along which wooden palisades were erected; the *pa* on these hills may have boasted hundreds of warriors 200 years ago.

"Tamaki of 100 Lovers"

It was the bloody intertribal conflicts that gave Auckland its early Maori name, *Tamaki*, the word for "battle." The isthmus was also called, rather charmingly, *Tamaki makau rau* – "Battle of 100 lovers." This poetic description had absolutely nothing to do with love and romance but accurately portrayed *Tamaki*

102

as a very desirable region longed for and fought over by many tribes.

Events leading to the British settlement of Auckland began with the visit of the adventurous missionary, Samuel Marsden, in 1820. Marsden was aboard the sailing ship *Coromandel*, which ventured into the Hauraki Gulf seeking masts and spars. While timber was being felled, the intrepid preacher covered about 900 km (some 550 miles) along rough tracks, by whaleboat and in canoes offered by the friendly Maori of Mokoia village, near the site of the present Auckland suburb of Panmure. Marsden is credited with being the first European to cross the Auckland isthmus (November 9 and 10, 1820).

The last recorded tribal battle in Auckland was in 1827, then the Ngati Whatua Maori attacked the Ngapuhi tribe and seized control of the territory. The fighting had reduced the Maori population such that 13 years later, on October 20, 1840, the British found it much easier to win Auckland from the fierce Ngati Whatua. They purchased the area now comprising the heart of Auckland city for a shopping list of groceries and hardware: 50 blankets, 20 trousers, 20 shirts, 20 waistcoats, 10 caps, four casks of tobacco, one box of pipes, 100 yards of gown material, 10 iron pots, one bag of sugar, one sack of flour, 20 hatchets and a cash sum of £50 sterling, with another £6 paid the following year. Their prize: 1,200 hectares (3,000 acres) covering three bays from Freemans Bay to Parnell and inland to Mount Eden. Today just one acre of land in downtown Auckland is worth at least NZ$12 million.

Plonked ignominiously on a traffic island in downtown Auckland, at the entrance to **King's Wharf**, is a piece of rock and a greening metal inscription marking Auckland's birth on September 18, 1840. The shabby memorial is hardly a tourist attraction, but nonetheless, it marks the spot where Auckland's founder and New Zealand's first governor, Captain William Hobson, declared the settlement to be the capital of the country.

On a point about 30 metres (100 feet) above the plaque, but long since demolished during harbour reclamation, the Union Jack was hoisted up a flagpole. Those assembled drank toasts and cheered while two naval ships in the harbour saluted with cannons. The first

Historic Queen Street.

Auckland Regatta then took place, comprising a race for Maori canoes and two for rowing boats from the anchored ships.

A pioneer settler of the time described the settlement as consisting of "a few tents and huts and a sea of fern stretching as far as the eye could see."

Urban Sprawl

Today there is a sea of suburbs stretching as far as the eye can see. It's no accident that Auckland and Los Angeles have sister city status – both are gateways to their respective nations and both sprawl over huge areas.

Auckland and its urban area occupy 1,016 sq km (378 sq miles) and are spread 80 km (50 miles) along the coast from Whangaparaoa and Torbay in the north, to Papakura and Drury in the south. This is partially due to the Kiwi's penchant for a house and garden on a "quarter-acre section" (lot) and the abundance of easy building land. On the positive side, this has created a decentralised city with plenty of wide, open spaces; few highrise apartment blocks; and outlying communities served by numerous shopping centres and the satellite cities of North Shore City in the north, Waitemata City in the west and Manukau City in the south. Such disseminated settlement once prompted an irreverent mayor of Wellington to slate Auckland in a scurrilous magazine interview as "a desperate collection of little villages."

From the tourist's viewpoint, Auckland's sprawl has not made it the easiest place to stroll around, with the exception of the central city.

Taxis are not cheap. One of the most economical deals is the Auckland Regional Council's "Bus-About" ticket which takes a visitor almost anywhere in the region – to Waiwera in the north, Helensville in the west, Panmure in the east and Manukau City in the south.

"Bus-About" tickets are valid for one day and can be purchased from bus drivers. A booklet detailing attractions such as museums, beaches, parks and historic buildings also includes explanations about which bus to catch to reach them. It is available from the ARC Bus Information Centre at 131 Hobson Street in the central city.

Alternatively, daily coach tours leave the city on sightseeing excursions ranging from three to eight hours in duration with commentaries en route about places of interest. Information about various tours and rental car rates can be obtained from the Auckland Visitors' Centre in Aotea Square, half-way up Queen Street, or the New Zealand Tourist and Publicity Office in Lower Queen Street.

Paua and Possum

Lower Queen Street is Auckland's "Golden Mile," offering the best range of shopping in New Zealand. Souvenir and sheepskin shops sell hand-made woollen garments. Maori carvings, greenstone (jade) ornaments, *paua* (abalone) shell jewellery, opossum fur coats and woolly car-seat covers. Queen Street is complemented by arcades and side streets containing traders in antiques, rare books, stamps, second-hand jewellery, New Zealand paintings, pottery, crafts and assorted knick-knacks.

Kiwis are a sporty mob and sports shops can hold intriguing items like gaudy New Zealand trout flies, woollen fishing jackets, snug hunting caps, foot-

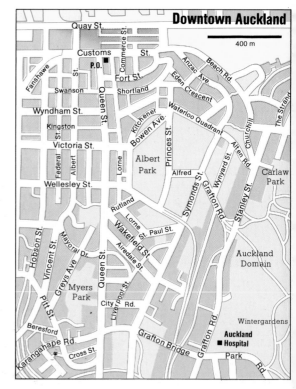

ball jersey and knee-high rugby socks.

Pausing briefly at the intersection of Queen and Fort streets, it's hard to imagine waves once lapped the shore at this spot. Little more than a century ago, Fort Street was the beach front, Shortland Street in the next block was the main street of early Auckland Queen Street in the 1840s was a bush-covered gully.

The bottom of Queen Street is occupied by **Queen Elizabeth Square** containing the Central Post Office, Downtown Complex and Air New Zealand.

The square is a favourite haunt of lunchtime office workers, soapbox orators and protest marchers bewailing grievances ranging from visits by nuclear ships to stingy kindergarten funding. A gaily coloured fruit barrow offers kiwifruit, feijoas, tamarillos, pepino, kumara and other fresh New Zealand produce while a Danish ice-cream parlour tempts the sweeter tooth. Across the road, the blue and white sails of the "Pride of Auckland" invites one to sail on Auckland's Waitemata Harbour. Visitors are encouraged to help in the sailing on these regular cruises.

Bounded by Customs, Albert and Quay streets, the **Downtown Complex** contains a variety of stores and boutiques and bookshops to interest the tourist. Further along Quay Street, a short walk east, is the oriental market which has over 140 stalls selling food, clothing and handicrafts. The airport bus terminal is across the road adjoining the Travelodge Hotel.

Historic Shops

Sitting majestically opposite the Downtown Complex on the corner of Customs and Albert streets is the **Old Customhouse** which was the financial heart of Auckland for more than 80 years. Designed in French Renaissance style, the building was completed in 1889 and is one of the last remaining examples of monumental Victorian architecture to be found in the central business district.

Turn-of-the century liberal Prime Minister Richard Seddon, better known as "King Dick," preferred to sleep in the cramped, top-most turret of the Customhouse where he could watch the ships coming and going on his visits to Auckland and shunned repeated requests to stay in the best hotels.

Harbour bridge.

The Customhouse cost NZ$30,732 to erect but more than NZ$3 million has been spent on its restoration. Open every day, it houses gift shops, a restaurant, tavern, coffee bar, and shops selling books, wood and woollen products.

Ten minutes' walk to the west are the **Victoria Park Markets**, located on the disused site of the city's former rubbish destructor. Completed in 1905, the yellow brick buildings were opened by Mayor Arthur Myers, who was hauled to the top of the 40-metre (131-foot) chimney in a ship's bo'sun chair to lay the final brick. In a pioneer conservation move, heat from the old destructor was used to generate electricity in 1908 and 94 horses were stabled to haul 10,000 tonnes of garbage from around the city to the furnaces. The historic site now offers seven-day buying at fruit, vegetable and craft shops or hawkers barrows and food stalls.

In addition to harbour cruises, both the Customhouse and Victoria Markets can be a godsend to an overseas tourist booked into a downtown hotel on a quiet Sunday. A well-worn wisecrack tells of the tourist who landed in New Zealand on a Sunday and "found it closed." Ingrained business tradition is gradually bending and every weekend now sees more shops open.

Junk and Hotdogs

Halfway up Queen Street is **Aotea Square** dominated by the monolithic Auckland City Council administration building and the old Town Hall, built in 1911, forming the eastern boundary. On the western side of the square is the city's new cultural complex, the Aotea Centre, which was built amid much controversy for a total of $120 million. It has a 2,300 seat multi-purpose theatre, a convention centre, exhibition foyers, meeting rooms and a restaurant.

Central Queen Street is the city's Cinema Centre, housing a dozen movie theatres – now accompanied by the latest in electronic bleeps and blurps emanating from the nearby video parlours which feed off the waiting hours of film patrons and street kids.

A block away, in Lorne Street, is the public library's reading room – popular with homesick travellers and immigrants devouring newspaper pages from the foreign press. Off the "main drag" and up Wellesley Street East is the city **Art Gallery**, occupying a French Renaissance styled building opened in 1887 and containing the biggest collection of New Zealand paintings in the country. They date back to works by John Webber and William Hodges, who accompanied Captain Cook on his South Pacific voyages in the late 18th century.

Griffins and Muskets

Above the Art Gallery is picturesque **Albert Park** – once the site of Albert Barracks, built in the 1840s against attacks by warring Maori tribes. Remains of the barrack walls containing musket holes can be seen in the **Auckland University** grounds behind the main library on the eastern side of the park.

The intricate clock tower of the university's Old Arts Building, completed in 1926 in "New Zealand Gothic" style, was dubbed "The Wedding Cake" by locals because of its decorative pinnacles and original white-stone construction. Grinning griffins and gargoyles created by German engraver Anton Teutenberg adorn the exterior walls of the castle-like Supreme Court in nearby Water Quadrant, built in 1868.

Also within the university confines, a stone's throw from the gargoyles and directly opposite the Hyatt Kingsgate Hotel, is the **Old Government House**, erected in 1856 and now used as a common room.

A few steps away is Parliament Street, another vestige of Auckland's former glory as New Zealand's capital. The first meeting of an elected General Assembly was held in 1854 in a parliament building constructed with great haste at the corner of Parliament and Eden streets on a site destroyed in the formation of Anzac Avenue. Due to complaints from European settlers in the gold-rich South Island about the distance they had to travel for sittings of government, the capital status was arbitrarily wrenched from Auckland in 1865 and transferred 660 km (410 miles) south to Wellington.

This "short-sighted and high-handed" action by the government in removing the capital to "a wind-swept, earthquake fault line in stormy Cook Strait" was a bitter blow to Auckland's pioneer community,

Downtown architectural contrast.

resulting in a population decrease over the next decade. With half of New Zealand's population now living within a 300-km (186-mile) radius of Auckland, it still remains a bone of contention.

South along Symonds Street, opposite the Sheraton Hotel, lies the body of Captain Hobson who selected Auckland as the site of the nation's capital following the signing of the treaty of Waitangi.

Hobson chose Auckland because it was strategically placed between two main areas of Maori population (Northland and Waikato) and was central for the main European settlements (Russell and Wellington). He named the fledgling capital after the Earl of Auckland, George Eden, Viceroy of India – a personal gesture on Hobson's part because it was Lord Auckland who, as First Lord of the Admiralty, gave Hobson captaincy of the naval frigate *HMS Rattlesnake* in 1834, his first command after a long retirement. Hobson's patron is also remembered by his family name "Eden" in Mount Eden, Eden Park and other place names.

Hobson did not live long to see his newly founded capital develop for he collapsed and died in Auckland two years later. September was a month which played a big part in Hobson's life and it still figures in his memory: he was born September 26, 1793; founded Auckland on September 18, 1840; and died on September 10, 1842. Each year a wreath-laying ceremony attended by Auckland's mayor and the naval commodore is held at his graveside on the third Sunday of September.

Hobson is also remembered in city streets and landmarks like Mount Hobson (overlooking Hobson Bay) and the township of Hobsonville (15 km northwest of the city). Hobsonville was actually the site Hobson first selected for the capital but he rejected it in favour of the city's present location on the advice of his surveyor-general, Felton Mathew.

K-Road

Opposite **Grafton Bridge** – the biggest ferro-concrete span in the world on its completion in 1910 – is Karangahape Road, known to locals as "K-Road." Home to Polynesian Airlines, Air Nauru and Pacific consulates, it is the shopping place of the Pacific Island community of

Westhaven Marina with Queen Street in the background.

Samoans, Fijians, Tongans, Nuie and Cook Islanders. Shops display brilliantly coloured cloth, *taro*, yams, papaya, mangoes, green bananas, coconut products and other tropical foods.

Auckland is the biggest Polynesian city in the world with 99,500 people tracing Maori ancestry and 82,000 Pacific Island inhabitants.

The "K-Road" vicinity is also Auckland's mecca for culture and crudity. Situated off the main street is the Mercury Theatre and centre of the performing arts featuring local and overseas plays; while in "K-Road" proper, strip shows and massage parlours attract a less discerning clientele. The city has a number of mainly disco-styled nightclubs.

There are literally hundreds of restaurants throughout Auckland, each with its own New Zealand or ethnic specialties and standards ranging from fast, fried takeaways to silver service. Some of the best are in the Ponsonby Road "restaurant strip" off "K-Road." Parnell, Symonds Street and the central city all offer – excellent, if sometimes pricey, eating but the ownership and chefs of Auckland's restaurants change with such regularity it is impossible to make lasting recommendations. For the latest restaurant ratings, cuisine standards and dollar value, seek the advice of a local or consult a popular entertainment guide. Highly recommended for the visitor is the strongly critical *Eating Out: The Guide to New Zealand Restaurants* which is updated annually and, according to its author Michael Guy, "makes just enough money to pay the restaurant bills and lawsuit defences."

Touring the Suburbs

On wheels by either car or coach, there is much more to Auckland.

A short drive east of the city centre is historic **Parnell**, the city's first suburb, where pioneer homes like Ewelme Cottage (1864) and Kinder House (1858), both in Ayr Street, are open to the public. In Judge Street is tiny St. Stephens Chapel (1857) with its pioneer cemetery, and the wooden Gothic Church of St. Mary's (1888) stands in Parnell Road. Farther south in Gillies Avenue is the 15-room Highwic dated 1862.

Parnell Village on Parnell Road is a

One Tree Hill.

favourite weekend shopping area with its quaint Victorian-styled shops, restaurants and boutiques. The Village is one of the successes of millionaire property developer Les Harvey, bane of the town planners, who was awarded an M.B.E. from Queen Elizabeth for protecting Auckland's few remaining historical buildings from the "bulldozer vandals."

Harvey buys up single and double-storied buildings, restoring and leasing them for business enterprises in keeping with their character – thus foiling "hideous, high-rise development" much to the chagrin of modern architects. He usually makes his purchases on the northern side of downtown streets to preserve low-level structures and allow Aucklanders to "keep walking in the sun."

Big Boat, Big Bird

To the south of Parnell, overlooking the city and harbour, is the **War Memorial Museum** located in the rambling grounds of the Auckland Domain. With the appearance of a Greek temple, it houses one of the finest displays of Maori and Polynesian culture in the world with exhibits of artefacts dating back to A.D. 1200. A highlight is the 30-metre (98-foot) war canoe, *Te-Toki-A-Tapiri* ("The Axe of Tapiri"), carved in 1836 from a single giant *totara* tree and used to carry 80 Maori warriors on their patrols in the Gisborne area.

The hall of New Zealand birds is another unique feature of the museum incorporating skeletons and a reconstruction of "Big Bird," the now-extinct, 4-metre, flightless moa.

East from Parnell, along the Tamaki Drive seafront, are Judges Bay, Okahu Bay, Mission Bay, Kohimarama and St. Heliers – luring weekend hotdog vendors and family fun-seekers with soft sands, saltwater baths, mini-golf and bicycle, yacht and windsurfer hires. Kelly Tarlton's Underwater World is on the waterfront between Okahu Bay and Mission Bay. Visitors enter a huge perspex tunnel to be entranced by dozens of varieties of fish swimming around and above them in the first aquarium. In the second are sharks and stingrays. At Mission Bay stands the **Melanesian Mission** building which was constructed in 1859 to be established as a mission school. It now houses a restaurant and museum of Melanesian artefacts.

A half-hour east of Auckland, the coast road arrives at Howick and **Colonial Village** with 19 restored buildings. A feature is an 1847 "fencible" cottage – a survivor of four military village outposts built outside Auckland by the Royal New Zealand Fencibles to buffer the city against Maori attack.

Just south of the city centre, via Symonds Street or the Gillies Avenue motorway off-ramp, is the 196-metre (643-feet) extinct volcanic cone of **Mount Eden**, Auckland's highest point, affording a dramatic 360-degree panorama of the entire region. In an old lava pit, on the eastern side, Eden Gardens provides a dazzling display of more than 500 camelias, rhododendrons and azalias amid 1,000 trees and shrubs.

A short distance south again arises the landmark cone of **One Tree Hill**, carrying a lone pine tree and the tomb of "the Father of Auckland," Sir John Logan Campbell. Sir John set up a tent as Auckland's first store at the bottom of Shortland Street on December 21, 1840, and was the city's most prominent busi-

Stained-glass window from the War Memorial Museum.

nessman until his death in 1912 at the age of 95, by which time the city had swelled to 115,750 inhabitants. With his partner, William Brown, he built a house called **Acacia Cottage** in 1841. Now Auckland's oldest building, it is preserved in Cornwall Park at the base of One Tree Hill.

A philanthropist, Sir John presented his 135-hectare (335-acre) farm, encompassing One Tree Hill, as a park for the people of Auckland, in 1901, to mark the visit of the Duke and Duchess of Cornwall the same year. The obelisk beside his grave was erected at his request to record his admiration for the Maori people.

Off the Western Motorway at Western Springs is MOTAT – the **Museum of Transport and Technology** – containing working displays of vintage vehicles, aircraft and machinery. Volunteer enthusiasts operate many exhibits on the weekends and the static displays include an aircraft built by New Zealander Richard Pearse which may have flown in March 1903, some months before the Wright Brothers. Also at MOTAT is the Science and Technology Hall where visitors of all ages enjoy "hands-on" experience of a wide range of scientific equipment and phenomena.

A brief ride in an old tram or a pleasant walk around Western Springs lake leads to **Auckland Zoo**, starring New Zealand's unique, flightless kiwi bird and the *tuatara* lizard, a "living fossil."

A popular drive out west climbs over the forested **Waitakere Ranges** via **Titirangi**, home of ardent conservationists and woodland-dwelling "bush freaks." Tall *kauri* trees, giant ferns and *nikau* palms line the road to the rugged black-sand, surfing beach of **Piha** and the *kauri* park at **Swanson.**

Forest Hill Road provides an escape route from the trees, down into the grape-growing district of **Henderson** where visitors can choose from among 30 vineyard wine-tasting bars.

Just before Helensville, about 50 km (30 miles) from Auckland through the wine-growing centres of Kumeu, Huapai and Waimauku, is the thermal resort of **Parakai**, where tired or aching limbs can be soothed in hot mineral waters bubbling out of the earth into tiled pools then pumped down exhilarating water chutes.

Offering dramatic harbour views to the

Auckland Harbour.

motorist and coach passenger is the **Auckland Harbour Bridge**, the city's best-known landmark. Built in 1959 as a four-lane span, its capacity was doubled 10 years later when Japanese engineers built two more lanes ("The Nippon Clipons") on each side.

A bridge to connect the city with the North Shore was suggested as far back as 1859 when it was estimated a pontoon structure would be "be crossed daily by 110 people, 10 wagons, 20 horses, 10 cows, 12 sheep and 5 pigs." Today the Harbour Bridge carries 110,000 vehicles daily and up to 115,000 on peak days.

The North Shore can also be reached by ferry from the downtown waterfront. The *Kestrel*, launched in 1905, travels between the city and Devonport on Friday and Saturday nights, to the accompaniment of live music. At other times, the *Kea*, a sleek modern seabus, does the 10-minute journey at regular intervals.

At Devonport, the volcanic promontories of Mount Victoria and North Head gives unobstructed views into downtown Auckland and across the harbour to the Eastern Bays. The two hills were honeycombed with fortified tunnels during a Russian invasion scare in the 1870s and were inhabited by Maori communities over a 700-year period through to 1863. A stone monument and plaques in English and Maori on the foreshore between the two hills commemorates the landing of the Tainui Maori canoe near the site around the 14th century.

North from Devonport the coastline is an endless procession of sheltered coves and white-sand beaches stretching to the tip of the North Island.

The Waiwera Hot Pools

Less than one hour's drive north of Auckland are the popular holiday resorts of **Orewa** and **Waiwera**. Waiwera means "hot water" and refers to thermal springs percolating up from volcanic layers onto a sandy beach in which the Maori dug holes and lay in pools of hot mineral waters.

The Waiwera Hot Pools are a good deal more sophisticated today with a number of public and private pools of varying temperatures, barbecue facilities, picnic grounds and devastating, stainless steel water chutes called The Choobs.

A customer in the Puhoi pub is attended to by proprietor Ron Seymour.

A few kilometres north of Orewa is the Puhoi pub, whose interior is a veritable museum of the pioneers of that area. The entertaining antics of the pub's proprietor and owner, Ron Seymour, provide an added attraction.

On a sparkling, calm day there is no substitute for a leisurely cruise to the offshore islands in the Hauraki Gulf. Cruise launches and ferries leave the wharves daily at the bottom of Queen Street to **Rangitoto, Motuihe, Motu-tapu, Rakino** and the holiday resort island of **Pakatoa.**

A more in-depth look at the islands can be gained by a weekend cruise to **Great Barrier Island**, 90 km (56 miles) northwest of Auckland. The *Gulf Explorer*, a 48-metre (157-foot) cruise ship which offers a variety of cabin accommodation for 80 passengers, leaves Marsden Wharf on Friday evenings and returns on Sunday afternoons.

The *Sea Flight*, a large modern catamaran, does the trip to Great Barrier in 2 hours. Those with less time can fly See Bee Air or those with all the time in the world can, in summer, do the trip on a restored scow called *Te Aroha*.

For a quick look at the harbour on "something different," the restored vintage steam tug *William C. Daldy* takes day-trippers on one-hour voyages from Marsden Wharf on Sundays and public holidays.

Leaving Auckland

Leaving for Northland, a diversion to **Sandspit** (at Warkworth) allows for a four-hour launch excursion to historic **Kawau Island** – site of the restored Mansion House built by controversial New Zealand Governor Sir George Grey, in 1862. Kawau is still the home of the parma wallaby, thought to be extinct in its Australian homeland.

Departing from Auckland in the south, train buffs can leave the motorway at Drury and follow the signs from Waiuku Road to the **Glenbrook Vintage Steam Railway** which operates on weekends and public holidays.

Having discovered the charm of "The Queen City," it is time to discover the rest of New Zealand. Despite what Aucklanders say, it is there, all right – beyond the Bombay Hills.

Mansion House, Kawau Island.

HISTORIC NORTHLAND

Tribal warfare, bloody clashes between Maori and Pakeha, debauchery, insurrection, missionary zeal, a treaty of peace and promises – all are part of Northland's historical backdrop.

This region is the birthplace of the New Zealand nation. Here, Maori Aotearoa succumbed to British New Zealand.

Early Polynesian adventurers and European colonists first settled in this sub-tropical region, leaving a legacy of hectic history and romantic legend. But Northland has more to offer the traveller than the past. It is a place to relax, to enjoy the sun, food, sights and a distinctive way of life. It is famed for its varied scenery – its pastoral, productive south and the wilder, remoter and legendary far north. It is noted for its game fishing, unspoiled beaches, pleasant climate, thermal pools and *kauri* forests. And it's a friendly place on top of it all.

The Winterless Northland

This irregular peninsula juts upwards some 450 km (280 miles) north from Auckland to the rocky headlands of North Cape and Cape Reinga, the topmost tips of the land. Its "winterless north" label means mild, damp winters; warm and rather humid summers. A feature are the *pohutukawa* trees, which in early summer rim the coast and decorate the hinterland with their dark red blossoms.

For those waiting to explore the region freely, it is best to work from a base at Paihia, a Bay of Islands township on the far northeast coast. Several air charter and small plane companies offer charter flights to the Bay of Islands. Eagle Air flies to Kaitaia and Whangarei daily. Mount Cook offers 4 daily flights to Kerikeri – and Great Barrier Airlines fly to Paihia from Auckland twice daily. Alternatively, it's a pleasant and easy (though sometimes winding) 3½-hour drive up Highway 1. There are no big hills or large cities, and traffic is light except at Christmas time and on long weekends.

The route from Auckland begins across the Harbour Bridge, proceeds along the Hibiscus Coast with its beach-

front resorts, then continues through the small farming towns of Warkworth and Wellsford and around Whangarei city, gateway to the far north. Drivers eventually leave the main highway at Kawakawa (where the main railway still runs down the main street) and snake down the harbourside resort of Paihia.

This is the Bay of Islands, the cradle of New Zealand. The bay's irregular 800-km (500-mile) coastline embraces 150 islands and is steeped in historical association with the country's early settlement. Looking across the harbour from Paihia towards Russell, the first capital of New Zealand, and the islands shimmering in the sun beyond, it is hard to believe this lovely, tranquil spot was once a sin centre of the South Pacific.

Legendary Polynesian explorer Kupe is said to have visited here in the 10th century followed by another canoe voyager, *Toi*, 200 years later. Captain Cook discovered the harbour for Europeans in 1769. Impressed he gave the sheltered waters of the Bay their name.

In the scattered group are eight larger islands and numerous islets. The biggest measures 22 hectares (54 acres). Many

Preceding pages, heading for the sands of Ninety-Mile Beach, which is actually 60 miles long. Left, Cape Reinga Lighthouse. Right, Kauri tree.

are uninhabited; two are privately owned; some are Maori reserves. About 4,000 people live permanently in the region, but in the summer holiday from Christmas to late January, up to 50,000 people head north to camp, boat, swim, fish, sightsee, relax and enjoy themselves. As most Northland visitors go to the Bay, this period requires accommodation reservations well in advance.

Since the 1950s, the small, sleepy township of **Paihia** has been revamped to meet the challenge of tourism. Modern motels have sprung up alongside a neat, expanded shopping centre. A variety of eating places, modest nightlife and a positive approach to visitors make it a worthy hub of Northland. The wharf, its focal point, caters for island cruises and fishing trips.

Paihia has marked its places of historical note with bronze plaques along the red-sand seafront. It has many firsts: New Zealand's oldest Norfolk pine stands here. A mission station was created on the town site in 1823. Missionaries built and launched the country's first ship, the *Herald*, from the beach in 1826.

From the first printing press, brought from England in 1834 by William Colenso, came the first Bible in Maori.

The **William Memorial Church**, a tribute to pioneer-missionary the Rev. Henry Williams, has a barrel organ in the vestry which played 11 tunes. Colonial history is etched in the graveyard.

Kelly Tarlton's **Shipwreck Museum** is like a visit to Davy Jones' Locker. The beached barque houses an intriguing array of relics salvaged from wrecks around the New Zealand coast – coins, gold, silver, bronze, precious stones and other souvenirs. Belowdecks, swinging lanterns, realistic sailing-ship sound effects, and the smell of ropes and tar create a seagoing illusion. The ship's owner was a diver, photographer and journalist. Kelly Tarlton died several years ago after completing his impressive "Underwater World" in Auckland – a vision he once offered Paihia but which the local council declined planning consent.

The Waitangi Treatment

The most significant act in New Zealand's early history took place on the lawn of the **Waitangi Treaty House**. In **Waitangi Treaty House.**

1840, with Governor William Hobson signing on behalf of Queen Victoria, Maori chiefs and English gentlemen inked a pact to end Maori-Pakeha conflict, guarantee the Maori land rights, give them and the colonists Crown protection, and admit New Zealand to the British Empire.

At the time the Treaty of Waitangi was signed, the house was the home of James Busby, British resident in New Zealand from 1832 to 1840. Later, the gracious colonial dwelling, with its commanding views of the Bay, fell into disrepair. When put up for sale in 1931, it was bought by the governor-general of the time, Lord Bledisloe. He gave it to the nation on the condition it be fully restored to its 1840 glory.

That condition was met and today the Treaty House is a national museum and a prime visitor attraction. About 2 km (1¼ miles) north of Paihia, it is reached across a one-way bridge which also leads to the **Waitangi Reserve** and a golf course.

Inside the Treaty House, with its artefacts and copy of the famous treaty itself, it is cool, quiet and full of the atmosphere of a slower, more gracious yet eventful era. Visitors are usually impressed by the splendour of an adjacent Maori meeting house and awed by a massive war canoe. Access is through a information-reception centre, which provides ample background plus an audiovisual on the treaty signing.

Deep-sea fishing for some of the world's biggest gamefish is a major lure at the Bay of Islands.

American Western author Zane Grey, a noted angler, was a regular visitor in the 1920s. His base camp was at **Otehei Bay** on Urupukapuka Island; it was popularised by his 1926 book, *Tales of Angler's Eldorado, New Zealand*. This single volume has reeled in thrill-seeking fishermen ever since.

The main fishing season is December through May or June when the huge blue, black and striped marlin are running. Many world records for marlin, shark and tuna were set here. Yellowtail kingfish, running on till September, provide good sport on light rods and tackle. Snapper, one of New Zealand's favourite table fish, is plentiful.

Fighting fish weighing up to 400 kg (880 pounds) are caught in the Bay, and

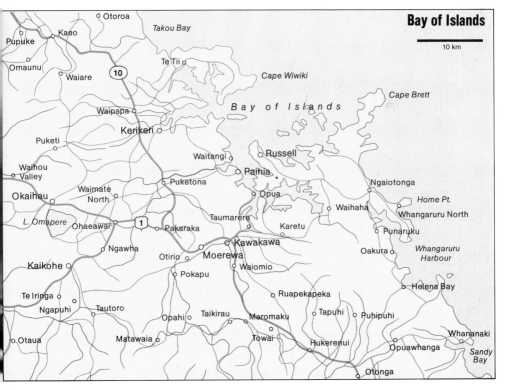

Bay of Islands

10 km

catch weigh-ins attract appreciative summer crowds. Competitions for line-fishing and surf-casting are frequently held, with big prizes arranged; the fore-most are in January.

Despite the "seasons," fishing is a year-round sport here. Charter boats are available at Paihia or Russell for half or full-day hire, and on a share basis.

Runaway sailors, escaped convicts from Australia, lusty whalers, promiscuous women of both races, brawling and drunkenness: **Russell**, formerly Kororareka, has known them all.

Colonists first arrived in 1809, making it New Zealand's first white settlement. Today it's small, quiet and peaceful. There's an aura of stored history, of romance, of skeletons jangling in those Victorian cupboards. But things liven up at Christmas and New Year when celebrating boaties and other visitors get the place rocking again. This former (but short-lived) capital of New Zealand is linked by a regular launch service to Paihia and Waitangi. A vehicular ferry serves the small peninsula from the deep-sea port of **Opua** south of the harbour.

Today's Russell services the needs of national and international yachts, as well as game fisherfolk and those visitors of historical bent. Strong efforts are made to retain the township's 19th century Victorian appearance.

In the early 1830s, the port was always full of whaling and trading ships and adventurers. Lust and lawlessness prevailed. Up to 30 grog shops operated on the tiny waterfront. Friction developed between Maori and European. Guns were traded, Maori shanghaied and badly treated. Shocked early settlers responded by building **Christ Church** in 1835, New Zealand's oldest church. Its bullet-holed walls are grim reminders of its siege in 1845.

Charismatic Maori chief Hone Heke reluctantly signed the Treaty of Waitangi in 1840, then grew discontented over government land dealings. In 1845, he defiantly chopped down the British flag-staff, symbol of the new regime, on **Maiki Hill** behind Russell. Meanwhile, chief Kawiti burned and sacked the town, sparing church property. Heke chopped down three more flagpoles that year. Two bitter battles for rebel strongholds resulted in defeats for British troops.

Kerikeri Old Stone House.

The showdown came in 1846 near Kawakawa, at Kawiti's *pa* Ruapekapeka. A strong Redcoat force captured this formidable fortress somewhat unfairly on a Sunday when the converted Maori were busy worshipping their new Christian god. Heke was eventually pardoned and his men freed.

Pompallier House, a Catholic mission house, was spared in the fighting. It is now an elegant, refurbished tourist and photographers' attraction.

Russell's new museum has a quarter-sized seagoing model of Cook's *Endeavour*. Its **Duke of Marlborough Hotel** is a hostelry and pub of much character.

The Cream Trips

The true beauty of islands in the Bay can best be appreciated from a position of comfort on the foredeck of one of the daily Cream Trips. These water tours out of Paihia and Russell retrace the voyages of bygone days when cream was regularly collected from island farms. Mail and provisions are still handled this way.

The Fullers launch cruise covers 96 km (60 miles). Passengers see the island

Digging for gum.

where Captain Cook first anchored on his 1769 voyage of discovery; the cove where French explorer Marion du Fresne, along with his 25 crew members, were slain by Maori in 1772; and bays where the earliest missionaries landed. A luncheon stop is made at Zane Grey's favourite Otehei Bay.

The catamaran *Tiger Lily III* offers a shorter four-hour cruise. This 230-passenger vessel also does a three-hour scenic trip to the **Cape Brett** lighthouse and **Piercy Island** and, weather permitting, passes through the **Hole in the Rock**.

"Sweet" Kerikeri

Kerikeri is the "sweetest" place in Northland. Twenty-three km (14 miles) north of Paihia by a pretty inlet, it is a township of unusual interest and character with a rich backdrop of early Maori and European history.

Today, Kerikeri's fertile land grows much of the country's finest citrus and subtropical fruits, including many hectares of luscious kiwifruit.

The township, with a population of 1,500, has become a thriving centre for handicrafts and cottage industries. Its climate and relaxed lifestyle have attracted many creative, artistic and personable residents.

Samuel Marsden established his second mission station at Kerikeri in 1819. The first plow in New Zealand dug into Kerikeri soil that year.

Down at the inlet are two of New Zealand's oldest buildings in a fine state of preservation. **Kemp House** is the oldest, built in 1822 of pit-sawn *kauri* and *totara*. It has been fully restored. Four generations of the Kemp family have lived in it, through turbulent times when pioneer womenfolk had to endure the grisly sight of decapitated heads stuck drying on the stake fence separating the property from the adjoining Maori *pa*. Tribal raids by fierce chief Hongi Hika meant souvenired heads to be dried and shrunken-part of Maori war games early last century.

Next door is the **Old Stone Store**, a national landmark. It was built by missionaries in 1833 of thick stone to protect their wares from marauding tribesmen. It is still a shop, with a museum upstairs.

Kororipa Pa should not be overlooked. This was Hongi Hika's forward army base between 1780 and 1828. Warriors were assembled here before launching gruesome raids on southern tribes (as far south as Cook Strait), whose primitive weapons were no match for muskets, bartered from the Europeans.

Not far from Kerikeri is **Waimate North**, the first inland settlement for white people and earlier inland mission station. Built in 1831-1832, the two-stored *kauri* mission house was the home of Bishop George Augustus Selwyn, New Zealand's first bishop, in 1842. He regularly walked the 16 km (10 miles) to his library in the Kerikeri Stone Store, and back. The house was built by Maori labour except for the English hearthstone and blown pane glass. It has been fully restored and is full of antiques.

In Maori mythology, **Cape Reinga** is where the spirits of the dead depart on their homeward journey back to the ancestral land of Hawaiki.

Coach tours now make their way up this legendary flight path, along the Aupori Peninsula to its northernmost point, and splash back down Ninety Mile Beach. Coaches leave Paihia daily at 7:30 a.m.-8 a.m. returning about 6 p.m. It's a tiring trip, but worthwhile, especially since the road north of Te Kao is too rough for an ordinary car.

The east-coast route traverses the worked-out gum fields north of Kerikeri, a relic of the huge *kauri* forests that covered this region eons ago. The dead trees left pockets of gum in the soil which early settlers found to be a valuable export for fine varnish. In fact, it triggered off a "gum rush." By the 1880s, more than 2,000 men were digging away. Most of them were from Dalmatia (now Yugoslavia); some made their fortunes. When the gum fields were exhausted, the Dalmatians turned to farming or came south to Auckland to found the city's vineyards (near Henderson).

In **Whangaroa Harbour**, a deep-sea fishing base, lies the wreck of the *Boyd*. The ship called in for *kauri* spars in 1809 and sent a party ashore. The party was murdered by Maori, who donned the victims' clothes and rowed back to the vessel to massacre the rest of the crew and set fire to the ship. This episode is said to have delayed Christian settlement in New Zealand for several years.

Sand dunes at Te Paki.

Further on is **Doubtless Bay**, named by Cook. It is favoured by a string of superb, gently sloping sandy beaches. **Coopers Beach**, lined with *pohutukawa* trees, is likewise attractive. So is **Cable Bay** with its golden sand and colourful shells. Both these beaches cater for tourists, with camping, motels and restaurants.

At **Awanui**, the coach heads north through **Te Kao**, largest Maori settlement in the far north, to Cape Reinga with its much-pictured lighthouse. At nearby Spirits Bay is the gnarled old *pohutukawa* from where Maori souls, homeward bound to Hawaiki, were said to take off on their way north. The whole district is rich in Maori lore.

Views from the Cape are impressive. You can see the turbulent meeting line of the Pacific Ocean and Tasman Sea; the **Three Kings Islands** discovered by Abel Tasman in 1643; neighbouring capes and secluded, lonely beaches. It is a desolate place with only gulls screeching, the wind howling, and waves crashing against jagged, foam-wreathed rocks far below.

Ninety Mile Beach is actually 60 miles (96 km) long. Its firm, sandy length is lined with dunes and hillocks of shell, the reminders of bygone feasts. The beach is noted for its shellfish, particularly the succulent, now-protected, *toheroa*.

The route back to Paihia is via **Kaitaia**, New Zealand's northernmost town, and the **Mangamuka Scenic Reserve** with its native bush.

The West Coast

Travellers can return to Auckland via a west-coast route where sleepy harbourside hamlets cling close to their pioneer past, and where forest giants live.

Objective No. 1 is **Hokianga Harbour**, 80 km (50 miles) across country. This long harbour, with its score of ragged inlets, is remote. The atmosphere is quiet, serene, rural. The scattered residents don't tout much for tourists: the harbour's perilous sandbar has already claimed 15 ships. Polynesian explorer Kupe is said to have left from here in A.D. 900 to return to Hawaiki.

Kaikohe, midway town, has a hilltop monument to chief Hone Heke (a descendant of the old renegade chief) who became a Member of Parliament. It has

spectacular views of both coasts. Nearby, **Ngawha Hot Mineral Springs** offer a tempting soak in their mercury-and-sulphur waters, claimed to be curative for rheumatism and skin troubles.

The tiny seaside resort of **Opononi** at the harbour mouth became briefly famous around the world in the southern summer of 1955-56, when a young dolphin began frolicking with swimmers at the beach. Opo, as she was called, played games with bottles and balls, let children ride on her back, and won her way into a nation's heart. Opononi had a three-month tourist boom. When Opo was found dead on March 9, stuck between tidal rocks, the nation mourned. She is remembered in a song and by a monument.

"Father of the Forest"

The road heads south through the **Waipoua Kauri Sanctuary** with its 2,500 hectares (about 6,100 acres) of huge, mature *kauri* trees, the largest pocket of *kauri* forest left in the land. Two giants (close to the unsealed road) tower above them all: Te Matua Ngahere ("Father of the Forest"), about 2,000 years old, and brother Tanemahuta ("Lord of the Forest"), 1,200 years old with a girth of 13.6 metres (44.6 feet). Further south at **Trounson Park** are more fine *kauris*, including one unusual tree with four stems.

Dargaville, 184 km (114 miles) from Auckland, was founded on the timber and *kauri* gum trade. The town museum has many fine gum samples and is a museum piece itself – built of clay bricks brought in from China as ship's ballast.

The highway turns east to **Whangarei**. This lightly industrialised city of some 40,180 is a deep-sea port and boasts a splendid harbour, glassworks, cement plant and a oil refinery. There is plenty of quality stopover accommodation. **Mount Parahaki** gives panoramic views of city and harbour.

Major visitor attractions are the Clapham Clock Collection (400 timepieces dating back to the 17th century), safe swimming beaches, the deep-sea fishing base of **Tutukaka**, and the city's handsome parks, reserves, picnic grounds and bushwalks.

Auckland is about 2 hour's drive away.

Coromandel And Bay Of Plenty

"Coromandel: Mine Today, Gone Tomorrow!"

The slogan reflects the strong feelings of its inhabitants that the Coromandel Peninsula's greatest asset is not mineral wealth but its natural attractions. It's time to save the area for its recreational potential, they say, and let it produce "treasure from tourism."

The Coromandel region once yielded treasures of gold, *kauri* timber and gum. Reminders of these bonanzas abound, and today one still gains a certain pioneer feeling with colonial buildings, old gold-mine shafts and *kauri* relics, and perhaps the sense of achievement at travelling some of the peninsula's rougher, more remote roads or walking its rugged tracks.

Seen from Auckland, the Coromandel Peninsula is a lumpy, irregular profile, almost a caricature of a theatre backdrop for some vast outdoor scene. "Outdoor" is the area's lodestone, whether visitors engage in driving, diving, fishing, boating, swimming, camping, tramping, hunting for history or fossicking for gemstones. Thousands visit the peninsula every year, reflecting the earlier thousands who flocked here – gold-seekers, gumdiggers and bushmen.

Gold Fever Territory

Thames – at the base of the peninsula – was officially declared a goldfield in August 1867. The ensuing gold rush swelled the town's population to 18,000 at its peak. In its heyday, Thames had more than 100 hotels. Today there are just four, the oldest being the **Brian Boru** built on the corner of Pollen and Richmond streets in 1868, now gaining fame as a venue for regular Agatha Christie-style "murder weekends."

To appreciate the town's past, one should visit the Mineralogical Museum and adjacent School of Mines. Nearby, at the old gold mine and gold-stamper battery (well-signposted at the northern end of Thames), members of the Hauraki Prospectors' Association demonstrate the technology used to retrieve gold.

Mercury Bay.

Kauaeranga Valley, also signposted in Thames, is the site of the Conservation Department's visitor and information centre, 10 km (6 miles) from Thames. The first *kauri* spars from here were taken in 1795; by 1830, *kauri* trees were being cut in greater numbers. The logging and milling lasted for a century.

Late in the 1800s, huge *kauri* timber dams were built across creeks and streams on the peninsula in order to bank up water and then float the logs down to the sea. About 300 such dams were built throughout the peninsula, more than 60 of them in the Kauaeranga Valley. Many of them are still there, slowly disintegrating. A working model of a *kauri* dam (made of pine, not of *kauri*) has been built near the information centre. In summer this is tripped to show visitors how the dams worked. Today Kauaeranga Valley is a favourite spot for camping and tramping. Along more than 50 km (31 miles) of tracks, visitors have access to the wilderness with overnight hut accommodation available.

The Thames area owes its name to James Cook, who chartered the Coromandel coast in 1769. What is now the

Timber craftsman with daughter.

Waihou River, he called the Thames; and while the river reverted to its Maori name, the tongue of sea lapping the coast remains the Firth of Thames.

"Square" Trees and Potters

North of Thames, heading for the town of Coromandel, one soon experiences a winding road and spectacularly changing views. The road hugs the coast for much of the way, passing bays where holiday homes huddle on the shore.

Tapu, 18½ km (11½ miles) north of Thames, is the junction for the Tapu-Coroglen road, a scenic route climbing to 448 metres (1,470 feet) above sea level. It passes south of an area known as the Camel's Back because of its double-hump profile. Near this road, 25 km (15½ miles) from Tapu, is the famous "square" *kauri* tree, more than 9 metres (30 feet) in girth. *Tapu* is Maori for sacred or forbidden; and while caravans are not forbidden on this road, drivers of these vehicles are advised to take the easier Kopu-Hikuai road across the range south of Thames.

On a clear night in **Coromandel** township, near the northern end of the peninsula, one can see the lights of Auckland shining across the Hauraki Gulf. Yet the two places are the face and obverse of modern life. Auckland is flash new with commerce. Coromandel is undeveloped old, offering an alternative life of quiet concentration for painters who farm, potters who garden, weavers who rear their own sheep for wool. Nationally known potter Barry Brickell, for example, loves trains and he has built his own small railway track into the ever-close hills to haul out clay and some of the fuel for his wood-burning kiln.

The town and region were named after the Royal Navy ship, *HMS Coromandel*, which called into the harbour there for spars early in the 19th century. The township was the site of New Zealand's first gold find by Charles Ring in 1852. More than 2,000 people dashed across the gulf from Auckland at the news, but they had little luck. It wasn't until 15 years later that a rich gold-bearing reef was found nearby and brought wealth to those who worked it.

Coromandel has an air of the past about it, and even at the height of the summer holiday season, the pace is slow and the lifestyle relaxed. It remembers its past with such institutions as the School of Mines with its collection of rock samples, mostly from the peninsula itself but some from around the world.

Mythical Turehu

Beyond Coromandel, 28 km (17 miles) north, is **Colville**, the last store for those venturing toward Cape Colville and the northernmost tip of the peninsula. Coromandel enthusiasts insist that visitors cannot experience the full spirit of the peninsula unless they travel right to the end of this road.

En route, the road skirts the **Moehau Range**, whose 891-metre (2,923-foot) peak is the highest point on the peninsula. According to Maori legend, it is home of the mythical Turehu or Patupaiarehe, a short, fair-skinned people. However, unlike the Himalaya's yeti or America's bigfoot, not so much as a footprint trace of the Turehu has ever been found. Today's visitors might, however, manage to see the small, rare, native frog (*Leiopeima archeyi*). A refugee from the remote past, it lives only on the Coromandel Peninsula and is sometimes seen in this vicinity.

The unspoilt beauty and isolation of **Port Jackson** and **Fletcher Bay** draw people to enjoy some solitude. Fletcher Bay, at the end of the road, is also the starting point for the Coromandel Walkway, a three-hour walk to **Stony Bay**. The more sedentary can visit Stony Bay by taking the road just north of Colville, across the peninsula to **Port Charles**, then returning via **Kennedy Bay** on the east coast to Coromandel.

Two roads lead from Coromandel to Whitianga on the opposite coast of the peninsula. The first, longer and less developed, leads east to **Whangapoua Harbour** and **Kuaotuna Beach**. (Here, make a point of travelling the Black Jack Road, renowned as the most hair-raising route in the region.) Another 17 km (10½ miles) southwest of Kuaotuna, just beyond the sheltered expanse of **Buffalo Beach** (named for a British warship wrecked there in 1840), is Whitianga. The second route, 15 km (9½ miles) shorter, climbs to 300 metres (984 feet) before descending to approach the town from the south, along the Whitianga Harbour edge.

Whitianga means "the crossing" in the Maori tongue. The town was exactly that for the first 20-odd years of European settlement, for it was located on the opposite side of the harbour – at a spot said to have been occupied for more than 1,000 years by the descendants of the Polynesian explorer, Kupe. Now the site, just 300 metres (984 feet) across the harbour from the present-day town, is known as **Ferry Landing**. A small ferry crosses the channel regularly and ties up at the historic stone wharf built in 1837.

A few paces from the wharf, a track leads up to the **Whitianga Rock Scenic and Historic Reserve**, a former headland Maori *pa* with a sheer drop to bush-clad cliffs below.

Kauri gum was shipped from Whitianga from 1844 onwards, peaking in 1899 with the shipment of 1,100 tons. From 1864, *kauri* timber was also shipped from the harbour and an estimated 500 million feet of the timber left the area in the next 60 years.

Today's visitors can enjoy fishing, swimming or rock-hunting. The latter hobby draws those in search of the area's semi-precious gemstones including jas-

Bovine runaway of Coromandel.

126

per, amethyst, quartz, chalcedony, agate and carnelian.

South of Whitianga lies **Coroglen** (formerly Gumtown). Eight km (5 miles) east is the access road to two areas which are "must" stops – **Cooks Bay** and Hot Water Beach. It was at the former location (also known as Mercury Bay) that Captain Cook first hoisted the British flag in New Zealand in November 1769 to claim the territory in the name of King George III. While here, he also observed the transit of Mercury; the occasion is marked by a cairn and plaque at the top of Shakespeare Cliffs.

Hot Water and a Tidy Resort

An absolute must on the peninsula is the unique **Hot Water Beach**, where thermal activity causes steam to rise from the sand in places and the visitor can dig a thermal hot pool on the beach, using "sand-castle" walls to keep the sea out or let it in to regulate the temperature. It is a great way to relax travel-weary bodies from the bumps and bends of the roads.

The new centre southward is **Tairua**, on the harbour of the same name. The area is dominated by 178-metre (584-foot) **Mount Paku**, whose summit offers good views of nearby Shoe and Slipper islands.

Across the harbour is the beach resort of **Pauanui**, billed as a "Park by the Sea" but described by some as almost "too tidy to be true." It provides a marked contrast to the haphazard development of many New Zealand beach areas.

Whangamata Beach, 40 km (25 miles) farther south, is well-known both as a popular family holiday spot and the prime surfing beach of the peninsula.

The road winds inland from here. Thirty km (19 miles) south is **Waihi**, where a rich gold and silver-bearing lode was discovered in 1878. Martha Hill mine was the greatest source of these minerals. Shafts were sunk to a depth of more than 500 metres (over 1,600 feet); in 60-plus years, more than NZ$50 million worth of gold and silver was retrieved. Further gold is being won by an opencast mining venture which has laid bare the original mineshafts on Martha Hill.

The bullion trail led through the Karangahake Gorge to Paeroa, from where the ore was shipped to Auckland. A walkway through part of the gorge between Waik-

Thames.

ino and Karangahake, where the relics of the Victoria stamper battery, has been developed.

The Bay of Plenty was named by Captain Cook; his description proved to be both immediate and prophetic.

Perhaps the greatest current evidence of plenitude is the phenomenal growth of the "furry" kiwifruit, which has made the township of Te Puke the "Kiwifruit Capital of the World." Just beyond Te Puke is Kiwifruit Country, an orchard park and information centre. It includes a restaurant, and a "kiwifruit train" taking visitors around the park.

Waihi Beach, just north of Tauranga Harbour, is considered the boundary point between Coromandel Peninsula and the Bay of Plenty. By road through the Athenree Gorge south of Waihi, one reaches **Katikati** – promoted as "The Gateway to the Bay of Plenty".

The coastal city of **Tauranga** is both a tourist focal point and an important commercial centre, served by a busy port at nearby **Mount Maunganui.**

Flax-trading began here 150 years ago; missionaries arrived in 1838; and in 1864, during the New Zealand Wars, Tauranga was the site of fierce fighting during the battle of Gate Pa. That battlefield was also the scene of heroic compassion when Heni te Kirikamu heard mortally wounded British offices calling for water, and risked death during the battle to take water to the wounded enemies.

The site of the original military camp, the Monmouth Redoubt and the mission cemetery holds not only the remains of the British troops killed at Gate Pa, but also the body of the defender of Gate Pa, Rawhiri Puhirake, killed during the subsequent battle of Te Ranga.

Among the leading attractions in Tauranga are Tauranga Historic Village (on 17th Avenue), giving the pioneer history of the area, and The Elms mission house (1847) in Mission Street.

Across the harbour from Tauranga is the Mount Maunganui holiday resort. It is built around the 231-metre (758-foot) "Mount," affording views of Tauranga and the surrounding area. Visitors who are reluctant or lack the energy to climb the "Mount" can simply laze on the beach or swim in the hot saltwater pools near the foot of the hill.

Te Puke is 28 km (17 miles) southeast

Mount Maunganui.

of Tauranga. Its subtropical horticulture has indeed brought prosperity. The kiwifruit, originally known as the Chinese gooseberry, was introduced to New Zealand from China in 1906, and thrived best in the Bay of Plenty. In 1937, Te Puke farmer Jim MacLoughlin planted an acre of the vines; this can be regarded as the birth of the now-highly successful kiwifruit industry. However, it was not until about a quarter-century later that the simple brown-skinned fruit began to gain prominence as an export item, marketed under the thoroughly New Zealand name of "Kiwifruit."

Acting as a Man

About 100 km (62 miles) from Tauranga and 85 km (53 miles) from the thermal centre of Rotorua is **Whakatane**, at the mouth of the Whakatane River and at the edge of the fertile Rangitaiki Plains. Until it was drained 70 years ago, the area was a 40,000-hectare (about 100,000-acre) tract of swampland.

Whakatane takes its name from the arrival of the Mataatua Canoe from Hawaiki at the local river mouth. Legend records that the men went ashore, leaving the women in the canoe, which then began to drift away on the incoming tide. Though women were forbidden to touch paddles, the captain's daughter, Wairaka, seized a paddle and shouted: *Kia whakatane au i ahau!* ("I will act as a man!") Others followed her lead and the canoe was saved. A bronze statue of Wairaka now stands on a rock in the river mouth. Above the area, known as The Heads, is Kapu-te Rangi ("Ridge of the Heavens"), reputedly the oldest Maori *pa* site in New Zealand, established by Polynesian explorer Toi in A.D. 1150.

Clearly visible from Whakatane and adjacent coasts is **White Island**, a privately owned active volcano 50 km (31 miles) from Whakatane. Scenic flights pass over the steaming island, which was mined for sulphur ore with varying success between 1885 and the mid-1930s. In 1914, 11 men lost their lives on the island during a violent eruption; the work camp's cat was the only survivor. Cardboard has been produced at the Whakatane Board Mills since 1939. Visitors may tour this plant and that of the huge Tasman Pulp and Paper Company mill at **Kawerau**, 32 km (20 miles) from Whakatane towards Rotorua.

Just over the hill, 7 km (4½ miles) from Whakatane, is the popular **Ohope Beach**, described by former New Zealand governor-general Lord Cobham as "the most beautiful beach in New Zealand." A visit to the beach on a sunny day might convince many travellers Whakatane is the sunniest location in the North Island.

The last centre of note between Whakatane and the eastern boundary of the Bay of Plenty at Cape Runaway is the rural centre of **Opotiki**. Here in 1865, missionary Rev. Carl Volkner was murdered by a Maori rebel leader, Kereopa, in a gruesome episode which saw Volkner's head cut off and placed on the church pulpit, and the communion chalice used to catch his blood.

Beyond Opotiki, the road to East Cape winds along the coast for 115 km (71 miles) to **Cape Runaway**. En route, it passes through the small settlements of **Te Kaha** and **Waihau Bay**, a popular camping area. Like the tip of the Coromandel Peninsula, this is the Bay of Plenty's own remote area, and it has a unique charm.

Kiwifruit.

WAIKATO AND TARANAKI

When the birdsong shrills into the dawn in the central and western region of the North Island, it climbs over the beat of an unusual accompaniment – the chugalug-chugalug of electric milking machines. Grass grows quicker here through the year than anywhere else in the world and the cows that crop it daily have brought prosperity to generations of farmers.

Twice a day for about nine months of the year, the "cow cockies" or dairy farmers, drive their docile stock to the milking sheds. There they relieve the beasts of their butterfat-rich milk from which New Zealand's famous yellow, mild cheddar cheese and milk powder are made.

Carefully bred dairy herds free-graze on Waikato or Taranaki pastures along fertile river valleys or on the volcanic plains around Taranaki's snow-capped Mount Egmont. The grass is fed by a mild, wet climate (rainfall averages 1,120 mm or 44 inches in Waikato's Hamilton, and 1,565 mm or 62 inches in Taranaki's New Plymouth) and liberally applied artificial fertilisers.

The steeper land supports sheep and cattle and, in the Waikato, the flats are also chequered with fruit and vegetable crops and opulent stud horse and cattle farms.

But not all of the people are farmers. The two regions contain New Zealand's most closely clustered farming population, yet most people live in one of the many small towns which service the country areas, or in the two major cities – Hamilton (population 97,600) and New Plymouth (population 44,000). The towns and cities are linked by the nation's tightest networks of sealed roads carrying some of the highest volumes of traffic.

A Landscape Flecked With Blood

This peaceful, productive landscape was entirely manmade by European settlers during the 20th century. Much of the now-green pastures were the spoils of land wars between Maori and Pakeha during the 1860s and were the scene of bloody bitter fighting.

The Waikato region was once comparatively highly populated by Maori tribes and its land communally owned, according to ancestry. It was a landscape of dense bush on the hills, peat swamp and *kahikatea* (white pine) forests on flat land and the low hills of the Waikato and Waipa river systems. By the 1840s and 1850s pockets of Taranaki and the Waikato were beginning to resemble a South Pacific England with their church spires, crops and villages.

The land wars disrupted it all; it took nearly 20 years for the British and colonial forces to defeat the rebellious Maori tribes who were intent on keeping what was left of their land. With the rebels driven out or dead, and the Waikato supporters of the Maori nationalist King movement pushed south, the lands of the Waikato and Taranaki were unlocked.

What land was not confiscated by the government was effectively taken through 1862 legislation which forced the traditional Maori group ownership to be individualised. Single owners were easy prey for land agents who plied them with alcohol and money to encourage them to sell. The way was then open for the gradual development, during the 20th century, of the natural wilderness into the intensively farmed land that it is today.

It was a long slow road for the early settler families. Years sometimes passed before they could afford to sow grass where the bush had been cleared, buy livestock and build permanent houses. Buckets and stools were carried into muddy paddocks to milk cows until primitive milking sheds were built.

One man who helped ease the transformation from pioneer hardship to the high-technology farming and processing of today was a pigtailed Chinese pedlar, Chew Chong. At first he created cash markets for butter in New Zealand; by 1884 he sent a consignment to Britain. Chew built a butter factory at Eltham, and to boost supplies of cream, he introduced share-milking, a system whereby dairymen could run their own herds on his land for part of their milk payment.

By the 1900s the dairy industry was growing fast. Butter and cheese production had moved from farm to factory and farmers had formed co-operative companies – which today still govern the milk payout, and process and market dozens of

Morokopa Falls, Waikato.

dairy products worldwide. Taranaki has become the world's largest exporter of cheese, while butter and milk powder are produced in the Waikato. In both regions hundreds of stainless steel milk tankers collect the milk from farms, each equipped with its own milk separator and milking machines to take much of the drudgery out of the dairy farmer's life.

Capital of the Waikato

Hamilton, the Waikato's capital, is an attractive and prosperous city straddling the Waikato River, 50 km (31 miles) inland in the heart of farmland. Like the grass and crops in the surrounding countryside, Hamilton's city trees and shrubs, in public parks and private gardens, thrive in the mild climate. Much of the city's riverbanks are parkland, a restful walk for strollers and a popular route for joggers.

The river was the reason for the establishment of Hamilton in the 1860s although the Maori had settled on the east bank. The first businesses grew up on the riverbank, today the main street and commercial hub of the city run parallel to

it. **Lake Rotorua**, in the centre of the city, is a boating and recreational park. The continuing rapid growth of the city has put it among the five largest in the nation. Its commerce, government offices and industries service the surrounding country areas. Hamilton has become an international known agricultural research centre. The Ruakura Agricultural Research Centre and soil research station, and the Meat Industry Research Institute of New Zealand, have been pioneering institutions in the fields of agricultural science, animal health, stock-killing methods and meat processing. The New Zealand Dairy Board's centre for cattle semen harvesting (artificial insemination is commonly used to improve herds) is nearby at **Newstead**. Waikato University, also on the eastern side of the city, is one of several large educational institutions in Hamilton. Southwest of the city is the white spire of the New Zealand headquarters for the Church of Jesus Christ of the Latter Day Saints, at **Templeview.**

The Waikato River is no longer the transport waterway it once was. But a replica paddle steamer and other tour boats offer meals and a leisurely cruise **Waikato River, Hamilton.**

through the city by river. The river's prime importance is in providing one-third of the nation's hydro-electric power. Eight power stations harness its waters upstream from Hamilton. Ribbon lakes lie behind each dam attracting boaters, fishermen and swimmers.

Racehorses and Spas

Upstream from Hamilton, following the main state highway, are idyllic treed pastures where many of the country's thoroughbred horse stables are located. Horticultural crops supply fruit and vegetables for the export and home market.

The quiet, pretty town of **Cambridge** sits on the river 24 km (15 miles) upstream from Hamilton. The town's charming Anglican church, tree-lined streets and village green – a popular summer cricket pitch – give it a very English atmosphere.

East of the river are the Waikato towns of Morrinsville, Te Aroha and Matamata. **Morrinsville** is itself a centre for the surrounding dairy land, with six large processing factories in the vicinity. **Te Aroha**, on the Waihou River farther east,

was once a gold town and fashionable Victorian spa sitting at the foot of 952-metre (3,123-foot) bush-clad Mount Te Aroha. The town domain has elegant bath houses and kiosks over fountains of mineral water. The world's only known hot soda-water fountain, the Mokena Geyser, is in the domain.

Matamata is known for its thoroughbred racehorse stables. As with Morrinsville, the surrounding land was once part of huge holdings of land speculators. Josiah Clifton Firth, took on the seemingly impossible task of clearing the Waihou River of snags to make it navigable. The three-storey blockhouse he built stands as a reminder of the settlers' insecurity after the wars. The Firth tower is now part of a reserve containing a museum.

From Matamata, the pine forests and farmlands of Putaruru and Tokoroa to the south are within easy reach. **Tokoroa** has grown from a village three decades ago to a town of about 19,000 people during the development of one of New Zealand's largest companies, NZ Forest Products Limited's huge pulp-and-paper mill at nearby **Kinleith.**

Cattle
mustering,
Taranaki.

Maori Stronghold

Down the Waikato River from Hamilton is **Ngaruawahia**, capital of the Maori King movement and an important Maori cultural centre. On the east riverbank in the town is the **Turangawaewae Marae**, its name meaning "a place to put one's feet." In the 1920s, Turangawaewae became the focal point for a revival in support for Kingitanga, inspired by Maori princess Te Puea Herangi. Her organisational abilities established a complex of buildings on 4 hectares (about 10 acres) of riverbank (this was later increased). Today the *marae* contains traditionally carved meeting houses and a modern concert hall which can sleep and feed 1,200 people. The *marae* is not open to the public except on special occasions, but can be seen from the river bridge on the main road a little downstream.

Mount Taupiri 6 km (3.7 miles) downstream is the sacred burial ground of Waikato tribes. Near here the river's lazy waters are used to cool a massive coal-and-gas-fired power station at **Huntly**. Its two 150-metre (492-foot) chimneys tower over the town which stands at the centre of New Zealand's largest coalfields, both opencast and underground.

Southwest of Hamilton is **Te Awamutu**, dubbed the "the rose town" for its fragrant gardens and rose shows. One of the country's oldest and finest churches, St. John's Anglican Church, stands in the main street, built in 1854. Another, St. Paul's, built in 1856, lies to the east of **Hairini**. Both are notable for their stained-glass windows. Near Hairini is **Orakau**, scene of the final battle of the Waikato land wars in 1864 when Rewi Maniapoto and 300 men, women and children fought for three days to defend a fortified *pa* against about 1,400 colonial soldiers.

Waitomo Caves and Maui Gas

In the northern King Country, to the south, are the **Waitomo** limestone caves and glowworm grottos. Three caves are open to the public – Waitomo, Ruakuri and Aranui. The area offers the choice of a tranquil boat ride to view the glowworms, a speleological (cave) museum, adventure caving, a model Maori village and bush walks. At **Te Kuiti**, 19 km (12

Mount Egmont, Taranaki.

miles) further south, charismatic Maori leader Te Kooti Rikirangi took refuge and built a meeting house, later gifted to the local Maniapoto people as a gesture of thanks for their protection. The carvings in the house are among the finest in the country; the structure has been restored or rebuilt five times.

The 169-km (105-mile) **Te Kuiti to New Plymouth road** shows the south-bound traveller rugged farmed hill country, the Awakino River gorge and beautiful coast with cliffs and placid sandy bays. Tiny river-mouth settlements are popular holiday and fishing spots. After a climb up the road over **Mount Messenger, Taranaki Mount Egmont** is in full view on a clear day. The road passes by a striking memorial to famous Polynesian anthropologist Sir Peter Buck just north of **Urenui**, his birthplace, and Motunui, a synthetic petrol plant. A visitor's centre at the main gates is open daily. Near New Plymouth, Taranaki's capital, the land flattens to fertile dairy plains encircling the dormant volcano of Mount Egmont, a near-perfect cone 2,581 metres (8,468 feet) high.

Among the tidy green fields southwest

Sir Peter Bucks Memorial, North Taranaki.

of the city are the well heads and processing plant towers of the **Kapuni** natural gas field.

The Heritage of New Plymouth

New Plymouth spreads down the coast with Mount Egmont as its backdrop. It offered a location, soils and climate immediately attractive to European settlers in the 1840s. As in the Waikato, the first missionaries and settlers found a Maori population depleted by inter-tribal wars, but nevertheless land troubles between the natives and newcomers beset the settlement from the beginning. War broke out in 1860 and eventually placed New Plymouth under virtual siege. The city has several historical buildings to remind of the past. St. Mary's Church is the oldest stone church in New Zealand, the remains of the church vicarage, built in 1845, have been restored by the Historic Places Trust. So has Richmond Cottage, the house of three of the first settler families, and Hurworth Cottage, built in 1855 and home of four-time New Zealand premier, Sir Harry Atkinson.

But it is New Plymouth's beautiful parks which are best known. **Pukekura Park**, once wasteland, has lovely lakes, gardens, a fernery, fountains and a waterfall, lit by night. The upper lake gives a postcard-like view of Mount Egmont.

In September and November, a 360-hectare (890-acre) park, 29 km (18 miles) from New Plymouth, provides one of the world's best displays of flowering rhododendron and azalea bushes in a native bush setting. The **Pukeiti Rhododendron Trust** is also a bird sanctuary, nestling between the Kaitake and Pouakai ranges. A loop road to the park passes the **Pouakai Wildlife Reserve** and zoo, where native and exotic birds and animals can be seen in a bush setting.

At **Egmont National Park**, skiers traverse the slopes in winter and in summer, climbers walk the bush tracks to discover waterfalls and enjoy native trees and plants, some unique to this park.

A climb to Egmont's summit is not difficult, but weather conditions change rapidly. On a clear day, the summit gives magnificent views across to the snow-capped peaks of the Tongariro National Park and over the dairy land to wild whitecaps of the Tasman Sea.

ROTORUA AND THE VOLCANIC PLATEAU

Of his visit to **Rotorua** in 1934, playwright George Bernard Shaw declared: "I was pleased to get so close to Hades and be able to return."

But Shaw was not the first to draw an analogy between Rotorua and the devil's eternal dwelling of fire and brimstone, for it was Victorian writer and war correspondent George Augustus Sala who, in 1885, christened one of the thermal areas "Hell's Gate."

To pious Anglican pioneers the region had all the hallmarks of Dante's Inferno – a barren wasteland of stunted vegetation, cratered with scalding cauldrons, bubbling mud pools and roaring geysers hurling super-heated water into a sulphur-laden atmosphere.

Today Rotorua represents pleasure and not torment, a place of thermal wonders, lush forests, green pastures and crystal clear lakes abounding with fighting trout. No fewer than 10 lakes are the playground of anglers, campers, swimmers, water-skiers, yachtsmen and pleasure boaters, comprising many of the 917,000 annual visitors from other parts of New Zealand as well as from overseas.

Rotorua is situated on a volcanic rift which stretches in a 200-km (124-mile) line from White Island off the coast of the Bay of Plenty to Lake Taupo and the volcanoes of the Tongariro National Park in the Central Plateau of the North Island. With a population of 59,000; Rotorua is an important forestry, farming and light industrial centre. The city has the greatest concentration of Maori residents of any New Zealand centre and is the national "hot spot" of Maori culture.

Rotorua was settled by descendants of voyagers from the legendary Maori homeland of Hawaiki, thought to be the Tahitian island group. Among the arrivals in the Te Awawa canoe around A.D. 1350 was the discoverer of Lake Rotorua, named in Maori tradition as Ihenga. Ihenga travelled inland from the settlement of Maketu and came across a lake he called Rotoiti, "little lake." He journeyed on to see a much larger lake which he called Rotorua, the "second lake."

The first European to visit "the disturbed districts," in 1830 was a Danish sailor, Captain Phillip Tapsell. On October 30, 1831, at the invitation of an Awawa tribal chief, missionaries Thomas Chapman and Henry Williams held the first Sunday service in Rotorua.

During the mid-1880s the Arawa tribe remained loyal to the British Crown and, as a result, were subjected to raids by warring Maori tribes. When the fighting ceased, the government decided to turn Rotorua into a tourist and health-spa resort. An agreement was reached in November 1880 for land on which to build a town to be leased from the Maori owners.

The state-controlled down settlement was administered by The Tourist and Health Resorts Department until 1923 when Rotorua finally achieved independent status.

Liquid Assets

The majority of Rotorua's biggest hotels and a large number of motels are located on or just off Fenton Street, running north-south across the city. It is only a short drive to the popular tourist attractions but some form of transport is essential. The Government Tourist Bureau in Fenton Street provides information on hire cars, coach excursions, trout fishing and sightseeing services.

East of the northern end of Fenton Street are the **Government Gardens** dominated by the magnificent **Bath House**. Built in 1908 as a sophisticated spa centre, the Bath House now houses an interesting local museum and art gallery. The scene is more English than England when white-uniformed bowls and croquet players compete on the lawns in front of the Elizabethan-styled building.

To the right of Bath House are the **Polynesian Pools**. Here are contained a number of thermal pools, each with its own special mineral content and varying temperatures. The Priest Pool was named after a Father Mahoney, who pitched his tent alongside a hot spring on the site in 1878 and bathed in the warm water until he reportedly obtained complete relief for his rheumatism. Other pools in the complex include the Rachel and Radium Springs.

Rotorua's world-famous thermal waters and their alleged miraculous healing properties were central to the European

development of the area. In 1874, former New Zealand Premier Sir William Fox urged the government to "secure the whole of the Lake Country as a sanatorium owing to the ascertained healing properties of the water." Bubbling with optimism, Sir William enthused that the district "might be destined to be the sanatorium not only of the Australian colonies but of India and other portions of the globe."

The building of the first sanatorium began in 1880 and, although Rotorua's sulphurous waters are still employed by Queen Elizabeth Hospital in the treatment of arthritis and rheumatism, they are viewed by tourists and locals alike as a pleasant form of relaxation – guaranteed to soothe frayed nerves and ensure a good night's sleep. Fronting the Government Gardens is the **Orchid Garden**, two temperature controlled glass houses filled with exotic blooms from around the world. Wander through to the theatrette where the Southern Hemisphere's only illuminated water organ dives and dances to an ever-changing music backdrop.

Along the lakefront from the Government Gardens is the historic Maori village of **Ohinemutu**, once the main settlement on the lake. On the site is St. Faith's Church built in 1910, with its rich carvings, Maori Christ window and bust of Queen Victoria, presented to the Maori people of Rotorua as a token of their loyalty to the Crown. An adjacent 19th century meeting house took 12 years to carve and is named after the captain of the Arawa canoe, Tama te Kapua.

Ohinemutu also has connections with Rotorua's Arawa discoverer, Ihenga. The names translates as "the place where the young woman was killed"; it is said that Ihenga's daughter Hine-te-Kakara, was murdered and her body thrown into a boiling mud pool where Ihenga set up a memorial stone, calling it Ohinemutu.

At the lakeside, float-planes, launches and the Lakeland Queen paddle steamer depart on flightseeing and sightseeing trips. A popular launch excursion is to **Mokoia Island** in the middle of Lake Rotorua, where visitors stop for a dip in Hinemoa's hot pool.

The Maori have a "Romeo and Juliet" love story connected with Mokoia Island. A young chieftain, Tutanekai, lived on the island; he fell in love with the maiden

Preceding pages, Whakarewarewa. **Below, Government Gardens, Rotorua.**

Hinemoa, who lived in a village on the mainland. Their marriage was forbidden by family opposition but Hinemoa secretly planned to follow the sound of Tutanekai's bone flute over the water during the night and join her lover. The plot was foiled when her people beached all the heavy canoes, so Hinemoa tied gourds to her body and swam across the chilling lake, following the sounds of Tutanekai's flute. Hinemoa recovered from her ordeal by warming herself in a hot pool that bears her name before being reunited with Tutanekai.

Mud and Geysers

At the southern end of Fenton Street is the **Whakarewarewa** thermal area, abbreviated to "Whaka" by the locals and a must for tourists. Unfortunately, too many visitors hurry down the main path, past a quiescent Geyser Flat and into the Maori settlement below, without savouring the attractions of the thermal area.

On Geyser Flat is **Pohutu** ("splashing"), the greatest geyser in New Zealand, thundering to a height of more than 30 metres (about 100 feet). The geyser is unpredictable but usually plays several times a day and sometimes almost continuously. As a warning, its eruption is often preceded by the playing of the Prince of Wales Feathers, a smaller geyser next to Pohutu. The big geyser is well worth waiting for.

At the entrance to "Whaka" is a model Maori *pa* incorporating a spacious meeting house, in which lunchtime Maori concerts are performed in a realistic setting. Maori groups also sing and dance at Ohinemutu and in major hotels.

Close to the top entrance is the **Maori Arts and Crafts Institute** where skilled Maori carvers and flax weavers can be observed at work. The intricately carved archway to "Whaka" depicts Hinemoa and Tutanekai embracing.

The bottom path exists past the Maori settlement where tribal people have, for generations, used the thermal waters for cooking, washing and heating.

In Tryon Street, colonial-styled shops in the **Little Village** sell sheepskins, furs, handicrafts and souvenirs. A greenstone carver can be watched at work. A fascinating but inexpensive item, which can be purchased from a small printery, is a

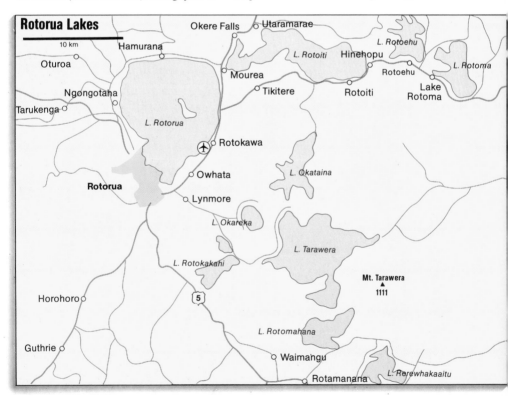

Rotorua Lakes

10 km

Okere Falls — Utaramarae

Hamurana

Oturoa

L. Rotoehu

L. Rotoiti — Hinehopu

Rotoehu

L. Rotoma

Mourea

Ngongotaha

Tikitere

Rotoiti

Lake Rotoma

Tarukenga

L. Rotorua

Rotokawa

Owhata

L. Okataina

Rotorua

Lynmore

L. Okareka

L. Tarawera

L. Rotokakahi

Mt. Tarawera
1111

Horohoro

5

L. Rotomahana

Guthrie

Waimangu

Rotamanana

L. Rerewhakaaitu

reprint of the *Hot Lakes Chronicle* of 1886 containing historical photographs and newspaper accounts of the devastating Tarawera eruption.

Departing via Froude Street, take a look at the **Arikapakapa Golf Course**, the only one in the world with boiling mud pool "traps" and hot pool "hazards."

Rainbow Country

Proceeding west from Rotorua on Highway 5, just 4 km (2½ miles) from the city, is the terminus for Skyline-Skyrides. Ride their gondolas mid-way up Mount Ngongotaha for a breathtaking view of the city, lake and surrounding countryside. For the more adventurous, plunge downhill again in a high-speed luge cart.

For a more relaxed stop-over, take in the fragrant delights of the neighbouring Herb Garden. Visitors will find **Rainbow** and **Fairy Springs**, containing natural pools crammed with thousands of rainbow, brown and brook trout among 12 hectares (30 acres) of native tree ferns and natural surroundings. Huge trout can be seen through an underwater viewing window and hand-fed along with species

of New Zealand deer, native birds and "Captain Cooker" wild pigs, introduced by the famous explorer himself. Live kiwis peck around in a nocturnal house.

Other trout springs are **Paradise Valley**, 11 km (7 miles) west of Rotorua and **Hamurana Springs** on the northern shore.

Brown trout from Britain via Tasmania were introduced to Rotorua in 1889; rainbow trout from Sonoma Creek, California, were released in 1898 and thrived.

To protect sports fisheries, it has been made illegal to buy or sell trout in New Zealand. But a trout dinner is an easy catch with fishing guides claiming a 97 percent daily "strike" rate. In fact no trip to Rotorua-Taupo is complete without a fishing expedition on the lakes. Guides supply all tackle (often including cups of "fortified" coffee) and will meet clients outside hotels, with trailer boats ready for action, or at the boat harbour.

Rainbow trout on most lakes around Rotorua and on Lake Taupo average 1.4 kg (3 pounds) but on Lake Tarawera, where they are tougher to catch, fish of 3.5 kg to 5.5 kg (8 to 12 pounds) are not uncommon. The icing on the cake after a

Fire watcher at Rainbow Mountain.

day of fishing is having a hotel or restaurant chef prepare the catch – a service specialty they are well used to providing.

Also west of Rotorua, through **Ngongotaha**, is the spacious **Agrodome** located in 40 hectares (100 acres) pasture. Twice-daily "sheep shows" are particularly popular with Asians. The one-hour show explains the merits of 19 obedient rams through a multiple sound system. Following a shearing and sheepdog demonstration, visitors gather handfuls of freshly shorn wool and have their photos taken with rams and sheepdogs.

A drive to the top of Mount Ngongotaha is rewarded by a breathtaking panorama of the entire region.

Along Central Road, past Ngongotaha township, the Farm House hires out ponies and horses for riding over 600 acres of bush-edged farmland. The west-shore road continues to **Okere Falls** and **Hinemoa Steps** where, after a short walk through native forest and down a cliffside, the Kaituna River can be viewed thundering through a narrow chasm into the swirling pool below.

Proceeding north and east around Lake Rotorua, past the Ohau Channel outlet into **Lake Rotoiti**, an eastbound turn onto Highway 30, towards Whakatane, takes visitors to the door of **Hell's Gate**. The Maori name *Tikitere* recalls the legend of Huritini, who threw herself into a boiling pool because her husband treated her with contempt. *Tikitere* is a contraction of *Taku tiki i tere nei*, "my daughter has floated away." The volcanic activity here covers 4 hectares (10 acres), highlighted by the Kakahi hot waterfall.

With time in hand, a drive farther down Highway 30 along the shores of lakes Rotoiti, Rotoehu and Rotoma, with a diversion to the totally unspoiled Lake Okataina, is well worthwhile.

For a dip with a difference, take a side road between lakes Rotoehu and Rotoma to **Soda Springs**, where hot water percolates into a clear stream bed. Bathers pay a few cents to local Maori to change in wooden sheds, then lie in the flowing stream of warm water surrounded by open sky, pastures and trees.

The Eruption of Tarawera

Southeast of Rotorua, heading for the airport, is the turnoff to the forest-clad

Silica Terraces, Waiotapu.

Blue and Green Lakes is a favourite stomping ground for joggers and a retreat for those who enjoy walking or riding the well-marked and graded trails through exotic pines and native bush. Horses and ponies are available for hire. From a scenic vantage point, on a fine day, Lakes Tikitapu and Rotokakahi reflect contrasting blue and green colours, giving rise to their European names.

The road continues to **Lake Tarawera** via the buried village of **Te Wairoa**, destroyed on June 10, 1886 when an awesome eruption of Mount Tarawera blasted rock, lava and ash into the air over a 15,540-sq km (6,000-sq mile) area and buried the villages of Te Wairoa, Te Ariki and Moura, killing 147 Maori and six Europeans. The Buried Village contains items excavated from Te Wairoa including the *whare* (hut) of a *tohunga* (priest) who foretold the disaster and was unearthed alive four days after the eruption.

From Te Wairoa, before the eruption, Victorian tourists had been rowed across Lake Tarawera to the fabulous **Pink and White Terraces** – two huge silica formations which rose 250 metres (820 feet) from the shores of **Lake Rotomahana**

and were billed as one of "the eight wonder of the world" by writers of the 1800s.

Mount Tarawera ("burnt spear") looms on the eastern shores of both lakes. Flights over the crater and the thermal areas are conducted by Volcanic Wunderflites from Rotorua Airport. A thrilling landing on the mountain's slopes allows for a close inspection of the 6-km long, 250-metre deep chasm caused by the volcanic explosion which rent the mountain in two.

Adding to Tarawera's mysterious aura is the verified account of a ghostly war canoe full of mourning, flax-robed Maori seen by two separate boatloads of tourists on Lake Tarawera on the misty morning of May 31, 1886. Returning to Te Wairoa, the tourists found the local Maori in a state of terror for no such canoe existed in the region. Tuhuto, the *tohunga,* prophesied the apparition was "an omen that all this region will be overwhelmed." On a chilly, moonlit night 11 days later, Mount Tarawera fulfilled his prophecy to the letter, blasting the Pink and White Terraces off the world tourist map forever.

Twenty km (12½ miles) south of Rotorua, on Highway 5 towards Taupo, is

Proud fisherman holds on to trout, at Turangi.

Waimangu Valley. This unspoilt thermal area contains the Waimangu Cauldron, the world's largest boiling lake.

An easy walk downhill from a tearoom leads past bubbling crater lakes, hot creeks and algae-covered silica terraces to the shores of Lake Rotomahana (a refuge of black swans), where a launch can be taken to the intensively active Steaming Cliffs and site of the lost Pink and White Terraces. The valley is also the site of the extinct Waimangu ("black water") Geyser which hurled black water and mud to an incredible height of 500 metres (over 1,600 feet) between 1900 and 1904, on one occasion killing four tourists who ventured too close.

Another 10 km (6 miles) south on Highway 5 is a loop road leading to the **Waiotapu** ("sacred waters") thermal area. This contains the Lady Knox geyser, which erupts daily at 10:15 a.m. (with the encouragement of a little soap). Other attractions include the boiling Champagne Pool, tinted silica terraces and the Bridal Veil Falls. A free treat is a diversion off the loop road (watch for the sign) to some intriguing boiling mud pools and the Waikite Thermal Baths.

"Taupo," an abbreviation of *Taupo-nui-Tia* ("the great shoulder cloak of Tia"), takes its name from the Arawa canoe explorer who discovered Lake Taupo. The lake covers 608 sq km (235 sq miles) and was formed by volcanic explosions over thousands of years. It is now the most famous trout-fishing lake in the world, yielding in excess of 500 tonnes of rainbow trout annually to enthusiastic anglers fishing from boats and along the shores.

The rivers flowing into the lake are equally well stocked and fishermen frequently stand shoulder-to-shoulder at the mouth of the Waitahanui River forming what has come to be known as "the picket fence." Arrangements for boat hires can be made at the picturesque boat harbour and information centre, where a restored steamboat, *Ernest Kemp,* departs regularly on lake excursions. Or see the lake from the decks of the *Taupo Cat* an up-to-the-minute catamaran.

About 40 km (25 miles) northwest of Taupo and 70 km (44 miles) south of Rotorua is the active and well-signposted **Orakei-Korako** thermal area. Maori chiefs once decorated themselves in mir-

Hopeful angler at Taupo.

ror pools here, giving rise to the name which means "place of adorning."

Special features are the jet-boat journey across Lake Ohakuri, the 40-metre (130-foot) Great Golden Fleece terrace, underground hot pools in Aladdin's Cave and a huge area of silica deposits pockmarked with hot springs.

Some 7 km north of Taupo, just below the junction of highways 1 and 5, is the dramatic **Wairakei Geothermal Power Station.** Super-heated water is drawn from the ground through a series of bores, enabling dry steams to be piped to electricity turbines in a nearby powerhouse. At the entrance to the field is an information office; a road to the left of the pipelines winds to a hilltop observation area.

A nearby loop road leads to the spectacular **Huka Falls** where the full force of the newly born Waikato River hurtles from a narrow gorge over a 12-metre (40-foot) ledge. Lit by bright sunshine, the ice-cold water takes on a turquoise-blue colour as it hangs in mid-air before crashing into a foaming basin. *Huka* means "foam"; the falls are best observed across the footbridge from the opposite side of the river.

Chateau Tongariro.

A short distance along the loop road on the banks of the Waikato River is the famous Huka Fishing Lodge and a small replica pioneer village.

Also between Wairakei and Taupo, on a gravel road, are **The Craters of the Moon**, a wild thermal area controlled by the Forest Service. Entry is free. Visitors can gaze into a frightening abyss of furiously boiling mud and walk around a track to see steam rising from natural fumaroles in the hillside.

The international golf course at Wairakei is among the best in New Zealand.

The Information Centre in Taupo's Tongariro Street will give advice on sightseeing, attractions for children, as well as on flight-seeing. Impressive scenic flights by floatplane from the lakefront, or by fixed-winged aircraft and helicopters from the airport south of Taupo, are made to snow-capped summits of the volcanoes in Tongariro National Park.

At the southern head of Lake Taupo is the 7,600-sq km (2,930-sq mile) **Tongariro National Park** containing the three active volcanic mountains of Tongariro (1,968 metres; 6,400 feet), Ngau-

ruhoe (2,290 metres; 7,517 feet) and Ruapehu (2,796 metres; 9,175 feet).

The most scenic route from Taupo leaves Highway 1 at Turangi heading for Tokaanu, not far from the Tongariro Power Station, and winds up through bush-covered mountains and around the shore of Lake Rotoaira. The alternative route is to turn off the main highway at Rangipo onto Highway 47.

A brief diversion to **Tokaanu**, 60 km (37 miles) from Taupo, reveals a small thermal area, the Domain Thermal Baths and the historic St. Paul's 19th century church. According to Maori legend the volcanic fires of the Tongariro National Park were kindled when the priest and explorer Ngatoro-i-rangi was in danger of freezing to death on the mountains. His fervent prayers for assistance were answered by the fire demons of Hawaiki, who sent fire via White Island and Rotorua to burst out through the mountaintops. To appease the gods, Ngatoro cast his female slave into the Ngauruhoe volcano – called by the girl's name, Auruhoe, by the local Maori.

Ngauruhoe with its typical volcanic cone is the most active of the three moun-

tains and occasionally erupts spectacular clouds of smoke and ash. A major eruption in 1954-1955 continued intermittently for nine months.

Ruapehu ("exploding hole") is a perpetually snow-capped, multiple volcano with a flattened summit stretching 3 km (1.8 miles) and incorporating an acidic, bubbling Crater Lake and six small glaciers. Ruapehu has blown out clouds of steam and ash a number of times in the past 100 years, raining dust over a 90-km (56-mile) radius in 1945.

The mountain was directly responsible for a train disaster in which 151 people died on Christmas Eve 1953. A *lahar* or violent discharge of water from Crater Lake roared down the Whangaehu River carrying large quantities of sand and boulders before it. The torrent slammed into a railway bridge at Tangiwai, 35 km (23 miles) away, sweeping it into the night. Minutes later, a Wellington-Auckland express train and five carriages careened down the track, plunging to its doom in the raging river below.

Tongariro is the lowest of the three mountains with a series of small craters and the Ketetahi hot springs on the northern slopes.

The mountaintops were sacred to the Maori of the Ngati-Tuwharetoa tribe. In 1887, hereditary chief Te Heuheu Tukino made a gift of the summits to the federal government as New Zealand's first national park in order to protect them from exploitation.

For the tourist with days to spend in the park, rangers at the national park headquarters near **Chateau Tongariro** will give full information on walking tracks and accommodation huts. For the tourist on a limited time schedule, however, it is reward enough to glimpse Ngauruhoe belching puffs of smoke on a clear day and snow-decked Ruapehu soaring as a picture-postcard backdrop for the wild, rocky rivers on the western slopes.

In the winter, Mount Ruapehu is the major ski area of the North Island. The Chateau Tongariro-Whakapapa skifield is New Zealand's oldest, but more recently, the Turoa and Tukino fields have been developed.

"Adventure tour" operators also offer thrill-seeking tourists the prospect of a white water raft journey down the Tongariro and Rangitikei rivers.

Left, raft ride at Aniwhenua Falls. **Right**, green acres; in the background are Mount Ngauruhoe (on the left) and Mount Ruapehu.

POVERTY BAY
AND HAWKE BAY

High on Kaiti Hill, overlooking the city of Gisborne and the sprawling countryside beyond, is a life-size figure of the British explorer, Captain James Cook, looking to the mouth of the Turanganui River where he first stood on New Zealand soil. The site is historic for that reason, although the occasion – October 10, 1769 – was marred by a fracas with native Maori. But the site is noted also for the ageless reason that Gisborne, situated on 178 degrees longitude, is the first city in the world to greet the rising sun each day. Hence, it is the Sunrise Coast.

Across the bay from Kaiti Hill is Young Nick's Head, a promontory named after 12-year-old Nicholas Young who was surgeon's boy in Cook's ship *HMS Endeavour*. Nicholas was the first to sight land as the ship sailed in from the east in fine sunny weather, but history does not record whether he drew the gallon of rum which the captain had promised to the first man to sight land.

Cook erred badly, however, in the region Poverty Bay, because "it did not afford a single article we wanted, except a little firewood." Poverty Bay today is sheep and cattle country with a leavening of food-processing crops, citrus and kiwifruit orchards. It runs all the way from Cape Runaway in the north to the Mahia Peninsula, which bleeds into Hawke Bay.

Hawke Bay – named by Cook after the then-First Lord of the Admiralty – is again sheep and cattle country, with orchards around Hastings and small cropping for the country's largest food-processing factory. The twin cities of **Napier** and **Hastings** are only 20 km (12 miles) apart, but each has its own newspaper, radio station, civic administration, tourist attractions ... and suspicions of the other. Napier is a seafront city, serving an urban area population of 52,100 and bidding lustily for tourists; Hastings is an island marketing centre, urban area population 55,400. Both cities have a reasonable industrial base, good shopping facilities and good holiday accommodation.

They share, too, and Gisborne to a much lesser extent, a moment of tragedy when New Zealand's worst earthquake struck on Feb. 3, 1931. Buildings crumpled under the impact of a 7.9 Richter scale quake. What the shock did not destroy in the inner city areas of Napier and Hastings, fire did. The death toll of 258 included a substantial number of people killed by falling parapets. Others died from fire or smoke fumes and many survivors were scarred for life. Heroic deeds were performed by impromptu rescuers and by naval personnel from a sloop which happened to be in Napier harbour.

Napier suffered the most, with women and children evacuated along with the injured. Relief camps were set up in both cities; medical and engineering teams came from other North Island centres; and two earthquake commissioners were appointed by the government to replace civic administration for a period of two years. Hastings fought its own post-earthquake battles. At other places throughout the province, and into Poverty Bay, the smaller communities and individuals worked to repair the damage – not least at the town of Wairoa, where three people died.

Left, "Hawkeye" – the world's largest rugby mascot. Right, Pania.

This was Depression time but a sympathetic government and a sympathetic world came to Hawke Bay post-earthquake aid. Funds were sought and found and the rubble cleared. A town-planning opportunity was taken to widen streets, and a strict earthquake-proof building code was enforced. A true community spirit was created, particularly in Napier where the only earthquake memorials exist.

One such is the seafront colonnade, built on earthquake rubble from the stricken city centre. The visitor should tread warily, for who knows what dreams lie buried here? Engraved on the colonnade is an earthquake requiem:

... Although his buildings crumble to a mound
Of worthless ruins, man has always found
The urge to build a stronger city there
...

And build they did, aided by a fortuitous 2-metre (6½-foot) upheaval of some 4,000 hectares (10,000 acres) of former marshland around Napier. This challenge

to rebuild, and build better, fired a special kind of community enthusiasm in Napier, evident today in private gifts down the years for a public good.

Marine Treasures

Napier's seafront **Marine Parade**, with its towering Norfolk pines, hosts many of these gifts including a Sound Shell colonnade (with its tribute to the sloop in harbour that earthquake day), a golden girl lifting her hands high to the sky (the "Spirit of Napier"), and Pania, another statue, of a Maori maiden of offshore legend.

Another sculpture – Napier is rich in sculptures for a place its size – of trawlermen hauling a laden net, stands outside the **Hawke Bay Aquarium**. It complements another impressive Marine Parade neighbour, **Marineland**, where performing dolphins and sea lions cavort before a captivated audience.

But Napier is much more than its Marine Parade. The **Waiapu Anglican Cathedral** rises white, severe, on the site of the former church destroyed in the earthquake. British poet laureate John

Napier after the earthquake.

Masefield composed hymns for this church: "… Grant to this Shrine its purposed end, Of greater Hope and Light and Praise."

More than 400 yachts sail out of the Napier Sailing Club's international complex, while from the nearby Big Game Fishing Club, launches seek marlin and tuna. The **Hawke Bay Museum and Art Gallery** is rich in Maori artefacts and colonial culture.

On the outskirts of the city is the **Marist Brothers Seminary**, better known to a lay public perhaps for its winery producing "Mission" wine of an acceptable standard. The Brothers are the oldest commercial winemakers in New Zealand. Visitors are welcome to stroll round the vaulted cellars and sample the products.

This is one of 15 wineries in the Napier-Hastings area. A "wine trail" is indeed a pleasant way to spend an afternoon, and it leads to the oldest winery in New Zealand, **Te Mata Estate** in Havelock North; or to the hospitable restaurant at **Vidal's winery** in Hastings, where the diner can sip wine produced on the other side of the wall.

Napier today.

Fantastic Hastings

Chief attraction in Hastings is **Fantasyland**, a make-believe Disney-type wonderland visited by some 50,000 people a year. They enjoy a full-size pirate ship with skull-and-crossbones flag, a two-storey castle with moat and drawbridge, the shoe in which lived the old woman with so many children, Noddy Town with miniature buildings for the delight of small children, and lots more in an escape from reality.

As "The Fruit Bowl of New Zealand," Hastings is surrounded by hectares of fruit trees which in spring throw showers of white, pink and green blossoms. A spring rite in years gone by was the Hastings Blossom Parade, succeeded now by an October Spring Festival, with a different theme each year. The orchards create the largest fruit-growing district in New Zealand. Apricots, cherries, nectarines, peaches, plums, apples, pears and various berries can be bought at wayside stalls in season, as can a wide range of vegetables. Good subsoils, a Mediterranean-type climate, water from underground aquifers, and growers ready to

test new methods are translated into hectare after hectare of crops – tomatoes and sweet corn, asparagus and kiwifruit, grapes and pipfruit – pushing greedily into pastoral farming land in the areas of high-yielding soil.

As with most New Zealand cities, Hastings has its "Scenic Drive, a signposted tour of suburbs, parks and major attractions. Oak Avenue is a magnificent 1½-km avenue of old-established oak trees which meet in shadowy canopy overhead. Also notable is wartime artist Peter McIntyre's outsize memorial mural in the public library. Nearby is **Havelock North**, the "village," in a sylvan setting in the shadow of Te Mata Peak, three-quarters of the way up which is a restaurant where one may enjoy a panorama reaching right to the sea.

Norwegians and Danes

Pastoral farming is the dominant industry in the East Coast region. Coastal farm development depended on service by sea, bullock wagons being used as late as 1942 to carry wool and bulk goods up and down the coast to rendezvous with ships offshore. Dense vegetation discouraged settlement in inland areas until the government attracted Scandinavian settlers. Today southern Hawke Bay has a Scandinavian heritage: **Norsewood** was settled by Norwegians, a fine colonial museum in a restored settler's house captures the pioneering past. **Dannevirke** ("Dane's Work") boasts a tree-dotted domain where native birds are kept in captivity, one of the few places licensed to do so.

South of the Central Hawke Bay town of **Waipukurau** is a hill which has the highly impressive name of Taumatawhakatangihangakoauauotamateapokaiwhenuakitanatahu, which translated means "The hill where the great husband of heaven, Tamatea, caused plaintive music from his nose flute to ascend to his beloved."

More than 30 Maori *marae* (meeting grounds) exist in Hawke Bay. That at **Te Hauke**, some 20 km (12 miles) south of Hastings, is among the more innovative, with a "language nest" for pre-school children where only the Maori language is spoken, while a work skills programme for 15 to 24-year-olds is also conducted. **Waipiro Bay**.

Much farther south is **Te Aute College**, founded in 1872 for the sons of Maori chiefs and still an educational force in Maoridom.

The Road to Gisborne

From **Wairoa**, halfway between Napier and Gisborne, begins the spectacular coastal vistas of white sand and sparkling blue summer waters which accompany the scarlet blossom of the *pohutukawa* tree, often called the "Christmas tree" because it is then at its best. The combination of sand, water and blossom gives postcard views. It's a pity that this 480-km (300-mile) coastal road leading up to and beyond Gisborne, all the way to Opotiki, is not a recognised tourist route. In the *pohutukawa* season, it surely deserves to be.

Some of this colour rubs off on **Gisborne** (urban area population 32,000), a city of sun and water, parks, bridges and beaches. Water sports are a recreational way of life, prompted by the everlasting beaches only minutes from any part of the city. To walk where Captain Cook walked, along Kaiti and Wai-

Pohutukawa trees, East Cape.

kanae beaches, is surely to tread in the footsteps of history.

Gisborne lingers over its association with Cook. His landing place is a green reserve with a memorial obelisk. Bicentennial celebrations in 1969 were held here, attended by members of the British, Australian, Canadian, United States and New Zealand navies.

Young Nick's statue stands at the northern end of Waikanae Beach, looking out over Young Nick's Head and Poverty Bay. A cannon from Cook's *Endeavour* is displayed at the Gisborne Museum and Arts Centre, while one of the wards in the Gisborne District Council is called Cook.

A wide collection of historic treasures from the East Coast is housed at the Museum, reflecting also the region's Maori tradition and culture and extensive Maori land holdings, much of which is leased to European farmers.

Not least among the Maori inheritance are Maori meeting houses with carved lintels, panels and beams done in traditional style, or the unorthodox folk paintings of patterned foliage, birds and figures. The largest meeting house in New Zealand, **Poho-o-Rawiri** ("The Bosom of Rawiri") at the base of Kaiti Hill, is richly carved in the traditional manner; but almost every Maori settlement along this coast has its treasured house. These houses are part of a tranquil scene today, with the large Maori population of the province engaged in farming, food-processing and meat-freezing works. But in times long gone there was fighting and bloodshed.

Te Kooti and the Hauhau

Hauhau religious fanatics fanned the flames of rebellion in the 1860s and after inevitable defeat by government forces, many of the rebels were exiled to the Chatham Islands. Te Kooti, lowly born but an inspired leader who founded a genuine religious movement (Ringatau, which still exists in Maoridom) escaped back to Poverty Bay, rounded up followers and, when pursued by troops, embarked on a campaign of mayhem and murder. He swooped on farmhouses, native villages and *pa*, ravaging whatever stood in his way with tomahawk and bayonet. Although relentlessly pursued he evaded the troopers time and again,

mainly escaping into the Urewera Range. One of the darker chapters of Poverty Bay's story, the Te Kooti saga nevertheless had a placid ending with his being pardoned in old age and allowed to live in the security of his faith.

Te Kooti did spare the **Matawhero church**, built in 1862 of pit-sawn timber and used at first as a storehouse. Now serving the Presbyterian faith, it is the oldest church in Poverty Bay.

A mostly rugged interior restricts most horticultural development to coastal areas, with some commercial forestry being undertaken.

Poverty Bay is the largest producer of sweet corn in New Zealand. Citrus fruits are a familiar part of the scene: is there anything so still and so pleasing as a citrus orchard, golden-yellow fruit against dark green leaves, the trees in ordered lines, and green grass beneath?

Gisborne is also white wine country. Denis Irwin's Matawhero winery is noted for a magnificent Gerwurtztraminer amid other award-winning wines, while the province is coming into prominence for premium Chardonnay grapes.

Father figures such as Thomas Nelson (freezing works) and James Wattie (food processing) in Hawke Bay are complemented in Poverty Bay by members of a remarkable pioneering family, the Williams. William Williams opened a mission post at Turanga (now Gisborne) in 1840; his descendants and those of his brother Henry developed large tracts of farmland. The family tradition of generous and widespread public benefaction is still carried on.

Much of Te Kooti's old haunts have been preserved in the untamed **Urewera National Park**, northwest of Hawke Bay, and west of Poverty Bay, a 211,700-hectare (523,000-acre) region of natural beauty in forest and lake. Here abound the shining and long-tailed cuckoos, moreporks, parakeets, *tui, kaka,* pigeons and some kiwis.

Lake Waikaremoana ("Sea of Rippling Water") is the star feature, a trout-rich reserve where the bush crowds down to the water's edge, except on the east side where cliffs rise almost perpendicularly. Chalet, motel and motor camp accommodation is available at Waikaremoana near park headquarters, with hunting and tramping huts throughout the park.

Left, gannet from the colony at Cape Kidnappers. Right, Lake Waikaremoana.

MANAWATU AND WANGANUI

Where does a square turn full circle? In **Palmerston North**, flourishing centre of rich agricultural Manawatu.

The city's most famous feature isn't round, but nowadays it is as the city settlers wanted it. They envisaged a central public park, but instead – for three-quarters of a century – the railroad ran through the middle of town. In 1962 the railway was shifted to the settlement's northern fringe, and **The Square** in New Zealand's second largest inland city has since changed quite dramatically.

Named in Maori *Te Marae o Hine* or "Courtyard of the Daughter of Peace," the Square commemorates a chieftainess named Te Rongorito who sought an end to inter-tribal warfare in the early days of European settlement. In spring and summer, city workers enjoy their lunches on the grass of the Square; frequent open-air displays, recitals and forums add to the informal atmosphere.

Standing in the Square, you are surrounded by the city's main retail area and civic and cultural amenities. Most evident is the **Civic Centre**, a controversial structure protruding into the 6-hectare (15-acre) Square. Designed in an architectural competition marking the city's centenary in 1971, the Centre features in its foyer a striking *pou whenua* (totem pole) skilfully carved from *totara* by young Maori artist Te Aturangi Nepia Clamp. On top there's a lookout – not high, but this is a flat city.

The Civic Centre extends back onto former railway land, which is also the site for a new art gallery, theatre and convention centre, and a not-so-new museum. The Opera House, other theatres and cinemas, and the Square Edge – a community arts centre – are handy as well.

Education and Research

Roads radiate outwards. Prettiest is tree-lined Fitzherbert Avenue leading to the **Manawatu River**, the city's other major focal point. The river is crossed by one bridge, featuring an afterthought bicycle lane to cater for the hundreds who cycle daily to **Massey University** and the

Jerusalem, Wanganui River.

156

research stations, **Dairy Research Institute** and **DSIR Grasslands**.

These institutions are world-famed for agricultural research, and themselves attract many visitors. Drive through Massey's bush and garden setting via the university ring road, or stroll leisurely through the campus, which serves 16,000 students each year. Palmerston North has gradually assumed the role of a university city, Massey contributing greatly to the economic and cultural well-being.

On the city side of the Manawatu River, the pride of Palmerston North is **The Esplanade**, a reserve catering for light recreation, simple pleasures or peaceful contemplation, depending on one's mood. Children can cavort in the playground, and adults can join them on the miniature railway. The Lido swimming complex (including an indoor pool) adjoins the motor camp. Mini-golf challenges skill, but not stamina. Don't miss the Rose Garden, which has a distinguished record of developing new varieties. Palmerston North justifiably calls itself the "Rose City."

The city is frequently chosen as the site of national sports tournaments, thanks in part to its **Sports Stadium**. Accommodating 4,000-plus spectators, it is also a favoured venue for rock concerts. Also in Palmerston North, the **National Rugby Museum** is the best of its kind. The city has two racecourses and two nine-hole public golf courses.

Exploring Manawatu

The most dramatic road and rail approach to Palmerston North and the Manawatu region is from Hawke's Bay through the rugged **Manawatu Gorge**. The narrow, winding road requires careful attention. The growing country town of **Ashhurst** lies between the gorge and Palmerston North; travellers can detour here to **Pohangina** and **Totara Reserve**, an area of virgin native bush favoured locally for picnics and for swimming in the Pohangina River.

Less than 30 minutes' drive south of Palmerston North on Highway 57 is the **Tokomaru Steam Museum**; visitors can picnic and swim here at Horseshoe Bend. Highway 56 heads west to beaches at **Himitange** and **Foxton**. (They aren't great beaches, but they are well-

Dawn on the Wanganui.

patronised.) **Feilding** is 20 minutes north on Highway 54. This large town boasts two squares, a motor-racing track and racecourse, and a stock sale on Friday mornings. The surrounding region is perhaps the best place to fit in a stud-farm tour, certainly a worthwhile experience in Manawatu.

Historic Homestead

Highway 3 proceeds northwest from Palmerston North towards Wanganui, 70 km (43 miles) away. The first point of interest along this route is **Mount Stewart**, from which summit there is a fine view of the rich Manawatu pastures. A memorial near the road commemorates early settlers. It's a short hop from here to the historic homestead and gardens at **Mount Lees Reserve**.

The largest township en route to Wanganui is **Bulls**. Further your agricultural education by branching off here toward the coast to **Flock House**, an agricultural training institute. The house was built in 1895; it was purchased in 1923 by the New Zealand Sheepgrowers, which ran a scheme to train as farmers the sons of British seamen's widows. Just north of Bulls, pleasant detours can be made to **Duddings Lake Reserve** (where there is boating and water-skiing) and **Heaton Park** (with its fine old elms and oaks). But don't trespass in **Santoft Forest**. You can drive quickly through **Turakina** but if you have time, visit **Ratana**, a small township named after a famous Maori prophet and faith healer. A temple was built there in 1927.

Wanganui: The River City

The **Wanganui River** greets visitors on arrival at friendly **Wanganui**. The river, though not sparkling near the town as its muddy bed is stirred by the Tasman Sea, is the city's most remarkable asset and New Zealand's longest navigable river. Canoeists and jet boaters testify annually to its pleasures. Boat trips of various kinds operate from downtown Wanganui and from just outside at **Holly Lodge Winery**, Wanganui's fast-growing attraction.

Reminders of river history abound in Wanganui, particularly in **Moutoa Gardens**, where there is a monument to **Hazy, lazy...**

Maori who stood on the side of the British in the 19th century wars, and to the Maori chief Te Rangihuwinui (Major Kemp). In the superb **Wanganui Regional Museum** are a store of Maori artefacts and a war canoe, *Te Mata-o-Hoturoa*, once used on the river. The museum also boasts a remarkable collection of Lindauer paintings.

Before further exploring Wanganui, take the lift up the Memorial Tower on **Durie Hill**. The elevator climbs 66 metres (216 feet) through the hill. But if you want to walk up, the 176 tower steps are worth the trouble on a fine day, when you will get a magnificent view of the city and river – and may even sight the South Island.

Virginia Lake is a popular stop by day and night, when a fountain plays in colour. Spend some time, too, in **Sargeant Gallery** and **Putiki Church**. Children love the playground on Anzac Parade and White Stag Park. For evening relaxation, the city has some fine restaurants.

Chief attractions west on Highway 3 from the city are the **Bason Botanical Reserve** and **Bushy Park** scenic reserve, both reached easily with short detours.

... and just biding time.

Highway 4 north, through the Paraparas, is justly noted for its beauty. To the east of Wanganui and north of Palmerston North, the **Rangitikei River** – excellent in its upper reaches for whitewater rafting – links with Highway 1 near **Managaweka**. Enquire there or in Wanganui or Palmerston North about rafting. But book well in advance, and make your journey with an experienced member of the Professional Rafting Association.

The Road to Jerusalem

The highlight of any visit to the Wanganui area is the 79-km (49-mile) River Road. Contact the Visitors Information Centre in Wanganui and book a seat on John Hammond's mini-bus, which leaves the city at 7 a.m., Monday through Friday. This is your chance to sample a slice of remote New Zealand life as the driver delivers daily mail, bread and milk to the small settlements along the banks of the Wanganui River.

As you follow the narrow, largely unsealed road, you will learn something of Maori culture and family life today. You may also visualise the violence of the 1860s when the region's loyal Maori repelled the rebellious Hauhaus. As you approach **Jerusalem** (*Hiruharama* to the Maori), you will understand why Catholic missionaries established themselves at this bend in the river, and why poet James Baxter chose the serenity of this site for a commune in the early 1970s. If you want to see relics of this commune, however, you will be disappointed, as it disintegrated after Baxter's death in 1972. It will cost you $3 to view his grave, now on private property.

Top of the route is **Pipiriki**, once a thriving tourist town, now served by a solitary shop – Palmerston North's former piecart. Pipiriki remains beautiful, however, and its camping ground offers a base for tramping. There are many listed walks; **Mangapurua**, north of Pipiriki, enjoys increased fame.

The valley was settled after World War One by ex-soldiers. The Depression and farming difficulties forced them out by 1942. An eerie reminder of their former presence is the **Bridge to Nowhere**, a concrete bridge with its approaches now overgrown by regenerated bush. You can reach the walk by jet boat.

WELLINGTON AND THE WAIRARAPA

Tawhiri-ma-tea, the Polynesian god of wind and storm, fought many of his fiercest battles with his earthbound brother gods in the area now known as Wellington and the Wairarapa.

The stretch of Cook Strait separating this end of the North Island from the South Island was thus bequeathed by the aboriginal gods one of the most treacherous dozen miles of open water in the world, making for its citizens a spectacular, stark and somewhat nervy existence.

A Legendary Tale

In Maori mythology Maui, the frail fifth son of the first parents, was favoured by the gods with magical powers. Their most memorable expression is the famous story, which has many regional variations elsewhere in Polynesia, of fishing up the North Island of New Zealand as food for his brothers' families. The great fish was hooked by its mouth, Wellington harbour, and its eye was Lake Wairarapa.

The greed of Maui's brothers in cutting up the fish before he had had a chance to lift its *tapu* was a sacrilege that angered the gods and caused the fish to writhe and lash about, creating the steep mountains that divide the North Island. The repercussions are the earthquakes which have so often since caused massive convulsions across the head of the fish.

The Maori attributed much of this geological irritability to supernatural beings. Both the Ngai Tara tribe of Wellington and the related Rangitane tribe of Wairarapa record that turbulent *taniwha*, which seem not dissimilar to the dragons of European myth, burst out of Wellington and thus formed the entrance to the harbour.

The Maori had lived rather more peaceably around the head of the fish than their counterparts in medieval Europe until Captain Cook arrived to

Preceding pages, Wellington awakes. Below, Wellington Harbour.

explore the area in 1773. Cook failed to enter the harbour because of an unfriendly tide, but over the next 60 or so years, whalers from across Cook's Strait traded with and related to local Maori in what is now called *de facto* fashion, until the New Zealand Company arrived in 1839 to try out the planned colonisation theories of Edward Gibbon Wakefield.

The Glass Capital

Today the mouth of the fish is as pretty a little capital city as any in the world. Wellington's great blue bowl of harbour is only mildly scarred by port reclamations and a clutch of high-rise office buildings set below steep green hills which are dotted with white wooden houses. The favourite romantic image of the locals is the best-selling print of New Zealand Company draughtsman Charles Heaphy, depicting the first sailing ships at anchor in this fledgling Victorian colony. However, if you are someone who is suffi-

ciently high up, things have not changed that much.

It is a different matter at street level. Over the decade from the mid-1970s, an architect mayor, Michael Fowler, has shaken up the downtown area, encouraging demolition of the quaint plaster wedding-cake Victorian premises in the name of earthquake safety. The new skyscrapers, which look equally vulnerable, are so canopied with glass verandahs over street-level glass boutiques that locals have dubbed the downtown "Glass City."

Wellington is quite often compared to San Francisco, and indeed the former's inner-city gentrification of old wooden houses is producing some of the same painted ladies for which San Francisco is renowned. Paint manufacturers must have breathed a sigh of relief after several decades of dull concrete structures.

Like San Francisco, Wellington has a cablecar zooming straight out of its belly to a fine lookout point, beside the ivy-clad original red-brick university building which local conservationists have persuaded the authorities to retain, retention still being the exception. Unlike San Francisco, Wellington has replaced, at its feisty mayor's urging, the old open-seated and brass-railed Victorian cablecars with shiny enclosed bullets from Switzerland, known to local users as "flying coffins."

Mayor Fowler received a knighthood from Queen Elizabeth and stepped down. His most controversial promotion, the Michael Fowler Centre, is an auditorium which stands in contrast alongside the old town hall. Most of last century Wellington was dismissed as a mere fishing village, until it overtook the field as the principal port in the colony.

A Productive "Sleepy Hollow"

Its central position and excellent deep-water harbour ensured such status, but Wellington itself does not really appreciate the contribution of the region around it.

As far as most Wellingtonians are

Wellington and Vicinity

20 km

Cook Strait

Waikanae Beach
Waikanae
Paraparaumu 1
Reikorangi
Raumati
Paekakariki
Akatarawa
Pukerua Bay
Plimmerton
Mana I.
Kaitoke
Paremata
Birchville 2
The Plateau
Titahi Bay
58
Porirua
Tawa
Upper Hutt
Stokes Valley
Johnsonville
Ohau Point
Lower Hutt
Wairarapa L.
Makara
Wainuiomata
C. Terawhiti
Eastbourne
Wellington
Orongorongo R.
Sinclair Head
Baring Head
Lake Ferry
Turakivae Head
Palliser Bay

concerned the **Wairarapa**, an area of hundreds of thousands of acres, is a place you drive to over the 300-metre (1,000-foot) high Rimutakas to get away from city bustle. This is sleepy hollow, a vast plain with a few declining towns and old houses that can be snapped up for a song, to be used as weekend retreats.

True, there is the nationally famous Golden Shears competition every year in the area's one sizable town of **Masterton**, but that is simply symptomatic of a vast valley fit for sheep, a few cattle, not much else. Oh, except for **Lake Wairarapa** in the duck shooting season. Otherwise the hills between and the rivers beyond are for the birds, and the 2,000 or so persistent trampers, canoeists, rafters, botanists, conservationists and hunters.

The indifference is probably explained by numbers – over 327,000 packed into the Wellington area; in the Wairarapa half a dozen towns around the 2,000 mark. It's little wonder that a history of the Wairarapa once spoke of its exports as being primary produce and young adults.

Buzzing Around The Beehive

Built in the late 1970s the modern **Beehive** contrasts sharply with the nearby marble **Parliament Buildings** (1922) and the Gothic **General Assembly Library** (1897). The parliamentary chambers are precisely modelled on those of Westminster; there are conducted tours.

Other notable buildings nearby are the **Government Buildings** (1876) on Lambton Quay, built entirely of native woods, the second largest wooden building in the world; the **Alexander Turnbull Library**, which boasts a remarkable collection of New Zealand and Pacific history; and the **Old St. Paul's Church** (1866), an impressive Gothic cathedral.

After work many people travel a few miles home into the foothills, or along the motorway built around the harbour, directly on the earthquake fault line to

Lambton Quay in 1903.

the **Hutt Valley** and the **Eastern Bays** – an area with one of the finest marine drives in the world.

After the Quakes

The Maori found these areas uninhabitable because thick native forests plunged to the water's edge and the Hutt Valley was largely swamp. The great quakes of 1848 and 1855 raised the land about 1½ metres (5 feet), just enough to show the Pakeha that it was safer to build in wood, and the reclamation of the sea was the answer to lack of space. So far, more that 120 hectares (600 acres) have been added by reclamation, half as much again as the original plan for the colony.

The Maori preferred to live on an island that was linked by a subsequent earthquake to the rest of Wellington. Today this suburban peninsula is called **Miramar**, Spanish for "behold the sea," and the sandy strip linking it to the city is the airport.

Hundreds of years before Cook, the great Polynesian explorer, Kupe, landed on Miramar and cultivated crops there, and that is where the tribe of his son Tara settled. There were enough fish and birds, and sunny north-facing slopes to cultivate the delicate *kumara* (sweet potato) so that Tara's tribe could share the area with migrating tribal groups. Occasional marauders were repelled by fortifications developed around the headlands. For more than 600 years, there was a relatively peaceful occupation of the harbour.

The Pakeha musket ended all that. In 1820, Te Rauparaha and other warrior chiefs led a savage assault on the local tribes around Tara, wiping out people who stood there, unable to comprehend why they were falling. The victory cannibal feast lasted 3 weeks. But the new occupiers had enemies on all sides and thus welcomed the arrival of the white tribe in 1839; they were good for both trade and protection.

After the *kumara*, the potato was easy to cultivate. The Maori gardeners kept the early settlers supplied with food.

The Cabinet Room.

The settlers, however, had contempt for the Maori, and were unsympathetic to their requests that cultivation, living and burial grounds be protected. Such indifference is still apparent, for the viewing platform on **Mount Victoria** overlooking the harbour was built after bulldozing an ancient burial ground. (The summit of Mount Victoria, 643 feet, is reached by road. Another viewpoint at **Kelburn**, above the Botanical Gardens, is reached via a cable-car which rises 400 feet straight up from Lambton Quay.)

Wakefield's Settlement

Mind you, the citizens of Wellington have shown no great respect for founding father Edward Gibbon Wakefield either. They prefer to confer the title "father of Wellington" on one of the early migrants, John Plimmer, who complained that a place represented to him as "a veritable Eden" proved "a wild and stern reality." In fact, Wellington has always been both. Plimmer did well, converting one of the many early shipwrecks into a trading enterprise on the beach, adding a wharf like many of his fellow entrepreneurs, becoming one of the most solid citizens of the new colony.

There is no memorial to Wakefield in Wellington, partly (no doubt) due to lingering disapproval that he should have served a prison term for abducting an heiress. It was in Newgate Prison that he saw first-hand the miserable lot of England's poor and thereby devised his scheme to attract money from wealthy idealists to invest in a chance abroad for those with none at home. John Stuart Mill, the great libertarian thinker and writer, was among the admirers of the plan.

Quick Deals

The practice was a mess. Idealists were thin on the ground, speculators thick as shovels in a gold rush. Wakefield's brother, William, was in charge of acquiring land for the new

Below left, Kelburn cable-car. Below, the "Beehive".

emigrants, but he was given only 4 months to do it. He made some quick deals with the Maori, buying the site of Wellington for 100 muskets, 100 blankets, 60 red nightcaps, a dozen umbrellas and so on and so forth.

Wakefield claimed to have bought for £9,000 the "head of the fish and much of its body," a total of 8 million hectares (about 20 million acres). He failed to understand the Maori concept of communal ownership; he was not helped by the pidgin English and pidgin Maori of his translator, whaler Dicky Barrett, a rotund and cheery fellow who later set up the first pub in the new colony and hired out part of it to government offices.

The early settlers had little for which to thank Wakefield when upon arrival they were dumped on the beach, at the bottom of the Hutt Valley. After their tents flooded, they moved to a narrow but drier part of the harbour, the site of the present city.

Lambton Quay was where Plimmer and company set up business, but the narrowness of the site soon led to reclamations which have continued ever since, and which have beached Lambton Quay several streets away from the present water's edge. Brass plaques set along the golden business mile mark the 1840 beachline.

The first generation of wooden houses along the golden mile went up in smoke. The second generation have been mostly tumbled over the last 10 years, with millions of dollars a year being spent on glass and steel replacements, a building boom unprecedented in this country. The current fashion among insurance houses for reflecting glass premises makes it a dazzling downtown on a fine day; skulking below are a few curious relics of the more decorative eras.

Wellington's Wharves

The streets are narrow and windswept with few parks, but Wellingtonians are rarely more than a stone's throw from the wharves, which so far retain

Express leaving Wellington's Thorndon Station for Auckland in 1914.

their decorative buildings. The old bond store is now a **Marine Museum**, and down the wharves a bit, an old ticket office with the hole in its middle sells nautical ephemera, stirrings of new uses for old wharves.

The wharves are among the few in the world open to the public. Among the lunchtime joggers around the waterfront, you can spot national politicians and top civil servants. Goodness knows what the Russian and Korean fishing crews make of it all. A waterfront development scheme will see many changes in this area over the next few years too.

Wellington's compactness is one of its chief charms. On the wharves, chunky red tugs are crammed together with fishing fleets and container ships. The **Overseas Passenger Terminal** was built just as passenger ships were terminating, but it is an agreeable spot beside the elegant marina of the **Royal Port Nicholson Yacht Club**. Next to that is a huge indoor swimming pool leading into the sweep of the **Oriental Bay** beach, created by the dumping of sand ballast from ships. A line of mature Norfolk pines makes an attractive promenade; set behind them are medium-rise flats and old wooden houses peppered up the slopes. Above Oriental Bay is the green belt of pines that encircles the city, preserving in perpetuity one of Wakefield's best plans. This suburb is often called a mini-Riviera, for it faces the setting sun. Here Maori once cultivated *kumara;* now Pakehas cultivate suntans and watch the ships go quietly by.

Gorgeous Gardens

Across the bay is the country's oldest suburb of **Thorndon**, where the little wooden workers' and soldiers' cottages are getting the gentrification treatment, enjoying New Zealand's first historic zoning. Historic walks head towards another city landmark, the gorgeous **Botanic Gardens**. The motorway cut through this old suburb and impaled the heart of the settlers' cemetery before coming to a full stop in the town centre.

Schoolgirls on their way home.

The hills arrange Wellington naturally into village units. Thorndon has trendy young professionals, fighters for good causes like the enchanting little wooden Gothic ex-cathedral, consumers who like French restaurants and antique shops. Over on the other side of town, **Aro Valley** is a community which won a victory against council plans to demolish their wooden cottages in favour of concrete.

Over the hill, the stern grey **National Museum** and **Art Gallery** glower in the enclosed suburb of **Newtown**. There is an interesting collection of Maori artefacts and relics of Captain Cook in the museum. There is also a section devoted to 19th century European life in New Zealand and fine geological and botanical collections.

Newtown's narrow streets teem with migrants from Europe, Asia and the Pacific. At school, students are speaking 20 languages, while at shops with high clapboard facades like Wild West Hollywood sets, migrants sell exotic foods from a dozen lands. Another valley over

Island Bay is losing the Italian fishermen who gave it the Little Italy image, but Indian shopowners are redefining its identity. In these older suburbs you can find a Presbyterian church that holds services in Niuean, an extraordinary Greek Orthodox temple and a Polish clubroom. As it once was for tribes migrating south, Wellington has traditionally been a place where immigrants can start their new lives, and it has benefitted in terms of cosmopolitan colour.

Valley of the Hutt

Until the enthusiasm for the city became established, families used to make a great trek to the suburbs in the Hutt Valley and over the hills to Porirua and beyond. At weekends, many still go a few hills farther northwest to their cottage on the Gold Coast, or to the Paremata area for underwater sports, yachting and pleasure launches. It is a blander environment than Wellington's, and it is shared up the long valley of the Hutt,

Wellington's suburbia.

the flat suburbs that blend seamlessly into each other. Here are homes for the thousands of city workers, and the site of the nation's television complex. It is a lifestyle away from the 10-minute drive along the motorway to the city.

A 10-minute drive the other way to the Eastern Bays leads back to small communities folded into steep bush-clad hills. The principal settlement of **Eastbourne** consistently commands some of the highest market prices for houses in the country. New Zealand's most famous writer, Katherine Mansfield, lived and wrote here, and a more appropriate place for a writer is hard to imagine.

"A second Italy"

The Wairarapa was a triumph for the tree fellers, some of the early settlers were bitterly disappointed in the hollow promises of the New Zealand Company about land. While Miss Riddiford wrote back to England that Wellington looked like "a second Italy," those with no interest in anything but land drove sheep around the coast, paid Maori to canoe them across the lake, and proceeded to set up the country's first sheep stations.

Other settlers, led by Joseph Masters, opposed the Wakefield plan and developed the concept of small farms, which Governor Grey backed. These were mostly established in the Wairarapa; **Greytown** was named after the governor who persuaded the local Maori to sell, Masterton after the inventor of the scheme.

At that time, Pakehas were assuming the Maori was a dying race. Today the Maori are in a period of renaissance, rebuilding their language and their meeting houses and relearning their history. They are being joined in their concern for the environment by many Pakeha conservationists.

The Pakehas have developed a taste for colonial museums – not just in Wellington, but in many of those declining settlements in Wairarapa. **Carterton**, for instance, with a population of 3,900, proudly displays the mythical canoe from which Maui fished up the North Island.

The growing awareness of the considerable recreational and tourist value of unspoiled nature may yet save the eye of the fish, the place the Maori called "glistening waters," and also that lumpy forest nose that separates the eye from the mouth.

As for Wellington, the mouth itself, the marvellous thing is that despite the crude human cosmetics applied to its edges, it is still not much different from the place Lieutenant Colonel Mundy described in 1848 as a "crystal bay in its bronze frame of rugged hills."

The next great earthquake – which occupiers of the head of the fish feel is long overdue – may one day restore the mouth to a state which Kupe would recognise. Dodgy flights into Wellington and violent storms (like the one in 1968 in which an inter-island ferry foundered at the heads with 51 lives lost) remind locals that Tawhiri-ma-tea has not yet made his peace with his fellow gods around the head of the fish.

Left, providing cheer at the Raft Race, Wellington. **Right**, entrance to Victorian-style Antrim House.

NELSON AND MARLBOROUGH

Nelson and Marlborough smugly see themselves as a glittering sun belt round the midriff of a country which boasts about its climate from top to toe. But this metaphoric belt must surely be elastic to cope with the great summer influx of holiday-makers to the popular beaches and bays of the two provinces.

Nelson City's usual 44,000 population is said to double during the Christmas-New Year holiday period, and at popular beach resorts like Kaiteriteri, numbers jump from a few handfuls to thousands. They pour into hotels, motels and motor camps in cars full of children, towing caravans or boats or with tents strapped to roof-racks. Other younger and fitter travellers, often from overseas, arrive by bus or plane or with the help of a hitch-hiker's thumb, bringing boots and backpacks to add to the summer scene.

The approach to Nelson and Marlborough can be by road from the south, by scheduled Air New Zealand and small operator services into Nelson or Blenheim airports or, perhaps most dramatically, by one of the road/rail ferries that make the three-hour crossing of Cook Strait from Wellington.

Straight Through the Strait

Cook Strait is a natural wind funnel for the "Roaring Forties" and can be one of the most unpleasant short stretches of water on earth on a bad day. But the moment you enter the **Marlborough Sounds** through the narrow entrance of **Tory Channel** you enter a different world, a world of myriad inlets and bays with steep hills plunging so quickly into the sea that in most places you could anchor an ocean liner within spitting distance of the shore.

There used to be a whaling station at the entrance to Tory Channel, the last in New Zealand when it closed in 1964, ending more than 50 years of pursuit of the migratory humpback whale by the Perano family. The channel has been the sole highway for the Peranos, and for most owners of the many holiday homes and farm properties of the Marlborough

Preceding pages: Milford Sound; Southern Alps. Below, ferry leaving Picton for Wellington.

Sounds, for the better part of a century. Launch, speedboat or tug have been the means of conveyance; only a few enjoy the luxury of road access, if indeed luxury is the right word for the few narrow, tortuous and dusty (or muddy, depending on the season) tracks that serve as roads in this part of the country. Boats of one sort or another are everything here – the main means of recreation and (telephones and the occasional helicopter excepted) almost the only means of communication. The doctor does his rounds by launch; the mail is delivered by launch.

The hour-long journey down Tory Channel and **Queen Charlotte Sound** aboard the big rail ferries gives only a glimpse of it all. A full exploration of the various sounds would take months.

The most famous of all Pacific explorers, Captain James Cook, visited New Zealand three times; he visited the Marlborough Sounds five times, spending something like 100 days in and around **Ship Cove**. He first hoisted the British flag in New Zealand there on January 15, 1770, and on a subsequent visit beached his ship *Resolution* there for some weeks. A monument has been erected at Ship Cove, near the entrance to Queen Charlotte Sound, to commemorate Cook's visits.

The commercial centre for almost all activity in the Sounds is the bustling little town of **Picton** in one of the bays near the head of Queen Charlotte Sound. Picton is the start (or finish) of the South Island section of Highway 1 and of the main trunk railway. It is the terminal for the Cook Strait ferries and the base for the assorted launches, water taxis and charter boats on which locals and visitors rely for transport. There is also a float plane providing scenic flights, as well as a short-cut to guest houses or the Portage resort hotel in adjacent **Kenepuru Sound**. It is a mere 10 minutes' journey by float plane against a minimum of two hours by car and probably two days by sailing boat.

An old trading scow, the *Echo*, is drawn up onto the beach on one side of Picton Bay, where it acts as a clubhouse for the local yacht club. It was one of the last of New Zealand's old trading scows to remain in service, though ironically these flat-bottomed sailing craft were designed for shallow river harbours rather than the deep waters of the Sounds.

A shipping relic of far greater antiquity lies across the bay. The teak-hulled *Edwin Fox*, much vandalised and only just recognisable as a ship, is the only remaining East Indiaman – or ship of the British East India Company – in the world. The *Edwin Fox* came to New Zealand as a 19th century immigrant ship and ended its working life as a storage hulk for meat-freezing works, which operated at Picton until killing was moved in 1983 closer to the centre of pastoral farming in Marlborough.

Blenheim and Kaikoura

Blenheim, 30 km (19 miles) south of Picton, is the administrative centre of sparsely populated Marlborough. Sitting squarely on the Wairau Plain, it is a pleasant if unspectacular farm service town. One of its main claims to fame is the production from the extensive Montana vineyards established in the late 1960s. They have turned Blenheim into one of New Zealand's main wine-producing areas.

Grapes, apples, cherries, sheep – all take advantage of the Marlborough sun-

Special delivery: mail by boat, Marlborough Sound.

shine to grow and grow fat. But nothing needs the province's hot dry days of summer more than the salt works at **Lake Grassmere**, where sea water is ponded in shallow lagoons and allowed to evaporate until nothing is left but blinding white salt crystals.

The coastline in the southern part of the province, in marked contrast to the Sounds, is exposed, rocky and generally inhospitable to small boats. Near **Kaikoura** the sea and the mountains meet head-on leaving merely a narrow beach past which the road and railway must squeeze. In some places even that disappears and the road and railway with it, delving into the mountains themselves.

The town of Kaikoura nestles at the base of a small peninsula which provides at least limited shelter for the fishing boats based here. This is crayfish coast and for miles on either side of the town, roadside stalls offer them for sale fresh from the pot. Sperm whales spout just offshore from the town and can be visited by launch for a close encounter.

Inland from Kaikoura, two parallel mountain ranges thrust impressively skywards, reaching their acme in the peak of **Tapuaenuku**, 2,885 metres (9,465 feet) above sea level. Beyond that again is the Awatere Valley and **Molesworth**, New Zealand's largest sheep and cattle station. The Wairau and Awatere Valleys have been described as "the cradle of South Island pastoralism." They were also places where some of the most destructive overgrazing of the country's erosion-prone high country took place, until a derelict Molesworth was taken over by the government in the 1930s. Much of its 182,000 hectares (450,000 acres) has been painfully rehabilitated and the station now runs 10,000 heads of cattle. Safari tours by four-wheel-drive vehicle through Molesworth to the North Canterbury resort of Hanmer Springs can be taken from Nelson.

Mussels and Gold

The road from Blenheim to Nelson takes you down the attractive Kaituna Valley to **Havelock**, a fishing and holiday settlement at the head of **Pelorus Sound**. Havelock is like a smaller Picton, without the bustle of the inter-island ferries, but with the same feeling that all the

Montana Vineyards, Blenheim.

important business of the town is water-borne. Pelorus and Kenepuru sounds have developed the new industry of farming New Zealand's meaty green-lipped mussel; it is at Havelock that these marine farmers base their work boats, and to Havelock that they bring most of the shellfish they grow on thick rope lines hanging from buoys. Visitors with the best part of a day to invest can see the mussel farms close up by joining the mail boat *Glenmore* on its daily trip up the Sounds.

Just beyond Havelock is **Canvastown**, named for the tent town which popped up mushroom-like when gold was discovered on the Wakamarina River in the 1860s. It was a short-lived rush with most of the diggers going on to the more promising Otago goldfields but, nevertheless, Canvastown remembers its brief heyday with a memorial of old mining tools and equipment set in concrete. Visitors can hire pans and still get a "show" of gold on the Wakamarina.

Rai Valley is now little more than a rest stop for buses travelling the 115 km (72 miles) between Blenheim and Nelson, though once it boasted a cheese factory of

high repute and a bakery which achieved national fame for the length of its loaves. A road turning off here leads to **French Pass** at the outermost edge of the Sounds. This is a narrow, reef-strewn waterway between the mainland and **D'Urville Island**, named after the 19th century French explorer, Dumont d'Urville who discovered the pass in 1827 and piloted his corvette *Astrolabe* through in an extraordinary feat of seamanship.

Nelson: A City Apart

Nelson, with its busy fishing port sheltered behind a 10-km (6-mile) long boulder bank, is a city apart from the rest of New Zealand. It has never been linked with the country's railway network, and this has tended to breed a feeling of isolation which better than average air services to Wellington have failed to alleviate. Even the acquisition of the city status (by royal charter in 1858 as the seat of an Anglican bishop), 16 years after the New Zealand Company landed the district's first settlers, sets Nelson apart from new and bigger cities. The normal New Zealand requirement for city status is a popu-

Graham Valley, Nelson.

lation of 20,000, a bureaucratically magical figure not achieved in Nelson until the 1950s.

The city owes more than that to its bishop. Andrew Suter, Bishop of Nelson from 1867 to 1891, was a keen artist and art collector who bequeathed what is considered to be country's finest collection of early colonial water colours to the people of Nelson. They are housed in a gallery which bears his name and which, since its enlargement in the late 1970s, has played a dominant role in the city's cultural activities.

Churches (of all denominations) also contribute to the architectural atmosphere of a district which retains much from colonial days, including the pioneer homestead, Broadgreen. The city's churches are presided over by the Anglican cathedral on Church Hill, while a view from the Grampians Hill shows the Roman Catholic, Presbyterian, Methodist and Baptist churches all in line a little to one side, for all the world like a row of communicants.

Some of the prettiest churches, though, are in the settlements of the Waimea Plain – at **Richmond**, **Waimea West** and **Wakefield**, where the parish church of St. John's was built in 1846, making it New Zealand's second oldest church and the oldest in the South Island.

Nelson's image has been built on its sandy beaches and extensive apple orchards, though apples are only one of many crops grown in the district. The region also produces most of the hops and all of New Zealand's domestically grown tobacco. Intensive cropping is carried on even in the city, and many streets have vast tomato glasshouses tucked in behind what appear to be ordinary suburban gardens.

The city has attracted a new class of settlers – city dwellers who apparently fancy themselves turning one hand to farming a small holding while turning the other to a potters' wheel or some other handicraft. The availability of suitable rural retreats, along with the fact that Nelson is one of the country's major sources of potters' clay, has given the district such a concentration of these talented craftspeople that they have become a tourist attraction with trips to selected potteries promoted by the Nelson Visitor Centre.

Preserved beauty: a colonial lounge, Broadgreen.

Golden Bay Alternatives

The availability of relatively cheap small holdings has made Nelson province, like the Coromandel Peninsula in the North Island, something of a centre for alternative lifestyle communes. They dot the valleys of the Motueka River basin and of **Golden Bay**, where settlers try theories of holistic living along with the patience of local government administrators whose rules were never designed for such activities.

If Nelson feels isolated from the rest of New Zealand, Golden Bay is isolated even from Nelson. A single bitumen road over the marble and limestone **Takaka Hill** is the only way in – or out – for anything but birds, fish, or people with stout boots and sturdy legs. All people and produce go over the steep, winding hill, whether it be heavy trucks or holiday traffic heading for **Pohara Beach** or the **Abel Tasman National Park**.

A memorial to Abel Tasman, the 17th century Dutchman who discovered this island for Europe, stands at Tarakohe on the road to the park which bears his name. It was here that the first rather inauspicious encounter between Europeans and the Maori of New Zealand took place in December 1642, when Tasman anchored his ships *Heemskerck* and *Zeehaen* only to have one of his longboats attacked. As a result he lost four of his men, named the area "Murderers' Bay" and made no further attempt to land in New Zealand, thereby leaving the Maori in ignorance of the questionable delights of European civilisation for another 130 years.

These days there is very little apparent Maori presence in Golden Bay or elsewhere in Nelson and Marlborough, something due in part to the depredations of the great warrior from Kapiti Island, Te Rauparaha. Sometimes known as "the Maori Napoleon," he almost annihilated local tribes in his raids on the northern shores of the South Island in 1827-1828.

Farewell Spit, at the western tip of Golden Bay, is a naturalist's delight. The 25-km (15-mile) long spit of sand curves round the bay like a scimitar, growing each year as millions of cubic metres of new sand are added by the current, which sweeps up the West Coast and then dumps its load upon meeting conflicting tides and currents of Cook Strait.

Togetherness in a kitchen at Graham Valley Commune.

More than 90 species of birds have been identified on Farewell Spit. They fly by the tens of thousands from the Siberian tundra to enjoy the southern summer. The spit is classed as a wetland of international importance and is managed by the government with strict limits on access, particularly by vehicle. However, you can take a five-hour sightseeing trip by four-wheel drive vehicle from **Collingwood** out to the lighthouse near the spit's end. Departure time each day depends on the state of the tide.

Deer, Trout and Trampers

South of Golden Bay, even four-wheel drive vehicles are of no use. A large part of the North West Nelson Forest Park has been gazetted a wilderness area and not even helicopters or low flying aircraft are allowed in to disturb the backpackers who come here to commune with nature.

Helicopters are used by some fishing guides round the periphery of the wilderness to fly anglers in to mountain rivers where only small trout are rare.

Helicopters are also used occasionally (though cheaper hire services are avail-

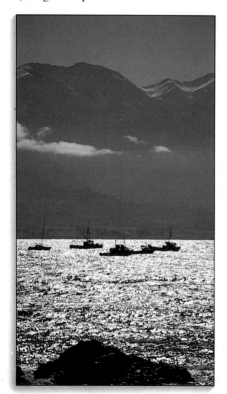

able) to drop off or pick up trampers walking the popular **Heaphy Track**. This is a tramp of two to four days along a track which starts a little way south of Collingwood and heads through the mountains, then down the west coast to **Karamea**. Overnight accommodation along the way is available in huts provided by the Forest Service, but like most parts of Nelson and Golden Bay away from the coastal plain, this is "backpack country," where what you sleep in and what you eat are what you carry on your back.

The limestone hills around Golden Bay contain some of the most extensive cave systems in the Southern Hemisphere and often attract expeditions of "pot-holers" from the other side of the world. **Harwood's Hole** on Takaka Hill is more than 200 metres (650 feet) deep and was regarded for many years as the deepest cave in New Zealand, until exploration of the Nettlebed cave system under Mount Arthur started. Although Nelson itself enjoys a generally dry climate, vast deluges quite often occur in the western ranges of Golden Bay, the water seeping through the soft limestone to create the underground network of caves and rivers. A walk of 400 metres (¼ mile) from the end of a road up the Riwaka valley, on the Nelson side of Takaka Hill, will take you to the visible source of the Riwaka River where it emerges in full spate from its invisible source inside the hill.

There are other oases, too, where people of softer feet and softer muscles can experience some of the thrill that backpackers get in the mountains of Nelson province. A restored 1920s fishing lodge on the shores of **Lake Rotorua**, 90 km (56 miles) south of the city in the **Nelson Lakes National Park**, boasts "blue-chip" fishing water within 50 metres' walk of the front door, and 26 top-class fishing rivers within an hour's drive. **St. Arnaud** village on the shores of **Lake Rotoiti**, the other glacial lake which gives the Nelson Lakes park its name, also offers comfortable accommodation and (for winter visitors) two skifields nearby.

It also offers another route down the Wairau valley and back to Blenheim (if you do not want to go on through the mountains to Christchurch or the West Coast) and away from the slightly dilatory life that Nelson seems to engender.

Left and right, contrasting views of the mountains of Kaikoura.

CHRISTCHURCH: JUST LIKE ENGLAND

A street map of Christchurch is an unusually useful document. It tells much about the origins and aspirations of a peculiarly English city.

You can start at the centre, and the centre is easy to find – **Cathedral Square**, smack in the middle. There, a lofty neo-Gothic Church of England cathedral presides, as if placed in its eternally rightful position by some great divine hand. Around it, a rectangular grid of streets is well laid out on the plains. The central streets assume the names of English bishoprics – minor ones, unfortunately, because by the time the city was planned in the early 1850s, the best-sounding names had already been taken for other communities of the Canterbury province.

At the limits of the city centre run four broad avenues. They enclose a square mile that echoes the "City of London." Within their bounds are tidy, tree-lined parks with names like Cranmer and Latimer. Sweeping through the entire city is the serpentine **Avon River**.

Locals like to believe the stream got its name from the river which runs through Shakespeare's Stratford. In fact, it was named after an obscure Scottish stream by the home of one of the city's pioneering families. Along with the Port Hills to the southeast, it is the city's greatest natural asset. It relieves the rectangles. Its grassy banks are wide and well-planted in trees. The willows along one stretch allegedly grew from slips brought from Napoleon's St. Helena grave. But Christchurch is full of stories like that.

Precision Planning

Returning to our street plan, you will see the massive **Hagley Park** to the west of the four avenues. The planners set it aside as a barrier between the city and the farm owned by the pioneering family who brought the Avon's name with them. It is filled with playing fields, open stretches of parkland modelled, Christchurch boasts, on the classic style of English landscape gardening, and botanic gardens.

Christchurch, you may have gathered by now, did not happen by accident. A city does not become more English than England without really putting its mind to it. It was a planned Anglican settlement, masterminded largely by a young English Tory with the delightful name of John Robert Godley.

Repelled by 19th century egalitarianism, Godley was rather more keen on a medieval notion of harmoniously blended church and state, presided over by a benevolent gentry. He got together the Canterbury Association, with no fewer than 2 archbishops, 7 bishops, 14 peers, 4 baronets and 16 Members of Parliament as its original backers. The idea, of course, was to drum up money and find settlers for the new little corner of England.

Only the best sort of migrant needed apply. They were to represent "all the elements, including the very highest, of a good and right state of society." To qualify for an assisted passage halfway around the world to the new colony, a migrant had to furnish a certificate from his vicar vouching that "the applicant is sober, industrious and honest, and that he

Preceding pages, golden bubbles – Christchurch from afar. **Left**, the Wizard spins his tale at Cathedral Square. **Right**, remembering Captain Scott.

and all his family are amongst the most respectable in the parish."

From such stock came the Canterbury Pilgrims, rather more solid and modest folk than the association may have dreamed of. The First Four Ships – Christchurch's *Mayflower* – berthed at the neighbouring port of Lyttelton in 1850. By 1855, a total of 3,549 migrants had made the journey, and the city on the plains was growing.

Unfortunately, something went wrong. Dreams of an ecclesiastical utopia crumbled a bit under the hard facts of colonial life. The Canterbury Association foundered. It was as difficult to revitalise Anglicanism in the New World as it was anywhere else. Christchurch's growth from the mid-1850s became less ordered, less ideal.

Yet dreams endure. To be of First Four Ships material is still worth dining out on today in Christchurch.

A City of Godley-ness

By city planning statute, no high-rise building is allowed to go higher than the Anglican cathedral's spire. Godley-ness

reigns. Any schemes to touch even a tiny chunk of Hagley Park for a re-routed road or new carpark meets with determined public opposition; the ensuing civic squabbles can get nasty.

And there are gardens – miles and miles of them – both public and private. Somebody, at one time, call Christchurch the "Garden City," and the citizens have been living up to it ever since. Gardening is certainly the biggest leisure-time activity in the city. It makes for some extremely pleasant drives and walks. Come to this city during late summer and you will easily spot countless prize-winning gardens.

Slowly, it has dawned on Christchurch that it is a city many tourists want to visit. It boasts at least two first-class hotels – The Parkroyal and the Chateau Regency. Some of the best restaurants and souvenir shops have geared themselves up with menus and window displays in Japanese. One tour company is doing a thriving business bringing young Japanese newlyweds to Christchurch where they can have their marriage vows blessed in the cute Gothic charm of **St. Barnabas Church** in the leafy, blue-chip real-estate

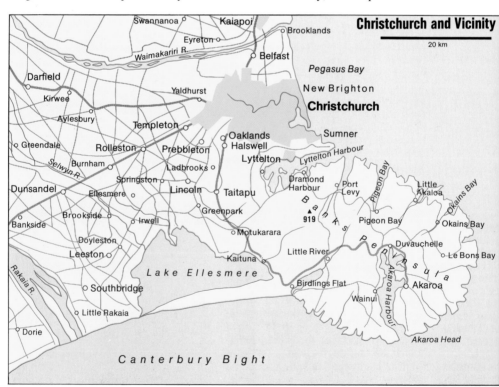

suburb of **Fendalton**. Organists, vergers and wedding party members are all provided as part of the service.

Christchurch is not without its share of interesting characters. Can that be a hangover of the city's utopian origins? Utopias anywhere generate a good number of mildly cranky individuals, do they not? Whatever the reason, take a city the size of Christchurch – which has a small population of about 320,000 – where everybody who is anybody knows everybody who is anybody, put it well away from the sea-lanes of world travel, and the result is a mixture that is a little inbred and, well, individualistic.

Denizens of the Square

Take a walk around the city centre and you will meet a few more of the public "cranks." Start your tour from Cathedral Square. Beautifully paved as a pedestrian area of grand but cosy dimensions, it is officially countenanced as a public speaking area.

Lunchtime on a sunny weekday is best. Star performer is The Wizard. An immigrant from Australia some time in the early 1970s, he has been haranguing bemused crowds ever since. Dressed nowadays in a fetching sackcloth-and-ashes number, and heavily tanned, he delivers an impassioned line on Queen and country, the virtues of the Established Church and the perils of liberated women. No one quite knows whether to take The Wizard seriously. Is he giving Christchurch and its Anglican antecedents just what they deserve? He has a more-or-less official status as the city's Lord of Misrule.

Also in the Square, you will find one or two speakers who take themselves a bit more seriously. The "Bible Lady" is one. She describes herself as a Jewess converted to Christianity and accompanies her evangelising with quite wacky numbers on her faithful violin. The little lady is something of a tolerated embarrassment to the distinctly laid-back authorities of the cathedral which serves as her backdrop.

During the summer months, the Square comes alive with frequent festivals of fun, food and frolics. There are stalls offering arts and crafts for sale, and tasty ethnic foods from a dozen countries. Lunchtime shows and dances fill the Square with music during the Summertime concerts that run through December and January.

Sadly however, Cathedral Square after dark takes on more sinister overtones and is not a safe place to walk alone during those hours.

A Stroll Through Town

For those more culturally minded, a walk around the Square and its environs by day can be rewarding. The cathedral itself is worth a visit. Construction began in 1864, and it is one of the Southern Hemisphere's finest neo-Gothic churches today.

Directly behind it are the offices of *The Press*, the city's morning newspaper. It isn't much of a building, but the paper is certainly worth a read for the nostalgia quotient alone. It is modelled unashamedly on *The Times* of London and is very much the paper of record for the Christchurch establishment.

South down Colombo Street from the Square you will find **Ballantynes** on the corner of the **City Mall**, a pedestrian's

Wet over needles and pins: fountains sprinkle in front of the Town Hall.

paradise. Ballantynes is very much the establishment department store of Christchurch. Farmers from the rich agricultural hinterland of the Canterbury Plains give the store their custom, making it a place to see and be seen. The assistants dress in black, and are notoriously helpful. Very other-worldly.

A stroll down the City Mall towards the Avon River and **Bridge of Remembrance** takes in some of the city's best shopping territory.

Across the bridge and north along Cambridge Terrace is the city's old library, one of Christchurch's architectural gems. Like many of the buildings around the city, this one has been exquisitely restored and now houses offices, a bank and a restaurant.

Along the Avon

A stroll along the Avon towards town reveals some of the river's attractions. Turn left down Worcester Street at the delightful Chamber of Commerce building and you will come to the **Christchurch Arts Centre**. A mass of dreaming spires, turrets and cloisters, it formerly housed the University of Canterbury. When the university moved out to the more spacious suburbs, its site was taken over by arts and crafts studios, theatres, restaurants and some prime downtown apartments. It's well worth a visit.

You're in Old Christchurch territory. Directly over Rolleston Avenue is **Canterbury Museum**. A charming building, the displays are for the most part unexceptional, except for a wonderful Antarctic wing documenting New Zealand's long and rich connection with that icy continent. Try showing a lot of interest, and the super-enthusiastic staff will show you some of the goodies they don't have on display. Behind the museum, all but hidden, is the municipal art gallery, the **McDougall Gallery**. It offers an early New Zealand collection with a staff trying hard, against the architecture, to be unstuffy.

Immediately north along Rolleston Avenue is **Christ's College**, dating from 1857. It is very Anglican, very English public-school and very proper for boys from Christchurch, and from all over New Zealand, who intend to go places in **Council Chambers**.

life. The buildings are marvellous. But in a shocking concession to modernity, straw-boater hats for the boys were dropped in the 1970s. They were very picturesque.

Past Christ's College you can enter the **Botanic Gardens**, within a loop of the Avon as it winds through Hagley Park. They are magnificent. A little electric vehicle takes regular tours, but if you've got time, take a walk. All the best specimens are signposted.

Centre of Civic Pride

Head back to town down Armagh Street and you'll pass Cranmer Square. On the far side is the old **Christchurch Normal School**. Like half of Christchurch's notable buildings, it is mock Gothic. It was long ago deserted by the educationists. Vandals had their way with the old folly for about 10 years, before a developer took over to transform the remains into luxury apartments. He had a big job on his hands.

Further down Armagh Street are the old **Provincial Council** buildings. They are modestly colonial, and lovingly kept

up by the Justice Department which uses some sections for court sittings.

Across Victoria Square is the pride of modern Christchurch, the **Town Hall**. It was opened in 1972 after the city had waited 122 years for a civic centre. Designed by local architects Warren and Mahoney, it is restrained and elegant, boasting an auditorium, concert chamber, conference rooms, a banquet hall and restaurant. The restaurant overlooks the Avon, making it one of the best settings in which to dine out in the city.

Christchurch's "splendid cathedral"

If you're interested in ecclesiastical architecture, you can seek out the city's other cathedral. It is the Roman Catholic **Cathedral of the Blessed Sacrament**, a high renaissance Romanesque basilica, built early this century. It is a wonderfully light and floating building, in a somewhat tacky part of town. George Bernard Shaw visited the city soon after it opened and praised Christchurch's "splendid cathedral." The pride of local Anglicans turned to chagrin when they realised he was referring to the basilica.

Far from the madding crowd: Dean's Cottage.

The Suburbs

Getting out of the city centre you can tour countless streets of fine homes – if you head in the right direction, which is northwest towards Fendalton and Merivale or up on to the Port Hills.

Christchurch is fiercely class conscious, real estate wise, along lines that are sometimes inexplicable. The inner city has been the slowest of any in New Zealand to become trendy again. **New Brighton**, by the beach, should be classy, but, unfortunately, is not. The **Port Hills** are the only area with a distinct advantage over the rest of the city. They escape the smog which can be quite difficult during winter.

The Summit Road along the top of the Port Hills gives spectacular view of the city, the plains and the Southern Alps; and on the other side, the port of Lyttelton and the hills of Banks Peninsula. It is worth taking a drive over the hills to **Lyttelton**, a sleepy, shady little port town with stacks of charming cottages. You can return through the road tunnel and head east to the seaside suburbs of Ferrymead, Redcliffs and Sumner. There is a transport museum at **Ferrymead**, which is splendid for train buffs, colonial enthusiasts and the like. **Sumner** has the air of an artists' retreat about it, now being carefully recultivated.

To the northeast of the city is **Queen Elizabeth II Park**. An athletic stadium and swimming sports complex, it was built for the 1974 Commonwealth Games. City rate-payers didn't want to get landed with a white elephant, so the park tries hard to promote itself as an all-around family attraction. There are water slides, a maze and sundry other diversions for amusement.

Lunchtime Joggers

If you are athletic, Hagley Park in the city is the best jogging area you could want. Thousands of office workers do it every lunchtime. Then there is cycling. School pupils and workers take to the flat streets on two wheels in hordes. You can get into the swing of things by hiring a bike of your own. If you do, beware of motorists. Familiarity breeds contempt. You can also boat on the Avon, for a fee that is downright peppercorn considering

Cathedral of the Blessed Sacrament.

192

the lovely perspective you get on the inner city.

The city has one professional theatre company, **The Court**, in the Arts Centre. The setting is intimate and the standards are uniformly high. Christchurch theatre-goers affirm The Court is the best in the country. A bar attached to a nearby vegetarian restaurant, also in the Arts Centre, provides a retreat after the performance. Christchurch's record for reputable nightclubs is however said to be poor. Therefore be on your guard if you should decide to visit any of the haunts which are operating.

Peninsula Excursion

If you've got time before you head south to the scenic mountains and lakes, you'll want to get out of town. **Banks Peninsula**, just beyond the Port Hills, is the best destination for a short trip.

It is the scene of one of just two bad blunders made by Captain James Cook when he circumnavigated New Zealand in the 18th century. He mapped the peninsula as an island. In fact, he would have been right if he had come several millen-

Sign of the Takahe.

nia earlier. The extinct volcanoes which formed the peninsula were once separated from the mainland. (Cook's other gaffe was Stewart Island, at the southern tip of the South Island. He linked it to the mainland.)

The hills of Banks Peninsula were once bush-covered, but they were long ago denuded for their timber. There are pockets of bush and plenty of delightful valleys and bays. Sheltered micro-climates support the growth of an array of horticultural products and flowers that cannot be cultivated anywhere else this far south in New Zealand. Kiwifruit is one. You'll also find some keen growers of exotic nut trees.

Seek out **Diamond Harbour**, **Okains Bay**, **Okuti Valley** and **Port Levy**. The last three are fertile, inviting and unspoiled. In many other parts of the world, they would most probably be bristling with condominiums.

About Akaroa

But the real gem of the peninsula is **Akaroa**, about 80 km (50 miles) from Christchurch. The little settlement began

its European life in 1838 when a French whaler landed. For a short while it flourished as a French settlement after 63 migrants set out to create a Southern Seas outpost. They arrived in 1840 and found the Union Jack flying.

During their passage on the ship *Comte de Paris*, British sovereignty over New Zealand had been declared. Piqued but not deterred, the French stayed. They built a community and worked the land, planting poplars from Normandy, tangled hedges and grapes. But the attempt to found a French colony failed. They were far outnumbered by the English settlers.

The dream lingers though, and of late it has been brushed up a little for visitors. Little streets wind up the hill from the harbour front, bearing names like Rue Lavaud, Rue Jolie and Rue Balgueri. A charming colonial style predominates in the architecture of the cottages, including some with a genuinely Gallic touch. Of most note is the **Langlois-Eteveneaux House**, now fitted out as a display with an adjoining museum.

Akaroa is a sleepy little village for most of the year. Many Christchurch people own holiday houses in the town, though, and the place can become crowded during January and February.

Akaroa's Churches and Cemeteries

Churches are among its notable features. The Roman Catholic **Church of St. Patrick** is the oldest in anything like its original form. It was built in 1864 and was in fact the third in the town built to serve Akaroa's French – and Irish, hence the name – Catholics. It is a cute and cluttered little edifice, the notable features of which include a Bavarian window on the east wall.

St. Peter's Anglican Church was built in 1863, but generously enlarged about 15 years later. It is a more austere building, in the Protestant style. Most distinctive of all is the tiny **Kaik**, a Maori church some 6 km (4 miles) south of the township along the foreshore. The church is in fact the only evidence of a Maori village or resting post.

Still with things churchy is Akaroa's town cemetery. Graveyards are perhaps an acquired taste, but this has to be one of

French Colonial Museum, Akaroa.

the best. On a spectacular terraced site just south of the town centre, its grave-stones are a wonderful document of the town's rich history.

The Old French Cemetery, on the other side of town, is a disappointment. It is the resting place of some of the earliest visitors, and after a hot slog up the hill it affords a good view of the harbour. But a benevolent government tidied the place up in 1925, turning it into a poor example of the war memorial-type monument to be found in just about every New Zealand town.

Food for Thought

Because it is a bit off the tourist track, Akaroa has been slow to realise its marketability, which is a virtue. The village town is now getting its act together, providing quite good accommodation and a few rather overpriced eating places. If you come for a day, pack a makeshift hamper and eat, as the French say, *a l'herbe*. However, if you prefer cooking and have the facilities for it, you should stroll down the wharf and buy some fresh fish from one of the boats in the fishing

fleet which fish the Canterbury coast from the port.

A day in Akaroa is a welcome contrast to the Englishness of Christchurch. Other environs of the city are far flung. You have to go a long way to reach any notable destinations, such as Hanmer Springs with its spa, the Southern Alps and their ski fields, and the wonderful coastline to the north around Kaikoura.

What you will see around Christchurch, however, are miles and miles of farmlands on the Canterbury Plains. They are New Zealand's biggest, richest cropping area, though prone to summertime water droughts. For that reason, local farmers have fought for years for rights to take irrigation water from local rivers, such as the Rakaia. Incidentally, you might be more interested in the rivers' salmon.

If you want an introduction to local farming practices, visit **Lincoln College**, about 20 km (12 miles) south of the city. It was founded in 1873 and is one of the world's foremost university colleges of agriculture. A telephone call beforehand will certainly help when arranging for a guided tour.

Apparently placid: Lyttelton Harbour.

CANTERBURY'S HIGH COUNTRY

Canterbury is nothing less than the marriage of mountain and sea, bound together by snow-fed rivers that cut braided courses across the plain to the coast. The Southern Alps, the Pacific Ocean, and two rivers (the Conway in the north and the Waitaki in the south) form the boundaries of this province distinguished by, but not noted for, its geographical diversity.

Popular imagination more readily grasps a stereotyped view of Canterbury as a patchwork plain where lambs frolic under a nor'west sky. This Canterbury exists. The plain, 180 km (110 miles) long and an average of 40 km (25 miles) wide, is the largest area of flat land in New Zealand. Canterbury lamb, bred for both meat and wool, and famous worldwide, is regarded as New Zealand's best. The Canterbury nor'wester is a notorious wind, a true *föhn* with its warm, dry, blustery weather east of the Alps whipping up dust from riverbeds and furrowed farmlands and receiving the blame for the moodiness of sensitive Cantabrians.

Yet Canterbury is much more. As well as being the largest plain, the province also encompasses New Zealand's highest mountains and widest rivers – not to overlook its pastoral and forested hills, fine beaches, and extinct volcanoes and sheltered bays of Banks Peninsula. Settlement is also diverse: Canterbury boasts one of New Zealand's four main centres, two fine ports, a secondary city, many small towns and large high-country sheep stations where, paradoxically, genteel English traditions are most vigorously upheld in the least probable of New Zealand settings.

Plain Fascination

The hallmark of Canterbury is not its plain; the great sweep of level land is merely the corridor to the province's special characteristic – its accessibility. In Canterbury you feel part of the main, near to sky, earth and sea, yet conveniently close to civilisation and to international air connections. From any point in the province one is never more than a

couple of hours from mountains, lakes, beaches, plains, rivers, cities and airports. The openness of the landscape and the ever-changing climate inspire an awareness of the surrounding environment. The traveller soon learns that a southerly wind invariably brings rain and a quick drop in temperature; a nor'wester dry heat and rising rivers from its high-country rainstorms; an easterly, a chill breeze to Christchurch and along the coast.

One hundred thirty-five years of European settlement have tamed the flat land. The treeless landscape that appeared so desolate to Canterbury's pilgrims is today a pastoral scene like no other: a patchwork of cropped fields dotted with sheep, divided by shelter belts of pines and macrocarpas, and sewn through with long straight roads that would have gladdened the hearts of the Romans.

From the air the view has a fascination. Patterned on the multi-coloured quilt of crops and pastures are vein-like shadows of ancient streams while the existing rivers gleam silver as they flow through their broad beds of shingle from the ranges to the sea. Towns, small or large, sprawl inelegantly along the roads like aphids clinging to sap-rich stems.

From the ground the plains create a less imposing sight. Travelling lengthwise in Canterbury is a comparatively monotonous journey, especially on the main highway between Christchurch and Timaru. Canterbury's finest scenery is inland, to the west along the foothills and valleys of the Southern Alps.

Three main roads provide easy access to passes through the mountains to Westland. Northernmost is the Lewis Pass, and its rewarding short detour to the tiny spa resort of Hanmer Springs; central is Arthur's Pass and surrounding national park of the same name; southernmost is Burke's Pass, which leads to the Mackenzie Country and the Mount Cook region.

Getting Healthy at Hanmer

Bypassed by conventional tourist traffic, **Hanmer Springs** survives as one of New Zealand's quietest resorts. This little village, an easy 136-km (84-mile) drive north of Christchurch, nestles in a sheltered, forested valley. Its hot mineral pools are set in a garden of giant conifers. Few experiences are more pleasurable than relaxing in the warm open-air pool on a winter's night, watching snowflakes dissolve silently through the steam or gazing, on a cloudless night, into the brilliantly starry heavens.

A European settler stumbled upon the springs in 1859; they were harnessed by the government in 1883. Since then their recuperative powers have been used to help rehabilitate wounded soldiers, the psychiatrically disturbed and, in more recent years, alcoholics. Although maintained by the Queen Mary Hospital they are open to the public. The complex includes several plunge pools for private hire, communal pools of varying (indicated) temperatures, and a fresh-water swimming pool.

Hanmer's forests and hills provide a number of invigorating walks. Several easy-going, well-defined paths meander through the forests which contain more species of exotic trees than any other plantation in New Zealand. This was the first exotic forest established by the government in the South Island; some of the oldest trees were planted more than 85 years ago.

More demanding walks to the summits of **Conical Hill** and **Mount Isobel** provide magnificent panoramas. The Mount Isobel track, which passes 200 different kinds of sub-alpine flowering plants and ferns, is a naturalist's delight.

Sporting opportunities abound: Hanmer's 18-hole golf course is one of the highest in New Zealand, while fishing, hunting, skiing and horse-trekking are also available, although not on the same thoroughly commercialised scale as in Queenstown.

Although Hanmer has accommodation in the form of a licensed hotel, several motels, guest houses, holiday homes and camping grounds, the main street has the low-key, subdued atmosphere of a typical rural township, rather than a resort. This very lack of self-consciousness or razzmatazz enhances Hanmer's pleasant aura.

Rugged Beauty

For those with cars, several excursions from Hanmer are worthwhile. The road over Jack's Pass to the isolated **Clarence Valley** is worth exploring for its rugged tussocked beauty, especially upstream. A word of warning, though: the road – originally built to provide access for electricity department workers to install and maintain the high-voltage transmission lines that weave their silver threads from the hydro schemes of Otago to Blenheim, Nelson and beyond – is an unsealed, often-steep track, suitable only in good weather and then requiring extreme care. It is not a through road and has locked gates at the Acheron River bridge (downstream from Jack's Pass) and at the Rainbow Station over the Main Divide. Hanmer, therefore, remains very much a "dead-end" town. Travellers have little choice but to backtrack 13 km (8 miles) to the Waipara-Reefton road (Highway 7).

Westwards this climbs up the Waiau Valley to **Lewis Pass**, Canterbury's most northerly gateway to Westland. This all-weather route (opened in 1939) offers a comparatively gentle, picturesque crossing at an altitude of 865 metres (2,838 feet) through beech-covered mountains. From the pass the highway descends to Maruia Springs and then on to the Rahu Saddle, Reefton and Greymouth.

Southwards from the "Hanmer turn-off," as it is locally known, Highway 7

Steely structures at Oahu B power station.

runs through the rolling hills of North Canterbury to its junction with Highway 1 at **Waipara**, passing along the way the small rural settlements of **Culverden**, **Hurunui** and **Waikari**. A historic pub is now Hurunui's chief claim to fame, thankfully saved from demolition and operated by local farmers. The road then passes through Waikari's limestone landscape in which keen-eyed observers might detect naturally sculpted animal forms in the cliffs – a dog, a seal and a frog, for instance.

A Touch of Switzerland

The quickest route between Christchurch and Westland is the West Coast Road (Highway 73) through **Arthur's Pass**. This, the South Island's most central pass, boasts New Zealand's version of a Swiss village. Although Arthur's Pass township, nestling in the heart of the Southern Alps 154 km (96 miles) west of Christchurch, lacks green pastures and tinkling cowbells, it does have a chalet-style restaurant and, in keeping with any self-respecting village in Switzerland, a railway station.

Arthur's Pass marks the eastern portal of the Otira Tunnel, the only rail link through the mountains. The 8.6-km (5.3-mile) tunnel, completed in 1923 after 15 years' construction, was the first electrified stretch of line in the British Empire – a necessary advance to save the passengers from being choked to death by the steam locomotive's sulphurous smoke. Today, as New Zealand ruthlessly closes ailing branch lines, the rail link between the West Coast and Canterbury remains a vital one. As an extra bonus, it is the most scenic rail journey in New Zealand.

Arthur's Pass is also the headquarters of the national park of the same name. Its close proximity to Christchurch and its many comparatively civilised tracks make the 100,000-hectares (247,000-acres) park one of the best utilised in the country. **Mount Rolleston**, 2,271 metres (7,451 feet), dominates the region in which there are 30 peaks over 1,800 metres (about 6,000 feet).

Hotel accommodation is non-existent. Motels and a youth hostel provide accommodation for visitors.

The 924-metre (3,032-foot) pass is named after Arthur Dudley Dobson, who

Rakaia River on course.

rediscovered the former Maori route in 1864. It marks the boundary between Canterbury and Westland, a boundary which is often graphically reinforced by the distinctive weather patterns of this area. During a nor'wester the traveller leaves a brilliantly sunny day on the Canterbury side of the pass and descends into heavy rain in the West Coast's Otira Gorge. Conversely, during a southerly, West Coast-bound travellers leave Canterbury rain behind to find a landscape bathed in sunshine.

In this savage and dramatic wilderness the ever-changing weather demands respect. Storms are often as intense as they are sudden, dropping as much as 250 mm (10 inches) of rain in 24 hours. The annual rainfall here is 3,000 mm (about 120 inches). Bad weather frequently forces the closure of the highway, which in the Otira Gorge is very steep with a series of hairpin bends requiring special care in wet weather and in winter. The road is not suitable for caravans. (Indeed, in bad weather, the Automobile Association often advises travellers to take the longer, but easier and safer, Lewis Pass route to Westland).

High Country Thief

A common sight in this vicinity is the *kea*, the inquisitive native parrot. This mountain species has criminal tendencies that surpass those of any thieving magpie, as the pioneer explorer Julius von Haast discovered when a vandalistic *kea* tumbled his valuable collection of native plants down a ravine, and as careless visitors discover today if they leave food or shiny belongings unattended.

Arthur's Pass, however, is not the highest point on the West Coast road. That distinction belongs to **Porter's Pass**, 88 km (55 miles) west of Christchurch, which traverses the foothills at 945 metres (3,100 feet). Porter's Pass is a popular winter destination for day-trippers from Christchurch for tobogganing, ice-skating at **Lake Lyndon** and skiing on the many skifields in the vicinity – the commercial field at **Porter Heights** and the club fields at **Craigieburn**, **Broken River** and **Mount Cheesman**.

Canterbury's most popular and best-developed skifield is **Mount Hutt**, 100 km (62 miles) west of Christchurch. This commercial field is serviced by the small

Staying close to the sheep.

town of **Methven**, 11 km (7 miles) away, which provides good accommodation.

Rooftop of New Zealand

The monarch of New Zealand's national parks is the **Mount Cook National Park**, where the highest peaks in the land soar above the crest of the Southern Alps. Supreme is **Mount Cook** itself, 3,764 metres (12,349 feet), the training ground for Sir Edmund Hillary, the first person to scale Mount Everest. The narrow park extends only 80 km (50 miles) along the alpine spine, yet it contains 140 peaks over 2,134 metres (7,000 feet) as well as five of New Zealand's largest glaciers.

The Mount Cook Line, which installed and operates the airport in the valley floor at the base of Mount Cook, runs daily air services to the park, only 35 minutes' flying time from either Christchurch or Queenstown. If the weather at the Mount Cook airstrip precludes takeoffs and landings, the airline uses an alternative airstrip near Lake Pukaki, and transports passengers between Pukaki and Mount Cook by road, a distance of some 60 km (37 miles).

Thieving eyes: the kea at Milford Track.

Paradoxically, although Mount Cook is almost due west of Christchurch, the journey by road is a circuitous distance of 330 km (205 miles). Getting there, however, is half the fun.

The main route follows Highway 1 south for 121 km (75 miles), marching easily across plain and river alike, casually belying the mighty challenges this journey once posed for Maori and pioneer. The wide rivers proved major obstacles to travel and settlement in the 1850s and difficult river crossings caused numerous drownings in Canterbury. Throughout New Zealand 1,115 people lost their lives in river accidents between 1840 and 1870 and it was suggested in Parliament that drowning be classified a natural death! Nowadays motorists speed over the bridges spanning the Rakaia, Ashburton and Rangitata rivers without a thought for the hazards that once confronted travellers.

Immediately past the Rangitata River the road to the Mackenzie Country (Highway 79) branches westwards from the main highway. It leads to the foothills and the tiny town of **Geraldine** which snuggles into them, offering detours to an historic pioneer homestead in the **Orari Gorge** and excellent picnic and fishing spots in the nearby **Waihi** and **Te Moana** gorges.

The Mackenzie Country

The road to **Fairlie**, a country town with a historical museum, passes the only elderberry wine cellars in New Zealand and a Clydesdale stud farm. The gentle, green countryside is left behind at Fairlie as the road, now Highway 8, rises with deceptive ease to **Burke's Pass**. At this gap through the foothills a different world stretches beyond – the great tussocked basin known as the Mackenzie Country, named for a Scottish shepherd who in 1855 tried to hide stolen sheep in this isolated high-country area.

Winding across the stark bronzed landscape the road reaches **Lake Tekapo**, a lovely turquoise glacial lake reflecting the surrounding mountains. By the lake's edge the simple stone **Church of the Good Shepherd** stands in harmony with its surroundings. Nearby the high-country sheepdog which has played an essential role in building New Zealand's agricultural prosperity is commemorated in a bronze statue erected by runholders from Mackenzie Country.

From the lazy lakeside town of **Tekapo** the road south continues across the tussocked quilt of the Mackenzie Basin – in summer, shimmering brown and parched in the windswept heat; in winter, barren and bleak with its frozen mantle of white. Winter sports are popular here, with skiing at **Round Hill** and ice-skating on the lake.

The road passes **Irishman Creek**, the sheep station where Sir William Hamilton perfected the jet boat to travel up, as well as down, the shallow rivers of the lonely back-country. Nearby, too, is the **Mount John Observatory**, previously used to help track United Stated satellites. The observatory is well-sited to take advantage of the pristine purity of the Mackenzie Country atmosphere and may be visited.

The road, for much of the way, follows the course of the man-made canal that drains Tekapo's turquoise waters to the first of the Waitaki hydro-electric scheme's powerhouses on the northern shore of **Lake Pukaki**.

Lake Pukaki today is twice the size it was in 1979 when its waters were allowed to flow unimpeded to Lake Benmore. Concrete dams now hold Pukaki in check, forcing its pent-up waters to rise to a new level for controlled use in hydro-electric generation. The dams have flooded forever the once-convoluted maze of streams of the broad river that flows into it from the Tasman and Hooker glaciers.

Travellers on the new highway that skirts the southern slopes of the Pukaki valley to the Mount Cook village might catch glimpses of the old road undulating above and disappearing into the still-rising surface of the lake far below. But its slow death by drowning draws little sympathy from those who knew it well, the travellers who rode its unsealed corrugations and choked in its dust. The new highway, sealed with an easy gradient, has halved the driving time to the Tourist Hotel Corporation's "hermit's abode" – **The Hermitage**.

The village lies within the Mount Cook National Park and the development of accommodation, therefore, has been limited. Nevertheless, in addition to The Hermitage hotel, there are also self-contained A-frame chalets, the Glencoe Lodge, a camping ground and well-equipped youth hostel.

Well-defined tracks lead from the village up the surrounding valleys. These eventually become "climbs" that are not for novices and should only be tackled by experienced climbers with the right equipment, and these only after consultation with the Park Board rangers.

Easier ways up the mountains are provided by ski-equipped scenic aircraft which land on the high snowfields. Skiing is available most of the year, the most exciting run being the descent of the 29-km (18-mile) **Tasman Glacier**.

The spectacular views of Mount Cook, especially when the last rays of the midsummer sun strike its blushing peak at late twilight, form the highlight of many a traveller's exploration of Canterbury. The mountain, named Aorangi ("Cloud Piercer") by the Maori, frequently shyly hides itself in a cloak of cloud, depriving sightseers of its face. But rain or shine, this alpine region is ever-masterful, ever-dramatic, a corner of Canterbury where people are dwarfed into insignificance.

Left, young talents at the Mackenzie Highland Show. **Right**, Tasman Glacier, Mount Cook National Park.

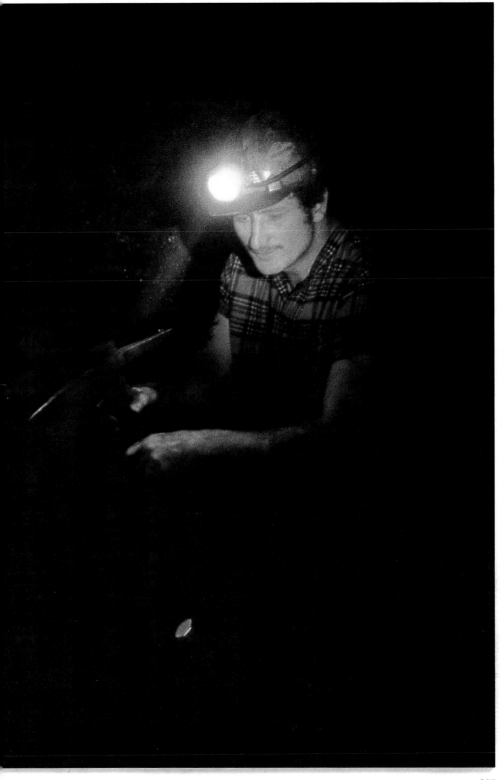

THE WEST COAST: A HERITAGE OF GOLD

Hollywood has immortalised the Wild West of North America's heritage, but no such fame has attached itself to the equally deserving Wild West Coast of New Zealand's South Island.

Maybe it's a reputation yet to be acknowledged. It certainly should be, for the coast and its coasters have a past as rip-roaring as that of the American West.

Today the visitor finds only ghostly shadows of the West Coast's former glory – of the gold rush days of the 1860s when dozens of towns with populations of thousands mushroomed around the promise of buried riches.

The hard-drinking, hard-fighting and hard-working men and women of those bygone days have left behind little more than a legend. The entire population of the 500-km (310-mile), coast is now less than it was in 1867 when it peaked at 40,000 – then 13 percent of New Zealand's total population. Today West Coasters number 30,000 – less than 1 percent of the country's 3.3 million people – and the land itself relentlessly reclaims sites where towns such as Charleston (with 12,000 souls and 80 grog shops) once boomed.

Nowadays, a few small claims, an old dredge and a Shantytown recreated for tourists, constitute scant evidence of the robust pioneering days when fighting in the street was a traditional Saturday night pastime and religious "wars" broke out between Irish Catholics and their Protestant brethren. It was a young, headstrong society with money to burn and an unqualified interest in booze. Men sometimes lit their cigars with £5 notes, but women who threw gin over each other were fined for their wasteful behaviour.

An Independent Character

Coasters are few in number, yet they have a strong identity distinct from the rest of the population. Proof of that strength resides in the strange fact that, officially, there is no such place as "the West Coast." The maps refer, authoritatively, to Westland; and they place the northern areas of Inangahua and Buller in the province of Nelson. Yet New Zealanders, with vague affection rather than strict authority, habitually refer to "the West Coast" in the general understanding that the term embraces the strip of land west of the Southern Alps.

The Coasters have a reputation for being down-to-earth, genuine, rugged, independent, aggressive and hospitable. On the West Coast, liquor licensing laws have been flouted with impunity for years. But the West Coasters' chief "enemy" nowadays is not central government, but a conservation lobby that wants to preserve intact the native forests and birdlife with which the West Coast is specially endowed. The locals, struggling to scratch a living from timber-milling and coal-mining, angrily oppose the conservationist concerns of those who live elsewhere.

The West Coast has never seduced its inhabitants with an easy life. And if it has proved wild and tough, it never promised to be anything else. It was settled late by the Maori, from about A.D. 1400, but even then only sparsely. Their main interest was in the much-coveted greenstone at Arahura, carried out with difficulty

Preceding pages, men at work in the Sullivan Coal Mine, Westport. Below, Fox Glacier.

208

first through a route north to Nelson and later across alpine passes in the Main Divide to Canterbury.

Early Explorers

Neither of the two great discoverers, Abel Tasman and James Cook, were enamoured when sailing past the West Coast in 1642 and 1769, respectively. "An inhospitable shore" was Captain Cook's description. "One long solitude with a forbidding sky and impenetrable forest" was the view, about 50 years afterwards, of an officer in a French expedition.

So forbidding was the West Coast that European exploration did not begin in earnest until 1846. And the opinion of one of those first explorers, Thomas Brunner ("The very worst country I have seen in New Zealand") served to discourage further investigation. His distaste resulted from the great hardships suffered on his 550-day journey through the region.

It was only in 1860 that the authorities responded positively to reports of glaciers in the south and of routes through the Alps to Canterbury: the central government bought the entire West Coast from the Maori for 300 gold sovereigns. Appropriately, European settlers then made determined attempts to find gold, and were successful. By 1865 the gold rush was in full swing and took another 5 years to reach its peak.

Glaciers and Rain

To the modern visitor, the West Coast appears more inviting than forbidding. It is a long, narrow strip of vigorous beauty, bounded on the east by the Alps and pounded on the west by the restless Tasman Sea. Glaciers, the largest anywhere in the temperate zones, grind their way down canyon-like valleys from about 3,000 metres (10,000 feet) to a mere 300 metres (1,000 feet) above sea level. Placid, fern-fringed lakes mirror the mighty mountains and dense natural forests. Rivers cascade through boulder-strewn valleys to the Tasman.

Rain falls frequently and ferociously: to travel in a typical West Coast downpour is to see the virgin forest in its full glory. Waterfalls, where there were none

West Coast; fury on the rocks.

before, burst in great torrents from mist-shrouded peaks; fern fronds bow graciously under the weight of raindrops; life is drenched, quenched, renewed. And when the rain is exhausted and the cloud rolls back from the mountaintops to reveal the sun, the bush becomes a sauna alive with birdsong and – the sole flaw in this other Eden – sandflies with their itch for human blood.

The West Coast can almost be guaranteed to switch on such a rainfall. This is the wettest inhabited area in New Zealand, Hokitika, for instance, averages almost 3,000 mm (118 inches) a year with rain falling on 144 days a year.

A raw savagery pervades the West Coast today. Days of hardship and disappointment are given mute testimony in the tumbledown weatherboard farmhouses and moss-covered fences. Tiny wooden churches, perched forlornly on hillsides, are now deserted outposts bereft of congregation. Everywhere the sense of decline, not seedy but sad, is tangible as heartbreak haunts each abandoned farm and dwindling village. New Zealand's past is frozen here in a land without a warped infatuation with the fashionable, the progressive, the modern. A time-trip back to the 1950s and beyond is an unheralded bonus for travellers in this naturally primeval and emotionally raw retreat.

Travelling Up the Coast

Four routes link the region with the rest of the South Island. The opening in 1965 of the most southerly, the Haast Pass, has enabled travellers to trace almost the entire length of the Coast as part of a round-trip through the South Island. This pass, linking Westland with the Southern Lakes of Central Otago, is also the most dramatic, providing a sudden contrast between the dry tussocked Otago landscape and the lush vegetation to the west. Irrespective of one's point of entry – south, north or east (via either trans-alpine pass from Canterbury) – Highway 6 offers a journey of spectacular scenery from Haast down in the south to Murchison up in the north.

Most famous of the West Coast's attractions are the world-renowned **Fox Glacier** and **Franz Josef Glacier**, about 120 km (75 miles) north of Haast. Like

Shades of the old West: at Glenmore Station...

many of the world's glaciers, these two have receded in recent years, but nonetheless still form a spectacular sight. Both are located, about 25 km (15 miles) apart, in the **Westland National Park**, which boasts 88,000 hectares (217,000 acres) of alpine peaks, snowfields, forests, lakes and rivers.

The main highway which traverses the park's western edge passes close to both glaciers. Narrow bush-clad roads provide easy access to good vantage points for visitors who want to view both the southernmost Fox Glacier and the more picturesque Franz Josef Glacier which is 11 km (7 miles) long.

Helicopter and ski-plane flights over both glaciers provide remarkable views of the greenish-blue tints and the infinite crevasses in the rivers of ice. For the energetic, guided walking tours over the glaciers are available.

Two small townships, each with a variety of accommodation, cater competitively for the needs of visitors to the glaciers. At Franz Josef, **St. James Anglican Church** sits hidden in a superb setting and is well worth a visit. Earlier this century its altar window framed the famous ice-flow but it has long since receded from view.

The national park headquarters at Franz Josef provides detailed information about the many walks available. These include the difficult, but rewarding, climb over the **Copland Pass** in the Main Divide to The Hermitage at Mount Cook. In fact, the park provides some 110 km (68 miles) of walking tracks through a sanctuary of varied native forest and birdlife, all dominated by the high peaks of Cook, Tasman and La Perouse. This trio is beautifully mirrored in **Lake Mathieson**, one of the park's three calm lakes formed by the glacial dramas of 10,000 years ago.

Whitebait and White Herons

The region south and north of the national park has a stunning coastline. Far to the south of Haast township is an especially lonely terrain, crossed by a secondary road leading to the fishing village of **Jackson Bay**, where it comes to an abrupt end. This small community is swelled in spring when keen whitebaiters descend en masse at the nearby river mouth to

...and down Shantytown, Westland.

catch the prized delicacy, an annual occurrence repeated beside swift rivers all along the Coast.

Fishing is a major preoccupation in this southern part of Westland. **Haast** in particular offers good surf and river fishing while, 45 km (28 miles) north at the quiet holiday spot of **Lake Paringa**, anglers are enticed by the prospect of brown trout and quinnat salmon.

A short detour west of Fox Glacier township is **Gillespie's Beach**, noted for its miners' cemetery and seal colony. Some 60 km (37 miles) further north on the main road, another detour leads to **Okarito Lagoon**, famous as the only breeding ground of the rare white heron. Okarito once boomed with 31 hotels; now only a few holiday cottages remain along with a monument commemorating the 1642 landfall of Abel Tasman.

Northwards, the main highway to **Ross** passes the idyllic **Lake Ianthe**. Ross was once a flourishing goldfield, producing the largest nugget (2,970 grams, or 104 ounces) recorded on the Coast. Nowadays, the town is a shadow of its former self, relics of its once proud history stored for posterity in a small museum.

Hokitika, formerly the "Wonder City of the Southern Hemisphere" with "streets of gold" and a thriving seaport with 100 grog shops, is 30 km (19 miles) north of Ross. It goes without saying that Hokitika is now a quiet town. However, it is served by the West Coast's main airfield and its tourist attractions include a historical museum, greenstone factories, a gold mine, gold panning and a glowworm dell. From nearby **Lake Kaniere** and the **Hokitika Gorge**, mountaineering routes lead to Canterbury over the Browning and Whitcombe passes.

Twenty-three km (14 miles) north of the town, at **Kumara Junction**, the highway is intersected by the Arthur's Pass Highway which links Westland and Canterbury. A few kilometres west of the junction this intersecting road enters the old gold.town of **Kumara**, from where a scenic detour of **Lake Brunner**, the largest lake on the West Coast, winds through native forest.

Gold Sluices and "Pancakes"

Towards Greymouth, about 10 km (6 miles) north of Kumara Junction, is **Pancake Rocks, Punakaiki.**

Shantytown, a reproduction of an early gold town offering sluicing and railway ride to old Chinese workings.

At **Greymouth**, the other trans-alpine route from Canterbury connects with Highway 6. The largest town to the Coast (population 7,000), Greymouth owes its commanding position to its seaport and its proximity to timber mills and coal mines.

Beyond Greymouth, the Coast Road to Westport hugs the coastline which, 43 km (27 miles) north at **Punakaiki**, takes on the extraordinary appearance of a pile of petrified pancakes. The "Pancake rocks" and their associated blowholes consist of eroded limestone. Reached by a short and easy walk from the main road, they are best visited when there is an incoming tide and the brisk westerly causes the tempestuous sea to surge explosively through the chasms.

Thirty-two km (20 miles) north is **Charleston**, site of the once-booming centre of the Buller district, with old gold workings nearby. At a junction 21 km (13 miles) farther to the north, the coastal road becomes Highway 67, leading to the nearby town of **Westport** and beyond to

the West Coast's northernmost town of **Karamea**, 88 km (55 miles) away. The road provides access to two acclaimed walking tracks – the **Wangapeka Track**, which traces the Little Wanganui River, and the 70-km (43-mile), **Heaphy Track**, a four-to-six-day tramp linking Karamea and Golden Bay.

Five km south of Westport, Highway 6 turns inland to follow one of the South Island's most beautiful rivers, the Buller, through its lower and upper gorges for 84 km (52 miles) to **Murchison**. At this point the West Coast is left behind and the road continues to Nelson and Blenheim.

Branching South

The West Coast section of this road, however, extends 2 branches southward, Highways 69 and 65, to connect with the Lewis Pass Highway. Highway 69, which turns off at the **Inangahua Junction** halfway between Westport and Murchison, traverses one of the most mineralised districts of New Zealand, 34 km (21 miles) south, it enters **Reefton**, a historic town named for its famous quartz reefs. This region was abundant in gold and coal, and the story of their extraction is unfolded in the township's School of Mines and the Black's Point Museum. Other old buildings of interest are the courthouse and churches.

The other route (Highway 65) to the Lewis Pass from Murchison is mostly unsealed and should be regarded as a secondary road. It joins up with the main Lewis Pass Highway at **Springs Junction**, 72 km (45 miles) south.

To travel well on the West Coast the visitor needs insect repellent, no-nonsense weather-proof gear, and a taste for a strong New Zealand brew – be it beer or a good cuppa tea.

Otherwise, however, extravagances (in clothing or conversation, for instance) are best avoided, becoming more than a little absurd in the Coast's raw surroundings. A sensitive exploration here will almost assuredly yield a sense of well-being and optimism.

The West Coast might be subject to cataclysmic earthquakes and floods, but, with today's growing awareness, it should never be subjugated by people. It will always be untamed and more than a touch wild.

Denniston Incline, Westport.

CENTRAL OTAGO: LAKE COUNTRY

Every traveller has a first magical journey embedded in his or her memory. For many adult New Zealanders, that first excursion came as children three or more decades ago into the heart of Central Otago, where the bronzed hills glaring in the summer sunshine and the chilling coldness of the lakes lent a mysterious incongruity to a series of unimaginable discoveries. The sole disappointing but nonetheless momentous surprise may have been that though the destination was Queenstown, the Queen did not, in fact, live there.

In recent decades, **Queenstown** has grown from a sleepy lakeside town for New Zealand summer holiday-makers into an all-year tourist resort, an antipodean Saint Moritz. Queenstown only lacks, by comparison, a certain architectural grandeur and, still, the presence of royalty (which, even if seasonal and minor, brings fame and glamour to Europe's playgrounds). Nevertheless, it reigns as the most sophisticated resort in New Zealand, a sophistication belied by its energy.

Within a radius of only a few kilometres, New Zealanders' ingenuity and mechanical wizardry have combined with the stunning landscape to provide a range of adventure activities unrivalled in such a concentrated area anywhere else. Indeed, an airport, ski fields, hotels and multiplicity of recreational facilities have transformed Queenstown into the tourism centre of Central Otago, a region that until the advent of air travel was one of the least accessible in New Zealand.

Landscape Burnished in Gold

"Central" possesses a regional personality quite distinct from other parts of the country. Some of the Southern Alps' most impressive peaks dominate its western flank, towering over deep glacier-gouged lakes. Yet its enduring impact lies with more subtlety in the strange landscape chiselled and shaved from Central Otago's plateau of mica schist rock. The rounded ranges of scorched-brown tussock resemble a blanket draped over the raised limbs of a reclining giant. Jagged outcrops of schist pierce the tussock near Central's core but elsewhere the slopes appear soft and pliant, as if a sky-jumper alighting on them would cause them to collapse in slow motion into a displaced hollow which would gently envelop the intruder.

Such fancies come easily among Central's hills as the day's ever-changing light casts new shadows and sculptures from the bronze forms. In the dry continental climate of the inland plateau, the pure atmosphere aids the play of light, evoking nuances few other landscapes permit. The overwhelming impression is of a stark, simple landscape burnished in glowing browns tinged with white, gold, ochre and sienna. The effect has attracted generations of landscape painters.

Once seen, the subtlety of those colour variations remain in the memory for ever; never seen, they cannot be imagined. The staff of an Auckland-based national magazine discovered this when publishing a colour shot of a Central Otago scene. The photo processor, dismayed at the absence of green in the rolling hills, employed technological resources and

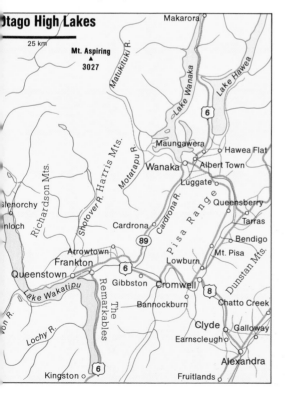

Otago High Lakes

dye to "remedy" the brown image. His conscientious efforts roused a negative reaction, however, from the magazine's editor – a former Southlander to whom the neighbouring hills of Central Otago were familiar and dear. The blunder was averted before the magazine went to print.

Yet idle fancies are not enough to lure people into staking out a patch of earth in arid, inhospitable country. Over nine centuries of sketchy human habitation, Central Otago's bait has been successively moa, jade, grazing land, gold, hydro-electric power and pleasure.

Hunters of Moa and Greenstone

The first humans to set foot in the region were Maori moa-hunters who pushed inland about the A.D. 12th century in quest of the vanishing ostrich-like bird. Against the hunters' disastrous use of fire, Central Otago could not offer the magnificent endangered moa lasting refuge. As fire ravaged native bush and forest, the moa and other birds disappeared forever. Some of New Zealand's best moa remains have been found in the banks of the mighty Clutha River as it winds through the plateau on its 322-km (200-mile) journey to the Pacific.

About the end of the 15th century, the moa-hunters were conquered by the now-mysterious Ngati-Mamoe tribe moving down from the north. This group, defeated in turn two centuries later by another invading Maori tribe, supposedly fled into the forests of Fiordland and thereafter into the mists of legend.

The victors, the Ngati-Tahu, took control of the supply of the Maori's most precious metal – the New Zealand jade known variously as *pounamu*, nephrite or greenstone. Hard, durable and workable, it was in demand among the Stone-Age natives for adzes, chisels and weapons. So desirable was the jade, in fact, that the Maori made epic expeditions through Central Otago and the alpine divide to bring it out from the West Coast, the only place it was found, via the head of Lake Wakatipu to the east coast. It was then "processed" and exported to northern tribes.

Today, the same jade that gave the Maori as good a cutting edge as any known to Stone-Age culture is a major **Queenstown.**

feature in New Zealand's jewellery and souvenir industries.

Despite the lucrative trade route, the Maori population of Central was never large. The extremes of temperature (the severest in New Zealand) were too harsh for the descendants of Polynesian voyagers from the tropical Pacific. In 1836, the last few remaining Maori settlements disappeared entirely when a war party from the North Island attacked on its way south.

Gold in Gabriel's Gully

For about 10 years trespassing man was absent and Central Otago slept in supreme silence. Forty seasons commanded sole possession of Central's solitude; the giant lonely limbs of the hills surrendered to slumber, as if gathering strength for the sudden stampede of people and merino that would soon disturb the deep peace.

The European era began in 1847 when a surveyor blazed a trail for pioneers in quest of country where they could establish large sheep runs. By 1861 these new settlers were squatting on most of the potential grazing land, willingly exiling themselves to a Siberia of their own choosing. In the face of the land's indifference the runholders persevered against the ravages wrought by winter snows, spring floods, summer droughts, fires, wild dogs, rats, rabbits and *keas*; they took in their stride obstacles such as dangerous river crossings, lack of roads, scarcity of food and supplies, and inadequate shelter; and all the while they toiled from dawn to dark, day in, year out. Release most often took the form of violent death.

These new settlers, predominantly of Scottish origin, had no sooner begun their self-imposed sentences than gold fever flared through Central Otago. In 1861 the first major discovery of gold "shining like the stars in Orion on a dark frosty night" was made in a gully along the Tuapeka River by Gabriel Read, a prospector with experience of the California gold rush of 1849.

Central Otago's gold boom had begun. In just four months, 4,000 men were swarming over the 5-km valley, probing and sifting each centimetre for glowing alluvial gold. A year on, the population of the Tuapeka goldfield was 11,500, double that of the fast-emptying provincial capital, Dunedin. Otago's income trebled in 12 months, while the number of ship arrivals quadrupled, many of the 200 vessels bringing miners from Australia's Victorian fields.

In Gabriel's Gully, all miners, regardless of social rank, wore identical blue shirts and moleskin trousers. The sentiment was reflected in a song:

On the diggings we're all on a level you know
The poor out here ain't oppressed by the rich
But dressed in blue shirts, you can't tell which is which.

This feeling of egalitarianism was echoed by a newspaper's praise of "the free and careless bluffness which is a great relief from the reserve and formality that prevail among all classes in the Old Country (England)."

"Richest River in the World"

New goldfields were discovered in quick succession in other river valleys –

Grand Old Lady on Lake Wakatipu, the Earnslaw.

the Clutha at the foot of the Dunstan Range, the Cardrona, Shotover, Arrow and Kawarau. In 1862 the Shotover, then yielding as much as 155 grammes (5½ ounces) of gold by the shovelful, was known as the richest river in the world. In one afternoon two Maori men going to the rescue of their near-drowned dog recovered no less than 11 kg (308 ounces) of gold.

But if gold was plentiful, "tucker" was scarce. Rationed flour and tea, augmented perhaps by a poached (and hard-boiled) sheep, kept many a miner barely alive. Several starved to death, especially those without the luck and boldness of one ravenous miner who, caught red-handed in the act of skinning a sheep, said in a defiant Irish brogue: "I'll kill any bloody sheep that bites me!" The joke went down well with the runholder who rode away laughing.

Today **Arrowtown**, 20 km (12 miles) from Queenstown, is the most picturesque gold-mining settlement in Central and arguably the prettiest small town in New Zealand. Its leaf and stone beauty has endured as if to compensate for the comparatively scant evidence of the esti-mated 80 goldfields that mushroomed, then wilted, in Central over one hectic decade.

Barmaid Bride

Ghost towns are scattered throughout the region, shadows of the calico, sod and corrugated-iron settlements that seemed "ugly" to visiting English novelist Anthony Trollope in 1872. To his eyes, though, the towns all shared one redeeming feature – libraries stocked with "strongly bound and well-thumbed" books. (Perhaps this was the first sign of New Zealanders' unequalled fondness for the written word.)

Two ghost towns, **Macetown** and **Cardrona**, haunt the hills above Arrowtown. **Bendigo**, near the Clutha River 25 km (15 miles) north of Cromwell (off Highway 8), is a dream ghost town, especially when the wind whistles through the tumbledown stone cottages at the bleak crossroads. A concentrated effort is required to visualise Bendigo's saloon on a Saturday night during the 1860s when "a hideous maniacal yelling … entirely overpowered and **Masonic Hall, Arrowtown.**

drowned every sound within a radius of a mile or so." Behind the imaginary bar, picture Mary Ann, probably the most successful novice barmaid in New Zealand's history. After being jilted on her wedding day, she fled Cromwell, the scene of her humiliation, to begin work the same day at the Bendigo saloon. In just 2 hours flat, the bar was drunk dry by miners eager to see the bartender bride in all her nuptial finery.

Several tiny gold-rush towns, with substance as well as atmosphere, have refused to die so easily. The original settlement – then Tuapeka, now **Lawrence** – still survives with a strongly Victorian flavour, a nearby monument in Gabriel's Gully marking the site of Gabriel Read's discovery. Pockets of old gold towns are stitched into the ranges, gullies, gorges and valleys elsewhere in Central. Some of them, particularly in Queenstown's rugged hinterland, attract specialised four-wheel-drive tours.

Today the river valleys are clear of the calico cities that sprouted during the rush of 1860s and the dredges that savagely exhausted leftover traces of gold during the early 1900s. Few dedicated prospec-

Panning for gold.

tors remain. Gold-fossicking is almost solely the preserve of tourists for whom it is a popular, but not (at least admittedly) very profitable, pastime.

Whitewater Adventures

The swift rivers near Queenstown also set the scene for whitewater rafting and jet-boating adventures. The latter is New Zealand's home-grown style of running rivers, upstream as well as down. Propeller-less power boats speed over rapid shallows barely ankle-deep. These nifty craft are thrust along by their jet stream as water, drawn in through an intake in the bottom of the hull, is forced out at high pressure through a nozzle at the rear. The typical river boat is powered by a standard automobile engine, handles 7 tonnes of water a minute, can skim over shallows no more than 10 cm (4 inches) deep, and can execute sudden 180-degree turns within a single boat length.

The Shotover jet, swerving up and down the Shotover River a hair's breadth from jagged cliffs, is probably the world's most exciting jet-boat ride and the most famous of some nine commercial trips in the Queenstown vicinity. Another, the Heli-Jet, offers a triple-thrill ride in helicopter, jet-boat and whitewater raft.

Other commercial water adventures on Queenstown's lakes and rivers include canoeing, yachting, windsurfing, parasailing, water-skiing and hobie-cat sailing, as well as hydrofoil and jet-bike rides. Traditional and sedate activities are also available – trout fishing in lonely rivers and streams, for instance, or an excursion in the aging steamship *Earnslaw*, a grand old Lady of the Lake that has graced the waters of **Lake Wakatipu** since 1912.

"Hollow of the Giant"

Perhaps the most haunting of Central Otago's lakes, Wakatipu has captured man's imagination with its strange serpentine shape, rhythmic "breathing" and constant coldness. According to Maori legend, the lake is the "Hollow of the Giant" (*Whakatipua*), formed when an evil sleeping giant was set on fire by a brave youth, melting the snow and ice of the surrounding mountains to fill the 80-

km (50-mile) long, double-dog-legged hollow.

In fact, the major lakes of Wakatipu, **Wanaka** and **Hawea** were all gouged by glaciers; and the peculiar rise and fall of the level of Wakatipu every 5 minutes is not the effect of a giant's heartbeat, as legend dictates, but of an oscillation caused by variations in atmospheric pressure.

But regardless of the origin of all three lakes, their appearance is indisputably handsome. "I do not know that lake scenery can be finer than this," enthused Trollope in 1872. "The whole district is, or rather will be in the days to come, a country known for its magnificent scenery." More recently, international television personality David Frost described the area as "one of God's triumphs."

Indeed, Wakatipu's beauty is so overwhelming apparent that New Zealanders, with their fondness for understatement, tend to downplay it in much the same way as a beautiful woman may be too determined to prove she is "not just a pretty face." And the variety of tourist drawcards, though entertaining and informative, often seem to serve as dis-

tractions from the natural beauty of Lake Wakatipu which then becomes most compelling in the mellow, half-awake moods of the early morning or evening hours.

By Foot, Water or Air

A thorough exploration of this magnificent region of snow-peaked mountains, virgin forest, uninhabited valleys and moody lakes is possible only for the traveller who takes to the air, the water, the open road and the narrow walking track.

Of the many tracks in the Wakatipu Basin, the most rewarding is the **Routeburn Track**. Trailing through splendidly isolated country at the head of Lake Wakatipu to the Upper Hollyford Valley, this 4-day trek is one of New Zealand's best, but requires a greater degree of experience and fitness than does the famed Milford Track in neighbouring Fiordland.

Passenger launches ply Lake Wakatipu to otherwise inaccessible sheep stations that give tourists a taste of high-country farm life and food, pioneering days, trout **Lake Hayes.**

fishing and seclusion. During the fishing season (October 1 to July 31) charters and safaris by way of jet-boat, helicopter or four-wheel-drive vehicle are available to remote pristine waters.

Some of the finest scenic flights anywhere in the world operate from Queenstown over lakes, alps and fiords. Subject to demand and weather, a number of flightseeing and charter flights are flown daily by tour airlines, including the Mount Cook Line, the company which pioneered easy tourist access to Central Otago and the Mount Cook region. Helicopter flights are operated by the Helicopter Line.

The Mount Cook company also controls two of the largest ski fields in the South Island. **Coronet Peak**, only 18 km (11 miles) by sealed road from Queenstown, has a ski season that extends from July through September. During the summer, sightseers can take a chairlift to the summit (1,646 metres; 5,499 feet), for a spectacular view, while thrill-seekers can enjoy a rapid descent in a Cresta Run toboggan. The company's other major ski field is **The Remarkables**. Other skiing opportunities exist in the Queenstown

district, with cross-country and downhill trips available at **Browns Basin**, **Mount Cardrona** and **Mount Pisa**.

Queenstown has a wide variety of accommodation, restaurants, après-ski entertainment and shops displaying quality handcrafted New Zealand articles such as suede and leather goods, sheepskin and woollen products, local pottery, woodcarving and greenstone jewellery.

Motoring the Back-country

Central Otago's network of roads is among the most interesting and challenging in New Zealand. Most roads are sealed, but some are not, and extra skill and caution are needed on narrower roads, particularly during the often hazardous conditions of winter. Rental-car companies advise their customers that if they drive on certain roads – through the **Skippers Canyon**, for instance – they do so at their own risk without the benefit of the company's insurance cover.

An especially attractive circuit is the 50-km (31-mile) round trip between Queenstown and Arrowtown, taking the "back" road past Coronet Peak and re-

turning via mirror-like **Lake Hayes**. Besides the pastoral charm of the countryside, one can also appreciate the recent emergence of New Zealand's own distinctive style of architecture in the thoughtfully designed farmlet dwellings where skilled craftspeople, artists, commuters and retired folk enjoy a gentle way of life once not possible on the same land.

New Zealand's Matterhorn

Northeast of Queenstown, Highway 6 follows the upper Clutha River to its source at Wanaka, a more modest resort gaining new importance (with two ski fields and a natural ice-skating rink) since the opening of the Haast Pass in 1965. This trans-alpine route, the lowest over the Main Divide, links Central Otago with the glacier-renowned region of the West Coast. It also runs through the **Mount Aspiring National Park**, which is a 161-km (100-mile) long alpine reserve dominated by New Zealand's Matterhorn, Mount Aspiring (3,036 metres; 9,961 feet). The park, together with the lonely valleys extending into Lake Wanaka, presents unrivalled opportunities for hiking, tramping and fishing in unspoilt wilderness.

An alternative fine-weather shortcut between Queenstown and Wanaka is the Crown Range road through the Cardrona Valley. The highest in New Zealand, this route is not suitable for caravans; it is closed in winter; and even in good weather, it merely reduces the distance to be covered, not the travelling time.

Directly south of Queenstown, Highway 6 skirts Lake Wakatipu to **Kingston** – home base for a vintage steam train, the *Kingston Flyer* – and continues south to Invercargill and the southern coast. Midway, before **Lumsden**, it is intersected by Highway 94, a well-trodden and rewarding scenic route which branches west out of Central Otago to Fiordland's Lake Te Anau, Eglinton Valley and Milford Sound.

One of New Zealand's best-kept secrets, however, is the **Lindis Pass** (Highway 8) which links northern Central Otago with Mount Cook and the Mackenzie Country. This inland route winds through some of the loveliest and most evocative hill country to be found in New Zealand.

Snow fun under the sun: Central Otago has excellent skiing facilities.

The main artery to the heart of Central Otago is the southern extension of Highway 8 as it runs parallel with the Clutha River, past the former gold towns of **Roxburgh, Alexandra, Clyde** and **Cromwell**. These prospering towns are still vital today through their connection with Otago's lifeblood: that same mighty Clutha. The river that once surrendered gold has since, through irrigation, transformed parched land into fertile country famous for its stoned fruit.

Now, through hydro-power projects, it is a major generator for electricity for the rest of the nation. A dam at Roxburgh, built in 1956, has formed a 32-km (20-mile) long lake between the town and Alexandra. When completed, a second dam at Clyde will alter the spectacular Cromwell Gorge forever, controversially drowning a small part of the historic Cromwell township.

Arrowtown holds an annual festival and Alexandra distinguishes itself by its colourful, blossom-parade tribute to spring. During the winter the townsfolk revive the good old-fashioned sports of ice-skating and curling on natural ice on the **Manorburn Dam**.

North of Alexandra, Highway 85 takes an easterly course through the **Manuherikia Valley** to the Otago coast. This road offers 2 worthwhile side trips, the first to **St. Bathans**, an old gold town, and the second to **Naseby**, a quaint atmospheric hamlet on a hillside at an altitude of 600 metres (about 2,000 feet). Another little-publicised, good-weather road worth travelling for its aura of solitude climbs **Dansey's Pass** to the North Otago town of **Duntroon** and the Waitaki River flats.

The intense seasons in Central Otago recreate a landscape through which chance wanderings reveal magical metamorphoses. In autumn, the settler-planted poplars glow gold and glorious; in winter, nature adorns the work of people, transforming power lines and crude wire fences into glistening lace-like threads of white across a frosty fairyland; in summer, the bronzed limbs of the tussocked hills sear the imagination. Central Otago bequeaths its grand legacy not to royalty or the privileged class, but to any humble traveller who simply dares to feel as vulnerable as a child before this land for all seasons.

DUNEDIN: OTAGO'S CONFIDENT CAPITAL

Dunedin reclines, all-embracing, at the head of a bay, a green-belted city of slate and tin-roofed houses, of spires, chimneys and churches, of glorious Victorian and Edwardian buildings, of culture, of learning. A sometimes quizzical air of *déjà vu* is backed by the belief of most if its 100,000 friendly citizens that this is as it should be, for here is a way of life, a peace and a tranquillity that few cities in the world can match. Growth may be stationary – gently in reverse, even – but the city soldiers serenely on, solid in its past, secure in its present, sanguine of its future.

How best to see this seductive city and its seven Rome-reminding hills? Surely as the first European settlers of 1848 did, from the haven of **Otago Harbour,** the 20-km (12½-mile) long, shallow-bottomed fiord where container ships and coastal traders now ply in place of Maori war canoes, whaling ships and canvas-topped three-masters.

Around the road-fringed harbourside sprout green-green hills, bumps and grinds and undulations stretching sharply up in a verdant and elastic girdle. Among them are the 300-metre (1,000-foot) dead volcano of **Harbour Cone** on the steep and skinny **Otago Peninsula** and the curiously cloud-carpeted cap of 676-metre (2,218-foot) **Mount Cargill**. Wood and brick houses, permanent and holiday (known as cribs here, and as bachs in the north), beribbon the harbour perimeter, some with stately sections of bush and trees, others the more basic homes of fishermen, wharf workers and city commuters.

Regular ferries once steamed this picturesque waterway. Sadly, there is none today, though often yachts, rowing skiffs and windsurfers. Short of borrowing a rowboat, the traveller can hardly put to direct test the proud words of early Dunedin poet Thomas Bracken (who also composed the national anthem, *God Defend New Zealand*):

> Go, trav'ler, unto others boast of Venice and of Rome,
> Of saintly Mark's majestic pile, and Peter's lofty dome;

Dunedin from Mount Cargill.

Of Naples and her trellised bowers, of
  Rhineland far away
These may be grand, but give to me
  Dunedin from the Bay.

A Peninsula Drive

The next-best thing to a Bracken's-eye view of Dunedin from the bay is to see it from that splendid peninsula. Take the "low road" and return via the "high." The 64-km (40-mile) round trip can take anything from 90 minutes to a full day and more. Much of Dunedin's history is illustrated on this drive; the sights are grand indeed, as Bracken noted. The narrow, winding road calls for careful driving, built as part of it was by convict labour for horse and buggy traffic. (The prisoners were housed in an old hulk that was dragged slowly along the seafront to keep pace with the work.)

Soon you will see Glenfalloch, 11 lovely hectares (27 acres) of woodland gardens; an ideal refreshment stop. At Portobello, visit the local museum (open Sundays 1:30 p.m. – 4:30 p.m. or by arrangement, call 780-294), then left to the wonderful Portobello Marine laboratory.

In aquariums and "touch" tanks you will see – and fondle – everything marine from a 6-metre (20-foot) shark to a one-inch shrimp, as well as sea horses, octopi and penguins.

Further on, at **Otakou**, the Maori church and meeting house appear carved, but actually are cast in concrete. In the cemetery behind are buried three great Maori chiefs of last century – the warlike Taiaroa, Ngatata (a northern chief said to have "welcomed the Pakeha to Cook Strait") and Karetai, induced by the missionaries to abandon cannibalism and take up the Bible. The *marae* here is sacred to local Maori and is still the most historic Maori site in Otago. The name "Otago," in fact, is a European corruption of "Otakou." There's a Maori museum, but to assure that it's open you must call in advance (780-252 or 780-466).

Just north lie remains of the whaling industry founded in Otago Harbour in 1831, 17 years before European settlement. The try works – bricks and ashes from the fires still there, together with stanchions used to tie the whales during flensing – are clearly visible and marked by a plaque. Another across the road commemorates the first Christian service held in Otago Harbour, by Bishop Pompalier, 1840.

Albatrosses and a Castle

As you crest the hill past Otakou and look towards lofty **Taiaroa Head**, the tip of the peninsula, glance up. Those huge sea birds hovering there, resting lazily on the wind like children's kites, are the world's largest birds of flight, rare Royal Albatrosses. Incredibly graceful, they dip, swoop, turn and soar with barely a bat of their 3-metre wings. Up to 20 pairs circle the globe (at speeds of up to 110 km) to roost here, pair-mating for life and usually producing a single chick every two years. One of these marvellous creatures, "Grandma", banded in 1937 as a breeding female, still returns every second or third year to breed. She is recognised as the oldest wild bird in the world. The Trust Bank Royal Albatross Centre opened in 1989 by Princess Anne has viewing galleries and display areas. Escorted groups observe most of the spring-summer breeding cycle and the pre-flight peregrinations of the fledglings. To visit

Dunedin and the Otago Peninsula

this only mainland Royal Albatross colony in the world, contact the Centre or the Dunedin Visitor Centre. Take in (for free) the antics of a southern fur seal colony at Pilot Beach, below the big birds.

Tour groups at Taiaroa Head also visit the unusual Armstrong Disappearing Gun, built in 1886 at the height of a "Russian scare." The 15-cm (6-inch) cannon is hidden in the bowels of the earth, rising only to fire (which it has done in anger but once and then only at a recalcitrant fishing boat during World War II); then sinking again for reloading.

A mile to the east, along a farm road, is Penguin Bay. Here, rare Chaplinesque yellow-eyed penguins strut in the surf. Contact the Dunedin Visitor Centre for viewing instructions or the landowner (call 780-286) for guided tours.

One has to return along the Taiaroa Head access road to Portobello to gain the "high road" back to the city. Up there is Larnach Castle, a century-old baronial manor that is New Zealand's only castle. It took 14 years to build (from 1871) as the home of the Hon. William J.M. Larnach, banker, financier and later Minister of the Crown, who had married the daughter of a French duke and apparently thought it necessary to house his young bride (and 44 servants) in the grand manner. An English workman spent 12 years carving the ceilings, along with two Italian craftsmen. Only the finest of materials were imported, all from Europe. The castle fell into disrepair after Larnach's bizarre suicide in Wellington's Parliament Buildings. It has now been fully restored and most of its 43 rooms, including accommodation, are open to the public. Perhaps not a grand castle on the European circuit, nevertheless Larnach Castle has a curious fascination in such a young country.

The "high road" back to suburbia has commanding views right down and up the harbour. On a fine day – there are many of them here – you can see forever (almost).

A Proud History

For this Otago Peninsula drive, the traveller has never left Dunedin city. It is the largest in area of any city in New Zealand, much to the chagrin of its more voluble northern counterparts. Once, it was New Zealand's most populous city,

too, and it does not forget that it was then the proudest and richest in all New Zealand. In the 1860s, with the discovery of gold in the Otago hinterland and a rush there that rivalled California's, Dunedin rapidly became the financial centre of the country. Immigrants flocked from around the world, head offices of national companies sprang up, industry and civic enterprise flourished. Here was the country's first university, medical school, finest educational institutions, first electric trams, then the first cable car system in the world outside the United States, the country's first woollen mills, first daily newspaper...

Even centuries before that, the coast of Otago was more densely settled than any part of the North Island. The moa-hunters lived here, groups of often nomadic Maori who thrived on fish, waterfowl and the moa, the giant flightless bird that resembled a huge emu and was easy prey to their stone and wooden weapons. At the height of the moa-hunter occupation, probably the 11th and 12th centuries, there may have been up to 8,000 Maori living in the estuaries and river mouths of **Larnach** Otago. As the moa were decimated, the **Castle.**

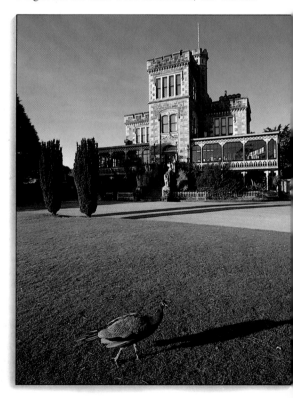

Maori followed them inland. Their fires destroyed much of the thick native bush that blanketed the land, leaving behind the bare tussock country which today covers most of the inland hills from behind Dunedin almost to the foothills of the Southern Alps.

When Captain James Cook sailed past Otago in 1770, he missed the Otago Harbour entrance, although noting the long white beaches now called **St. Kilda** and **St. Clair**. "A land green and woody but without any sign of inhabitants," he logged. There were Maori there, of course, but in small numbers in nomadic communities.

Fewer than 30 years later, sealers and whalers were in the Otago region. Soon, Europeans were quite familiar with the coastline, if not always popular with the locals. In 1813, four sailors were killed and eaten by Maori; in 1817, at what is still called **Murdering Beach**, just north of the harbour entrance, three sealers offended natives and were killed. In retribution, their captain, James Kelly, led a massacre of what some reports say was as many as 70 Maori.

Religious fervour on the other side of the world led to the European colonisation of Dunedin. Disruption in the Presbyterian Church of Scotland gave birth to the idea of a new settlement in the colony of New Zealand where "piety, rectitude and industry" could flourish. Free Kirk advocates Captain William Cargill, a veteran of the Peninsula War, and the Rev. Thomas Burns, nephew of poet Robbie, were the leaders. The ships *John Wickliffe* and *Philip Laing* landed 300 hopeful Scottish settlers in March 1848 to a site already chosen by the London-based New Zealand Company and purchased – for £2,400 – from the local Maori. Its first name was New Edinburgh; soon it became Dunedin (Edin on the Hill), Edinburgh's ancient name.

The settlement had been laid out from 19,000 km (12,000 miles) away, along the lines of Edinburgh, with a Princes and George streets, an Octagon and Moray Place; but with no regard for the contours of the land. This was to lead to tremendous physical problems. But the settlers, joined by later arrivals, stuck to their task nevertheless and hewed their township out of the invariably thick and often precipitous bush.

Otago University.

A Taste of the Wild West

Once gold was discovered inland, there was no holding Dunedin back. In two years, the population of Otago rose from 12,000 to 60,000 – 35,000 of them immigrant gold-seekers. Dunedin was the arrival point for the miners, the service centre for the goldfields and the bank for the gold. With its new prosperity came the trappings of a Wild West town – saloons, gambling dens, brothels, dubious dance halls. One local bishop set tongues wagging when it was learned that a building he owned was used by a bevy of irreverent young ladies. It was eventually accepted that no fault lay with the man of the cloth. Pubs there were aplenty, breweries too, and Dunedin to this day has retained a high reputation for its well-patronised licensed premises.

For a quarter of a century, Dunedin boomed. And where Dunedin went, the rest of New Zealand followed, until the gold ran out. Gradually, commercial and climatic attractions in the north led to the decline of the southern cities and provinces. For the last few decades, Dunedin has fought the inevitable drift north, especially through development of tertiary education facilities. Its greatly expanded university, teachers' college and polytechnic schools mean Dunedin remains one of New Zealand's leading cities of learning.

Dunedin is also known both as New Zealand's Scottish city and its Victorian city. Both appellations are true, but only to a degree. Founded by Scots it was, and many Scottish reminders there are. The giant statue of Robbie Burns the poet, for example, sits in the town centre, the **Octagon**, fittingly with the bard's back to the Anglican **St. Paul's Cathedral** and facing what was once a corner pub. Here, too, are the country's only kilt manufacturer, its sole whisky distillery, lots of highland pipe bands and regularly celebrated Burns' Nights – where, 'tis said, the Scottish liquid flows freer than the poet's couplets.

An Architectural Heritage

Dunedin folk are a little weary of continual references to the "Edinburgh of the South" but it is a title they have to put up with. The same goes for "Victorian City,"

which indeed its architecture makes it; but there are equally fine examples of Edwardian and later-style buildings that qualify the city as the most interesting and diverse architecturally in the country. The range is delightful, from full-fashioned ornate Victoriana through Edwardian splendour to impressive art deco and modern concrete-and-glass structures that have won national awards for excellence. But don't expect skyscrapers; in conservative Dunedin, churches stretch higher than offices.

Start in the easily locatable Octagon, which links Princes and George streets in the city centre. Tall, leafy trees, grass plots and comfortable benches make this a popular lunchtime gathering place. To the west is inspiring St. Paul's stone Gothic pillars rising 40 metres (130 feet) and supporting the only stone-vaulted nave roof in New Zealand. The four-manual organ has 3,500 pipes. The "new" sanctuary and chancel, consecrated in 1971, won a national design ward.

Next door are the century-old **Municipal Chambers**, designed by the noted colonial architect, R.W. Lawson, and behind it the 2,280-seat **Town Hall**, until

Denizen of the Albatross Colony at Taiaroa Head.

recently the largest in the country. The Municipal Chambers have been replaced by the adjacent **Civic Centre** as local government offices, although the modern, stepped design of the Centre has drawn criticism for its contrast with the Victorian Chambers.

The city's Visitor Centre (open every day), as well as conference facilities, are housed in the Municipal Chambers, whose imposing clock tower and spire were re-erected in 1989 amid an overall greening and spring-cleaning of the city centre.

Moving east, down Lower Stuart Street, one finds classic old buildings such as the **Allied Press** newspaper offices, the **Law Courts** and the **Police Station**, excellent examples of art in stone. Then comes the **Dunedin Railway Station**, perhaps the finest stone structure in the country. It earned the designer, George Troup, a knighthood and the nickname "Gingerbread George." Of Flemish Renaissance style, it features a 37-metre (120-foot) high square tower, three huge clock faces, and a covered carriageway projecting from the arched colonnade for passengers arriving and

departing in horse-drawn vehicles. Line up outside with camera-clicking tourists for exterior views, then enter the main foyer and study the majolica mosaic-tiled floor with the nine central panels showing a small English "Puffing Billy." The original floor consisted of 725,760 half-inch Royal Doulton porcelain squares. Other ornamentation is in original Royal Doulton china and church-like stained glass. Only two passenger trains a day now use this gingerbread house and the tourists easily outnumber the travellers.

On the Right Track

Actually, Dunedin has a fascination with trains. *Josephine*, one of the country's first steam engines (a double-boiler, double-bogey, double-facing Fairlie) is in a glass case on public display beside the Early Settlers Museum, together with *JA1274*, the last Dunedin-made steam locomotive to haul the main trunk-line trains. A weekend train enthusiasts' group operates all manner of steam machines along a private line between St. Clair and St. Kilda beaches. And the Otago Excursion Train Trust has reno-

Otago Settlers' Museum.

vated vintage carriages and rolling stock and operates New Zealand's only private-hire train.

During holiday periods, and on demand, the train makes harbourside runs or takes tourists into Otago's rugged hinterland through the spectacularly-bridged Taieri Gorge.It leaves the gingerbread railway station which may soon become home for the Otago Early Settlers' Association Museum, presently housed in what was Dunedin's first art gallery, just a few minutes' walk to the south. Next door to that again is the NZR Bus Station, a 1930s art-deco building regarded as one of the best of its era in the country.

The country's first skyscraper is nearby – the seven-storey **Mutual Funds Building** (1910). It lies close to the original centre of Dunedin, the **Stock Exchange** area, where the first settlers stepped ashore in 1848. Land reclamation has since pushed back the harbour edge with a proliferation of fine old office buildings, but movement of the city centre north has forced many into use as storage areas and some into demolition. A gargoyled "bride's-cake" monument in the Stock Exchange area pays homage to founder Captain Cargill. It once sat atop men's underground toilets until public opprobrium led to the conveniences being closed.

First Church, in **Moray Place**, was the founders' tribute to their Father in 1867. Its spire soars 55 metres (180 feet) heavenwards. The church, another R.A. Lawson design, is arguably the most historically significant building in the city.

Some of the banks and other churches in the central city area inspire praise, as does the Lawson-designed **Otago Boys High School** tower block, dominant above the city. It is situated just below the **Town Belt**, a 200-hectare (500-acre), 8-km (5-mile) long green swath that separates city from suburbs.

A walk or drive through the Town Belt offers some of the best views of a city and harbour in New Zealand. Hear the *tui* and the bellbird as you roam in peace above this city of serenity and seclusion. Observe, too, the many wooded reserves and sports fields, fine championship golf courses, *cotula*-turfed bowling greens, huge heated swimming pools and fine swimming and surfing beaches. Outdoor

sports live large here.

Olveston, "the jewel in Dunedin's crown," lies within the Town Belt. A Jacobean-style manor of double brick and oak, it was built in 1904 to the design of celebrated English architect Sir Ernest George for a local businessman, David Theomin. It was bequeathed to the city in 1966. The 35-room house and its magnificent furnishings and paintings, drawing thousands of visitors each year is rated the best example in New Zealand of the grand style of Edwardian living. (Call 773-320 for guided tours.)

To the northern end of Dunedin are the (almost) combined campuses of the University of Otago, Otago Polytechnic and Dunedin Teachers' Training College and some 15,000 students. Dominating the inspiring Gothic rockpiles of the university is the main clock-tower building beside the grass-banked water of the Leith.

Dunedin and Beyond

Dunedin visitors should not restrict themselves to the city. On and beyond the outskirts lie fascinating sights of natural and historic beauty. Eighty km (50 miles) north are the queer **Moeraki Boulders**, huge round stones that lie "like devil's marbles" on the seashore.

The food baskets of a wrecked canoe in Maori legend, they are septarian concretions that formed on the seashore 60 million years ago by the gradual accumulation of lime salts around a small centre. Several tons in weight and up to 4.3 metres (14 feet) in circumference, they gradually appear from the bank behind the beach as the soft mudstone is weathered by the sea.

Not many kilometres to the east of Dunedin, in the **Taieri River Gorge**, jet-boat and whitewater raft tours tumble more adventurous tourists between virgin bush-edged cliffs. For the less energetic, there are trout aplenty to catch.

Both north and south of Dunedin are coastlines of immense natural beauty, peopled by relatively few. They are still to be visited by the tourist hordes who are beginning to recognise this part of New Zealand for what it is – a majestically peaceful corner of Godzone (God's own country). Inland, to Central Otago, lies another world again.

Moeraki Boulders.

SOUTHLAND AND REMOTE FIORDLAND

Speak to the historical purist and you will learn that Southland is a contradiction. Officially, there is no such province. Question him further and you will find contradiction in his answers.

When Southland's early European settlers demanded provincial government in 1861, they forgot the canny nature of their Scottish background and in nine heady years developed town, country, rail, road and other signs of civilisation to such an extent that the provincial government of the rapidly increasing settler population was declared bankrupt. As a result, their province was legally and administratively fixed to their northern neighbour, Otago, in 1870.

Yet despite this, the future of the province was assured because the 107,900 people who call themselves Southlanders today have scant regard for the historical purist's arguments about their legitimacy. They live in New Zealand's southernmost land district – *Murihiku*, the last joint of the tail, as the Maori called it. The "province" takes in about 32,000 sq km (some 20,000 sq miles); its boundary starts just above Milford Sound on the West Coast, skirts the southern shores of Lake Wakatipu bordering Central Otago, and meanders its way through some of the lushest productive land in New Zealand to join the southeast coast near an unspoiled area called Chaslands.

Southland is a province of contrast. Signs of Maori settlement go back as far as the 12th century around the southern coast and since those days of rapid development in the 1860s, its people have developed a land of unlimited potential for agricultural purposes and regained the conservative reputation for which their largely Scottish forebears were known. Yet there is a grittiness in the Southland character, a strong determination to seek and to strive. It manifests itself in an agrarian excellence that would not have otherwise been achieved had conservatism dominated.

Contrast continues in the land itself. On the West Coast, deep fiords lap towering mountains and snow-capped peaks reach skywards amidst a myriad of vast bush-clad valleys in an area called, not surprisingly, Fiordland. Inland stretch the two massive plains on which the province's prosperity has grown to depend, surrounding the commercial heart the city of Invercargill, and eventually reaching the southern and southeastern coasts.

Tuataras and Aluminium

Invercargill and its 52,000 people reside along an estuary once plied by steamers and sailing ships. The city's Scottish heritage is well-reflected in street names; its original town planners were generous in the amount of space devoted to main thoroughfares and parks. Today, the city's Queens Park provides a wide range of both passive and active recreational pursuits, from sunken rose gardens and statuary by Sir Charles Wheeler to a golf course and swimming pool. This southernmost city in the British Commonwealth was the first to have built within its museum a "tuatarium" where lizards (*tuatara*) whose forebears survived the Stone Age can be viewed in a natural habitat.

Invercargill is where the traveller

Oyster fishing fleet at Bluff.

catches his breath. It is the main transport centre for Southland; from it, one can travel in any direction.

Twenty-seven km (17 miles) south is the port of **Bluff**. A journey there emphasises Southland's agricultural development. A massive fertiliser works, processing phosphate rock imported from various foreign lands, underpins the fact that Southland's soils need constant nourishment. Deer farms along both sides of the road are evidence of fast-developing new pastoral industry. Twenty years ago, deer were found only in the bush; today they are produced on farms by the thousands, rivalling at times the more traditional sheep, beef and forage crops for financial return. Their velvet, in particular, is keenly sought.

There is no mistaking Bluff as a port town. The air is dashed with salt; large vessels from around the world tie up at a massive man-made island within the inland harbour (cleverly created so that tidal flows were not disturbed); and workers toil around the clock. Aluminium-clad, snake-like machines, their tails buried in a large building and their heads in ships' holds, disgorge millions of tonnes of frozen lamb products for worldwide markets.

Across the harbour, three buildings 600 metres (2,000 feet) long, surrounded by other massive structures and dominated by a chimney stack 137 metres (449 feet) high, make up the **Tiwai Point** aluminium smelter, which produces 244,000 tonnes of aluminium a year. It stands in solid contrast on windswept Tiwai Point as a reminder that if, as John Donne said, "No man is an island," no province should rely wholly on a single industry for its continued well-being. Tucked away on the unproductive peninsula, where almost non-stop winds disperse effluent, the smelter has become a major employer in the south with 1,250 employed directly and maybe twice that number indirectly.

Yet Bluff is famous also for something that just lies there, waiting to be picked up. Thirty-five km (22 miles) across the sea is pristine Stewart Island the passage of water between is **Foveaux Strait**. Beneath the Strait lie beds of oysters which, between March and August, are harvested in a strictly regulated fashion by a 23-boat oyster fleet from Bluff. Tales

Bluff Smelter.

have it that many visiting football teams in Southland being taken to Bluff before their match and leaving the province beaten but craving for more of the delicious soft-bellied molluscs. Despite a ban on export, the reputation of Foveaux Strait oysters is worldwide.

Bluff leaves an impression. For New Zealand, it is the end of the road. From Bluff, the visitor gazes out to sea, taking in **Dog Island** and its lighthouse, Stewart Island, then the great emptiness of the Great South Basin, beyond which lie only a few sub-Antarctic islands and the vast white expanse of Antarctica. A signpost and restaurant have been erected at **Stirling Point**, not far from the port, stating the distance to London, New York and other faraway places. In a sense, it is comforting, because a visit to Bluff is as close as many people will ever get to the bottom of the world.

Brown Trout and Sheared Sheep

Southeast of Invercargill lies the small fishing port of **Waikawa**, reached by comfortable road through rolling countryside which not long ago was scrub and bush-covered. Vast areas of bush remain in Southland, well-managed and controlled. At the end of the road, 5 km (3 miles) from Waikawa, the curious can find the remains of a petrified forest buried millions of years ago at a place called Curio Bay. This freeze-frame of time has caught every grain of timber in the fossilised stumps; boulders which have broken open through some unknown force show patterns of leaves and twigs.

No dedicated angler could make the journey southeast without noticing, and probably stopping at, an unremarkable bridge. It crosses the **Mataura River** and it is, without shadow of doubt, among the very best brown trout fisheries anywhere. Anglers from around the world consider it their duty to fish the Mataura and some return annually for their pleasure. Space is not a problem. Nearly 500 km (300 miles) of fishing waters stretch along Southland's three main fishing rivers – the Mataura, the Oreti and the Aparima – which flow from the hinterland almost evenly spaced to the coast, cutting the province in three. In addition, there are at least eight smaller rivers (the Wyndham, Mimihau, Hedgehope, Makarewa, Lora,

One of New Zealand's rarest birds: the *takahe*.

238

Otapiri, Dunsdale and Waimatuku) and numerous streams well-stocked with brown trout. The angler who goes home without a fine trout or salmon has been holding his rod at the wrong end.

The Road to Fiordland

Flat as it is, there are few days in Invercargill when residents cannot raise their eye to the mountains, tens of kilometres away bordering Fiordland. For those in a hurry, this vast natural area can be reached in less than two hours across the central Southland plains via **Winton** and **Dipton**, over the **Josephville Hill**, through **Lumsden**, until rolling tussock country indicates land of a tougher nature. This journey through prime production country bearing several million head of stock, aptly proving how Southland has grown on the sheep's back, and the small towns which support this industry, passes in a blur.

But there is another more gentle route to Fiordland, a more interesting way. Head west from Invercargill past two of the province's four freezing works, which annually process more than 7 mil-

lion sheep and lambs. Find the historic town of **Riverton** nestling by the sea, 38 km (24 miles) from the city. Sealers and whalers made Riverton their home in 1836 and Southland's first European settlement still bears ample signs of those times. Preservation is a way of the life here; recently, the New Zealand Historic Place Trust offered a whaler's cottage for sale for the sum of just $1, so long as the new owner preserved it to the trust's specifications.

Ten km (6 miles) farther is Colac Bay, another historic area. Scrub-covered hills to the west once boasted a town of 6,000 people during the gold-rush days of the 1890s. Nearby is the town of **Orepuki**, where history merges with the present: what once was a courthouse is now a sheep-shearing shed.

Thundering surf follows the traveller between Orepuki and Tuatapere in what is probably the finest ocean view in the province. Looming darkly across **Te Wae Wae Bay** are bush-clad mountains, the first signs of what is to come. From the timber town of **Tuatapere**, where fishing and deer-hunting stories are as common as logs from the town's mills, the road

Prices at this deer sale soar up to NZ$2,000.

heads north, close to the recreational mecca of **Lake Monowai** and from there proceeds through the largely undeveloped countryside to **Lake Manapouri**. Fiordland stands majestically ahead.

A Lost Tribe and a Power Station

With an area of 1,209,485 hectares (nearly 3 million acres), **Fiordland** is New Zealand's largest national park and a World Heritage Park. That first glimpse across Lake Manapouri, to sheer mountains and remote deep valleys on the other side of the lake, gives the observer some understanding of why some Maori legends – such as that of the mythical lost tribe of Te Anau – never lose their romantic hold in this wild region.

Fiordland is a land of firsts. Captain James Cook discovered **Dusky Sound**, largest of the fiords, in 1770. He returned three years later and established, among other things, New Zealand's first brewery. Of course, he also established other important things while refitting his ship, such as a workshop and a smithy. In 1792, New Zealand's first residential home was built in the Sound for whalers and the following year the New Zealand shipbuilding industry was born in Dusky Sound when a 65-tonne vessel was floated.

Today, fishermen still manoeuvre small boats along the jagged coast where once sealers and whalers eked out an existence for markets which were located tens of thousands of kilometres away. Most of these isolated sounds can be reached only by sea or air, or by the hardiest of trampers.

But there are two glorious opportunities of experiencing the mountains, the sea and the bush together. One is by taking a launch across Lake Manapouri to its West Arm. Ponder man's folly, for once planning to raise this lake by 27 metres (90 feet) for hydro-electric purposes. Conservation eventually prevailed, although a massive power station, 200 metres (650 feet) under the mountains at West Arm, was built to supply power for the Tiwai Point aluminium smelter; and the lake level can now be controlled. But a necessary part of the construction was the building of a road from West Arm across the **Wilmot Pass**, through rainforest, to the Hall Arm of

Takitimu Mountains.

Doubtful Sound in an area known as **Deep Cove**. Here water from Lake Manapouri is discharged into the sea by a 10-km tailrace tunnel under the mountains. In spite of this development, it remains virgin country, as a boat trip to the open sea testifies.

Headquarters of this vast wilderness is the quickly developing tourist town of **Te Anau**, where hotels, motels and lodges mingle alongside **Lake Te Anau** with the homes of its 3,000 residents, who service both the tourist and agricultural industries. The wide open spaces and valley floors behind the town are the scene of perhaps the biggest land projects in New Zealand, with scores of new farms being developed.

"Eighth Wonder of the World"

The second way to the sea through Fiordland is via road to **Milford Sound**, world-renowned and described by no less a writer than Rudyard Kipling as "the eighth wonder of the world." Authors and artists have struggled to describe the beauty that unfolds as the road follows Lake Te Anau for 30 km (19 miles),

enters dense forests, and passes through such features as the "Avenue of the Disappearing Mountain" where the eyes are not to be believed. Forests, river flats and small lakes pass by as the journey through the mountains progresses, until the road drops toward the forested upper **Hollyford Valley** at **Marian Camp.**

From there, the road splits in two directions. One arm ventures into the no-exit Hollyford with its **Murray Gunn Camp**, a haunt for hundreds with one of the Fiordland's true characters. The main highway proceeds west, steeply up the mountain to the eastern portal of the **Homer Tunnel**. Named after the man who discovered the Homer Saddle between the Hollyford and Cleddau valleys in 1899, this 1-km long, tunnel was completed in 1940 after five years. It was not until 1953, however, that it was widened sufficiently for road traffic. Avalanches claimed the lives of three men; and in 1983, a road overseer was killed near the area. Homer can be Fiordland at its roughest.

From the Milford side, the road drops 690 metres (2,264 feet) in 10 km between sheer mountain faces to emerge into the

Sterling Falls, Milford Sound.

Cleddau Valley with its awe-inspiring chasm. Eventually it reaches the head of Milford Sound, where fine accommodation awaits to remind the traveller of life's contrasts. Boat trips regularly carry visitors 16 km (10 miles) to the open sea. The Sound is regally dominated by unforgettable **Mitre Peak** – a 1,836-metre (6,024-foot) pinnacle of rock – and several landmarks, notably the **Bowen Falls** (162 metres or 531 feet).

Discovering Mountain Tracks

There is another way to get to Milford Sound – by launch and on foot. A launch takes walkers from Te Anau to **Glade House** at the head of the lake. From there, through some of the most majestic scenery nature can devise, walkers take three days to reach the Sound via the **Milford Track**. They carry their own gear, but meals and sleeping accommodation are provided at huts along the way. It is a journey for the reasonably fit, with such obstacles as the 1,122-metre (3,681-foot) **McKinnon Pass**, but the track is not difficult. Mountain and forest scenery, including the well-protected flora and

fauna for which the region is famed; scores of waterfalls, including the spectacular 571-metre (1,873-foot) **Sutherland Falls**; lakes and spilling mountainside rivers can be viewed at close quarters. At night, a friendly international camaraderie exists at the comfortable **Pompolona** and **Quintin** huts.

The track is open from November until April. For the hardier, Fiordland National Park staff arrange trips for self-contained parties who can walk the distance and stay in park huts at lower rates.

Fiordland also boasts other world-renowned treks as well, including the Routeburn Track and the spectacular Kepler Track which meanders along mountain tops and through valleys across the Lake from Te Anau. Red deer shooting is encouraged in specified areas and wapiti shoots are held once a year. The park's native bird life – including the *takahe*, thought extinct until rediscovered in 1948 – is strictly protected. From park headquarters in Te Anau, numerous delightful bush walks can be recommended; similar hikes for the less energetic criss-cross the Manapouri area. Launch trips and scenic flights give the traveller a new perspective on many areas. A highlight is the **glow-worm caves** on Lake Te Anau which, although believed to have been known to early Maori explorers, were also only rediscovered in 1948.

Fiordland is to Southland, and to New Zealand, what the *Mona Lisa* is to the Louvre – an incomparable highlight.

Those departing Southland travel north towards Queenstown via Kingston, where a vintage steam train, the Kingston Flyer, recreates a transport mode of the last century between **Fairlight** and Kingston. Alternatively, motorists proceed northeast toward Dunedin via the Mataura Valley; Southland's second largest town, **Gore**; and the rich countryside of Eastern Southland. In the background stand the **Hokonui Hills**, which divide the two main plains of the province. In those hills, illicit whisky stills once produced a potent brew of varying quality before police and customs officers closed them down. Watch closely as you leave, and you may yet see a wisp of smoke, for there are yet one or two who claim the long arm of the law has not reached all the moonshiners.

Left, a reflection at Mirror Lakes. **Right,** Milford Track.

STEWART ISLAND: A "HEAVENLY GLOW"

A beautiful, peaceful island on the southern fringe of the world lies across Foveaux Strait, 20 minutes by air from Invercargill or 2 hours by ferry from Bluff. **Stewart Island**, lapped by both the Pacific and Antarctic oceans, rests easily as New Zealand's anchor.

Its early settlers left a wealth of history now gone – sawmills, whaling stations and tin mines included. Today, most of the 450 Stewart Islanders depend upon the industry of their forebears. Their small fishing boats venture into often-stormy waters around the rocky coast for the blue cod, the more lucrative crayfish (rock lobsters) and other marine species. Their main base, **Oban** and **Halfmoon Bay**, is on the north end of this triangular, 172,000-hectare (425,000-acre) island, but the land itself extends about 65 km (40 miles) north to south and 40 km (25 miles) east to west.

Many newcomers arrive on this island seeking tranquillity. On smaller isles around Stewart, meanwhile, Maori families still capture succulent young mutton-birds (sooty shearwaters), as did their ancestors. Maori who are longtime natives to this area have been granted exclusive rights to the isles where muttonbirds breed after a round-the-world migration.

Harsh Contentment

Stewart Island's harsh life is dominated by the weather and the sea. Nature has set a demanding course. Those who choose to live here must be determined; all too often they know premature loss and sorrow. But they live on a bush-clad island whose beauty breeds contentment. It was little wonder the Maori called it *Rakiura*, "heavenly glow."

The first impression to the visitor is one of peace. Here, road vehicles are subservient to pedestrians. There is no chance of life in the fast lane. Roads total a mere 20 km (12½ miles). Both the island's airstrip and its port are close to Oban, where most residents live. Comfortable accommodation there retains an individualistic approach to tourism. It's the island's way. The small museum in Oban illustrates

Below left, Paterson Inlet, Stewart Island.

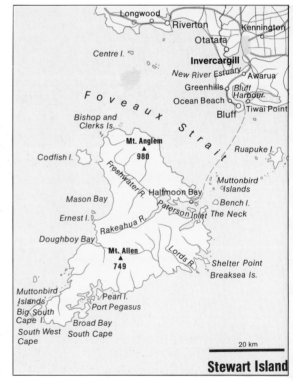

Stewart Island

well the island's history.

The South Seas Hotel, a 30-bed establishment in the centre of Oban, is the main community focus, but there are also a more up-market lodge, motels and backpacker accommodation catering for the island's growing tourist needs. The island now boasts its own electricity scheme but, perhaps because of the hard work required to live and work here, its way of life remains laidback and easy-going. For tourists seeking something different, a visit is a must. But even for those who feel like conserving their energy, the easy walks within reach of Oban deserve some attention.

Native bush and fern, and moss-carpeted glades, team with native bird life according to the season. In spring, the *tui* and bellbirds call out through the forest. In summer, the curious *weka* and the tomtit are present, while in winter, the fantail hovers about. Always, there is the swish of the wood pigeon as it flies from tree to tree. The island is a bird watcher's paradise.

Over the hill from Halfmoon Bay is the large **Paterson Inlet**, which juts deeply into the island's hinterland. Tracks and small roads take the walker to many of its beauty spots; launch trips are also available. A highlight is a trip to **Ulva Island** in the inlet's centre. Farther into the inlet are the remains of an old sawmill and whaling station. In **Big Glory Bay**, a salmon farm has been established.

Inland Wilderness

For the fitter visitor, longer and popular tracks meander around much of the island. They take in such exotically named haunts as **Port William**, **Christmas Village** and **Yankee River**. Off Stewart Island's western coast is **Codfish Island**, once a European settlement whose harshness of life eventually proved overwhelming; today it is a protected sanctuary for birds. Sea-fishing trips can be made, and most parts of Stewart Island are a deer hunter's dream. The white-tailed deer in particular is highly sought.

With daylight savings time in summer it is often light on Stewart Island until 10 p.m. At that time, on a clear night, it is worth standing on **Observation Rock** above Paterson Inlet to see why the Maori name for Stewart Island is so apt.

Stewart Islander opts for beer.

CHATHAM ISLANDS: WHERE DAY BEGINS

Flung in icy seas to the east of New Zealand and in the Southern Ocean on the way to Antarctica are several tiny islands all under New Zealand's sovereignty. The Auckland Islands, Bounty Island, Campbell Island, Antipodes Islands and Chatham Island are lonely, windswept places where whalers have been wrecked, sea mammals and sub-Antarctic birdlife have dominion, and where few mainland New Zealanders have ever ventured.

Scientific missions are the only regular visitors to most of them. They contain unique birdlife and they are valuable early warning posts for the winds, storms and frigid air flows that can sweep up to New Zealand from the ice-bound Antarctic continent.

Home of the Moriois

One group, the Chathams, has a resident population of 780. About 800 km (500 miles) east of Christchurch, the Chathams are world leaders in at least one respect – the three islands in the group are inched just inside the International Date Line. As a result, each day, every day, Chatham Islanders are among the first in the world to see the sun of a new day. The world's time zones begin here.

The Chathams were first settled about A.D. 1200 by Polynesian mariners from the eastern Pacific. Once on the islands, these settlers – known as Morioris – became stranded. The islands had no trees big enough to enable them to build canoes to sail onwards. So they remained, developing a culture of their own, evidence of which can still be seen in Moriori tree carvings.

The first European to sight the islands was Lieutenant William Broughton in 1791. Other Europeans came to settle in 1840, five years after a party of New Zealand Maori arrived to conquer and enslave the native Chatham Islanders. From an estimated peak of more than 1,000, the Moriori population dwindled to only 12 by 1900, wiped out by disease, massacres and desolation. It is believed that there are no pure-blooded Morioris alive today.

The last Moriori family of the islands, *circa* 1910.

More than anywhere else on earth, the Chatham Islands resemble the Falklands of the South Atlantic. The weather is wild, and communication with the rest of New Zealand is difficult. Sheep-farming and fishing are the main occupations. Crayfish is exported to the New Zealand mainland, Australia and United States. Meanwhile, honey is a hope of the future: after a string of failed attempts, New Zealand's Ministry of Agriculture and Fisheries has successfully established bees on the islands, bringing the potential for new jobs and spin-offs.

A World of its Own

An air service from Christchurch calls in the Chathams once every five days. Return air fare to the mainland is not cheap. A rusty old trader, the *Holmdale*, makes a monthly call. It brings nearly all the islanders' supplies – bread, groceries, petrol, and videotapes of television shows recorded on the mainland.

There is a telephone exchange, reached by cranking a handle on the phone. Islanders can call New Zealand through a two-line radio line. The biggest job of the Chathams' radio station is to broadcast daily navigational weather forecasts. The station, set up in 1913, also monitors distress calls from ships at sea. It has picked up calls from vessels in trouble all around the New Zealand coast; during World Was II its operators took calls from stricken vessels throughout the South Pacific.

Not all islanders are yet linked to the central diesel-supplied electricity system. Some must make do with backyard generators of their own. Experts are looking at ways of making the Chathams self-sufficient in their electricity production.

Life on the Chathams, the islanders say, is very much a matter of making your own amusement. You must be an outdoors person, and you must be able to get along with a small group of people for a long time. Rugby football, fishing and skin-diving are popular, and there is a nine-hole golf course in the main town, Waitangi. While there's a round of make-shift local concerts, cabarets and parties, some mainlanders who come to stay can't stand the isolation and they're back on the next sailing. You have to be a special breed to live on the edge of the world.

Albatrosses – a common sight in the the Chatham Islands.

THE COOK ISLANDS AND THE PACIFIC

During his trans-Pacific meanderings more than two centuries ago, Captain James Cook discovered Niue island and several uplifted atolls in the Cook Islands. He dubbed them "savage," his reception from the natives having been such that he really didn't care to return.

Today, in the New Zealand-administered islands of the South Pacific, nothing could be further from the truth. A warm "*kia orana*" welcomes visitors, and the towns and villages are reminiscent of sleepy trading ports out of the pages of Robert Louis Stevenson, Herman Melville, Jack London and Somerset Maugham.

New Zealand's South Seas consist of the Cook Islands, Niue and the three atolls of Tokelau. The Cooks and Niue are independent British Commonwealth nations in free association with New Zealand, which manages their external affairs and defence. Tokelau, although physically remote, is an integral territory of New Zealand.

The inhabitants of all of these islands are New Zealand citizens. English is commonly taught and spoken along with the local dialect. These factors have made it easy for many decades, particularly over the last 20 years, for the Polynesian islanders to immigrate to Auckland and surrounding areas. In fact, there are now more islanders in New Zealand than in their homelands. The money these people earn and send back to island-bound relatives has become a major source of family income.

New Zealand currency is used in all of its island enclaves (plus Cook Islands coinage up to $1 in that group only). New Zealand grants, loans, aid in education, postage-stamp sales and trade development keep the Cooks, Niue and Tokelau in a fiscally sound state. In each case, imports far exceed exports because the natural resources of each island are very limited.

A Future in Tourism

Tourism offers the best prospect to the islands of a steady cash income, both immediately and in the long term. The Cook Islands and Niue are easily accessible via Air New Zealand and Polynesian Airlines; Auckland is regarded as the major gateway.

With ferocious receptions of the 18th and 19th centuries now a thing of the past, there is nothing for visitors to fear but sunburn. Almost all the hazards of tropical places, such as malaria and poisonous land snakes, are absent. (There are sea snakes but they are rarely seen.) The facilities of hotels and motels are excellent. In the villages, life is clean and wholesome.

Visitors should be sensitive to local cultural mores, of course. All islanders refer to themselves as maori – a word meaning "natural to the place." There are New Zealand Maori, Cook Islands Maori, Niue Maori and so on. They possess a certain innocence, but are nonetheless keenly aware of the attitudes exhibited by visitors. You should smile, give the friendly greeting of "*kia orana*," and shake a few hands. Polynesians detest a sour face; they stay cheerful despite the hardships of their own lives. They don't like to haggle over a deal; outside hotels,

Left, musically-inclined village beauty. Right, young dancers present carefree images of island life.

most are embarrassed by tips. Small gifts are appreciated, but this does oblige the recipient to give something in return.

In spite of their happy-go-lucky nature, islanders take their Christian faith seriously. Protestantism was widely accepted early in the 19th century, Catholics, Mormons and other denominations followed. Today, Sunday is a day of church-going. Attending an island church service is a delightful thing to do, at least once in a visit. Neat and clean dress is expected, with hats for ladies and a tie for gentlemen.

Formal occasions call for formal attire. Harmless as bikinis may seem in this age of liberality, they should be worn with discretion. These island communities are still, to some extent, in the Victorian age.

A visit to the South Pole means that a lot of time will be spent in the water. A few words of advice might save some suffering. Swimmers should get local recommendations on where best to go into the water: reef currents can be dangerous. Those who walk on reefs should wear canvas shoes, as cuts or grazes from live coral are notorious for turning septic. Never put your hands in holes or niches in the reef: moray eels have sharp teeth, cone shells have lethal stingers, and other sea creatures lurk in unseen corners.

Rarotonga and the Cooks

The Cook Islands – particularly the main island of Rarotonga – are the most tourist-oriented destination in the New Zealand Pacific. Rarotonga, a high volcanic-origin island of about 32 km (20 miles) in circumference, is the site of the administrative centre of Avarua and the Cook's international port facilities. About 50 percent of the Cook Islands population of 19,500 make their home on Rarotonga.

From Rarotonga, you can visit all the other 14 islands in the Cook group. Nearby Aitutaki is developing a tourist trade, while Atiu, Mangaia, Mauke and Mitiaro offer some accommodation. Along with the other primitive southern islands of Manuae, Palmerston and Takutea, these are all uplifted coral atolls with reefs formed close against high coastal cliffs.

All of the southern islands are very fertile. Adequate rainfall and sufficient **Tropical boating.**

New Zealand's Pacific Family

Kiribati · Tuvalu · Tokelau · Penrhyn · Western Samoa · Vanuatu · Fiji · American Samoa · Cook Islands · Tonga · Niue · Aitutaki · Rarotonga

South Pacific Ocean

Kermadec Islands · Kaitaia · North Island · New Plymouth · Taupo · Motueka · Wellington · Haast · Christchurch · Chatham I. · South Island · Dunedin

DATELINE Monday Sunday

800 km

soils allow the cultivation of many tropical fruits and vegetables, including oranges and other citrus fruits, bananas, tomatoes, pineapples and *kumara* (sweet potatoes).

The northern Cook Islands – comprising the atolls of Manihiki, Rakahanga, Penryhn, Pukapuka, Nassau and Suwarrow – are lonely and remote.

For most of the year, the climate in the Cooks is balmy, with cooling southeast tradewinds, warm sunshine and occasional showers. In summer, from December to March, days can be cloudy and the weather sometimes oppressively hot. The months from April to June are most comfortable. From June to October, days and nights can be cool by island standards. Rarotonga is situated at 23 degrees South Latitude; it is east of the International Date Line, so when it is noon Monday in Auckland, it is 1:30 Sunday afternoon in Rarotonga, 3,000 km (about 1,900 miles) northeast of the New Zealand metropolis.

The first Polynesian settlement of the Cook Islands occurred about A.D. 700, probably by immigrants from the Society Islands. The first Europeans to see the northern islands were Spanish. Mendana passed Pukapuka in 1595, Quiros saw Rakahanga in 1606. However, it was not until Captain Cook visited the sizeable southern islands of Mangaia and Atiu in 1777 that knowledge of the group became substantial. Cook named the archipelago the Hervey Islands, but they were later renamed in his honour. Captain William Bligh of *HMS Bounty* discovered Aitutaki in 1789, then his *Bounty* mutineers, under Fletcher Christian, visited Rarotonga when seeking an isle refuge.

The Cook Islands became an internally self-governing country in 1965; local government is still based on the traditional system of island councils. Individual members of extended families give their allegiance to hereditary chiefs, or *ariki*, who sit on a legislative body called the House of Ariki. Land is held by registered title and is worked in communal fashion.

Rarotonga is an oval-shaped island, with a narrow coastal plain skirting the high mountains of the interior. It is encircled by a lagoon enclosed by an offshore reef, which varies in its distance from the shore. To the north and west, the

lagoon is broken and narrow; this is where Avarua and Avatiu Harbour are located. On the southern side of the island, the lagoon is broad and swimming is favoured. There are some channels to the open sea.

Ara Tapu: "The Sacred Way"

The coastal road – Ara Tapu, "The Sacred Way" – can be driven around the entire island in about two hours (or two days, for those who wish to dawdle). A short distance inland is the Ara Metua, a narrow, largely unsealed road which parallels the coast road but is broken into sections. The well-sealed Ara Tapu has many spokes leading to this inner road, from which several no-exit jeep tracks and footpaths head into the mountain valleys. A cross-island hike past the 412-metre (1,351-foot) needle of Te Rua Manga offers fine scenery.

Cars, mopeds and bicycles are available for hire in Avarua, where arrangements for horse rides, fishing trips, small-boat sailing and other recreations can also be made. In addition to acting as the Cook Islands' administrative hub, Avarua is the commercial centre and site of a fruit cannery, clothing manufacturer and handicraft workshops.

Nineteenth century architecture is one of Rarotonga's charms. The most impressive buildings are the Cook Islands Christian Church in Avarua and an old church at Titikaveka village on the southern coast. Opposite the entrance to the Avarua church are the ruins of the palace of Queen Makea Nui Ariki; they are tapu (forbidden) and should not be approached. In the church cemetery is the tomb of Robert Dean Frisbie, the Cook Islands' most famous literary figure, author of *The Book of Pukapuka.*

Just west of Avarua is the man-made harbour of Avatiu, where inter-island motor vessels, a fishing fleet and visiting yachts find haven. Offshore sits the wreck of the *S.S. Maitat,* which has somehow survived the pounding of waves since it went on the rocks in 1916. Only the boilers and engine are visible.

At Muri, there are offshore islands and the headquarters of the Rarotonga Sailing Club. Beyond Muri on the east coast is Ngatangiia Harbour, a beautiful place with a wide channel to the sea. Legend **Island couple.**

says it was from here that great Polynesia voyaging canoes set out for New Zealand and other Pacific destinations.

The Rarotongan, the island's leading hotel, is west of Avarua near the island's southwestern extremity. A Hawaiian-style lodging, it features sea and pool swimming, local dance entertainment and other amenities.

Niue Island

Niue elected to maintain a free association with New Zealand upon attaining independence in 1974. About 2,200 Niueans make their home on the 258-sq km (100-sq mile) island, plus a couple of hundred Europeans. More than 1,000 people live at the administrative centre of Alofi, and the rest stay in villages.

Niue was first colonised from Samoa, about 560 km (350 miles) to the north-west, in ancient times. Tongans also came to the island, The Polynesian dialect of Niue has affinities with Samoa; Samoan radio broadcasts, newspapers and travel link the two places. Local time is 50 minutes behind Rarotonga, or 23 hours and 20 minutes behind New Zealand.

There are no harbours on Niue. High coastal sea cliffs loom over close coral reefs. A canoe passage and lighter landing at Alofi allows the servicing of cargo and passenger ships that anchor offshore. To the south of Alofi is a good airstrip capable of taking intermediate jet aircraft. The internal road system consists of a 64-km (40-mile) road, which more or less follows the coast, and two cross-island roads.

Tourism is still at an early stage of development. The Niue Hotel – first on the island – has a limited number of rooms to go with its bar, swimming pool and magnificent view. Outdoor activities offered on the island include swimming, snorkelling, fishing, reef walking and cave exploration,

The island was discovered by Captain Cook in 1774. The London Missionary Society established teachers on the island from the mid-1840s onward. Today about three-quarters of the small population belong to the Ekalesia Niue (Niuean Church), a direct descendant of the London missionaries.

The Tokelau Atolls

Tokelau consists of the three atolls of Nukunonu, Fakaofo and Atafu. All are formed by islets set about reefs which together form expansive inner lagoons. Sitting between 8 and 10 degrees South Latitude and about 480 km (300 miles) north of Western Samoa, its time is 23 hours behind Auckland.

The resident population is about 1,700. The growth of the atoll population in the post-World War II period was too much for the limited resources of the prevailing coconuts-and-fish economy. The New Zealand government stepped in with the Tokelau Resettlement Scheme that carried hundreds of Tokelauans to live in New Zealand, mostly around Taupo and Rotorua.

There are no ports, and visits by small cargo vessels are infrequent. The lagoons can receive amphibious aircraft from Samoa.

Not surprisingly, there are few tourist facilities either. Those who undertake a journey to Tokelau should plan well in advance, making inquiries about entry, transportation, and what supplies of food and equipment should be taken along.

Polynesian shrine.

Names of Tatus

V shape centre [...]

Bands on foreh[...]
and temples   [...]

Where these
in inside
the eyelids

ornament on
of Tiwhana,
corner of eye[...]
          P

ornament ove[...]
between the
          KO

double spiral[...]
upper part [...]

notching do[...]
nose.   Wha

double spirals
nostrils   Pong[...]

pattern over
lip   H

Both Lips tal[...]
Ngutu pu[...]

Pattern on [...]
          Kau

8 Bands from
to chin patt[...]
          RER[...]

stab on the outer [...]
centre of the C[...]

SPIRAL on the upper cheeks
          KOWIRI —

lines of above, just under the eyes
                KumeKume —

lines between Kowiri and Ear

note 1/8 inch
brotl[...]

The classic art of New Zealand Maori is an unsurpassed Pacific tribal art. Many creative styles and much skilled craftsmanship yielded objects of great beauty. To appreciate the achievements of Maori arts and crafts an understanding of the materials used, the techniques of crafts, design and symbolism, and the economic, social and religious requirements that inspired the making of art objects, is invaluable.

Maori visual arts, the "arts and crafts," involved the artistic working of wood, stone, bone, fibre, feathers, clay pigments, and other natural materials by skilled craftsmen. Woodcarving was the most important of the crafts. Canoes, storehouses, dwellings, village fortifications, weapons, domestic bowls, and working equipment were made of wood; Maori culture was basically a wood culture.

Maori craft productions were of three distinctive categories: 1) those of communal ownership, such as war canoes made for tribal welfare; 2) intimate things for personal use, such as garments, greenstone ornaments, combs, musical instruments, and indelible skin tattoos. The things used in daily toil, the tools of the carver, lines and fishhooks of the fisherman, gardening tools of the field worker, the snares and spears of a fowler, were possessions usually made by the users and should be included in this category; and 3) the artefacts of ritual magic kept under the guardianship of priests (*tohunga*) – godsticks, crop gods, and anything else used in ceremonial communication with gods and ancestral spirits. Such things were often elaborate versions of utilitarian objects; an ordinary digging stick in its ritual form was ornately carved.

Periods of Maori art merge, yet there are four distinctive eras with characteristic features: Archaic, Classic, Historic, and Modern. First is that of the early settlers – the Archaic Maori or moa hunters, the immediate descendants of the Polynesian canoe navigators who first settled New Zealand. For centuries they survived by hunting, fishing, and foraging land and sea and are best known from archaeological evidence. Their art work, including

carvings and bone and stone work, is characterised by austere forms that, as pure sculpture, can surpass much of the later work.

Craft Specialists

In time, the cultivation of the sweet potato (*kumara*) and other crops, along with an advanced ability to exploit all natural resources of forest and ocean, allowed a settled way of village life. With it there came food surpluses, a tightly organised tribal system, and territorial boundaries. Craft specialists supported by

the community also became established. These people have been called the Classic Maori. They were well described by Captain (then Lieutenant) James Cook, some of whom he met when he landed on New Zealand soil from H.M. barque *Endeavour*, on October 9, 1769. Classic Maori culture was, in the 18th century, in full flower. Life and art seem to have reached their limits of development in the prevailing stone-age conditions. Great war canoes were then the focal point of tribal pride and warfare was an accepted way of life. The making of various weapons of wood, bone and stone with the glorification of fighting men by their tattoos, garments, and ornaments, was considered a matter of prime importance.

Preceding pages, inside a Waitangi meeting house; Haka party put up a show. **Left**, sketch of a Maori facial tattoo by General Horatio Robley, Hawke's Bay Museum. **Right**, Maori make-up.

The Historic period of Maori art underwent rapid changes due to the adoption of metal tools, Christianity, Western fabrics, newly introduced crop plants, muskets and cannon. After 1800 warfare became particularly horrible as the first tribes to possess muskets descended on traditional enemies still armed with clubs and spears. Palisaded villages (*pa*) were no longer defendable so they were duly abandoned. The great war canoes also became useless as the gunpowder weapons changed the strategy of battle. Large storehouses were built as the new potato crops and the acquisition of foreign goods ushered in a new type of economy. These structures became obsolete as Western-style sheds and barns proved more practical in meeting the needs of changing by the new social identity and new aspirations of the race. The roots of this Maori art resurgence reach well back into the 19th century, yet it was the early 20th century leaders, notably Sir Apirana Ngata and Sir Peter Buck (Te Rangi Hiroa) who advocated in a practical way the study and renewal of Maori art. The meeting house proved an ideal, practical medium in this endeavour.

Well-Dressed Warriors

Maori society and the arts have always been intimately associated with aristocratic fighting chiefs who exercised their hereditary rights in controlling tribal affairs. Always the best dressed, ornamented, and accoutred in the

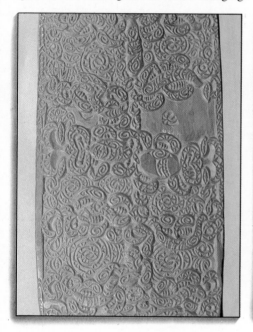 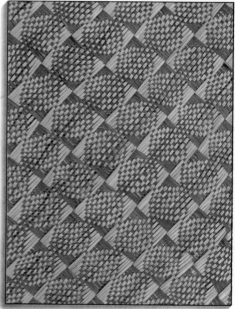

times.

Fine storehouses (*pataka*) of this era have been preserved in museums. One, named Puawai-o-te-Arawa (Flower of the Arawa), first erected at Maketu, Bay of Plenty, in 1868, is in the Auckland Museum. The great days of the *pataka* ended, yet communal meeting houses became increasingly useful during the Historic period. Indeed, they became the focal point of Maori social life and of a Maori art revolution.

The fourth period of Maori art, the Modern, was underway before 1900, and remains with us. The great rise in interest in Maori culture (*Maoritanga*) in recent decades is in step with a general renaissance of Maori culture inspired community, tribal prestige (*mana*) depended on these leaders.

Society as a whole was an autocratic hierarchy. Individuals belonged to extended families (*whanau*) which in turn clustered to form subtribes (*hapu*) which were allied as tribes through blood ties. Genealogical trees led back to ancestral canoes (*waka*), the names of which provided tribal names.

Society was divided into two classes that to a degree overlapped. The upper class was

Two close-up views attest to the sophistication of Maori design. <u>Left</u>, underside of a treasure box. <u>Right</u>, detail of basket.

composed of the highest nobles (*ariki*) and the military generals or chiefs (*rangatira*). The majority lower class was made up of the commoners (*tutua*). Outside these classes were slaves (*taurekareka*) who held no rights. These unfortunates did menial work and often died as sacrificial victims or to provide food when special events required human flesh.

People dressed according to rank, yet when engaged in daily routine work both high and low classes used any old garments. Men and women wore a waist wrap, plus a shoulder cloak when weather or ceremony required. Everyday dress was simply a waist garment. Pre-pubescent children usually went about naked. On attaining adulthood, it was an indecency to uncover the sexual organs.

The special indication of rank was facial tattoo. Tattooists were well paid in goods and hospitality according to their skill. Men were tattooed over the whole face in painful, deep-grooved cuts made by birdbone chisels dipped in a sooty pigment, which looked blue under the skin. Northern warriors often had additional tattoos over buttocks and thighs. Women were deeply tattooed about lips and chin, but the lips were made blue by the use of comb-type "needles." The remarkable art of the tattooist is best seen on Maori mummified heads in museum collections. Traditionally the heads of enemies were taken home to be reviled but those of kinsfolk were preserved to be mourned over. Mummification was achieved by a process involving steaming, smoking and oiling, and heads so treated remained intact and retained hair, skin and teeth. Out of respect for Maori feelings such heads are rarely shown in museums.

Tattooists and other craft specialists were generally drawn from the higher ranks and were respected priests. Skill in craft work was honoured by chiefs and commoners alike, and even the nobles turned their hands to creative art work. High ranking women enjoyed making fine garments and chiefs often filled in leisure hours with carving chisel in hand, working on a box or some other small item.

Wooden treasure boxes (*wakahuia*) were made to contain precious items such as greenstone ornaments or feathers. They were portable and were often collected by early visitors to New Zealand. These lidded boxes, designed to be hung from house rafters and possessing a variety of carving styles from many tribal districts, were ornately carved on all sides, especially on the underside as they were very often looked at from below.

The personal possessions of the Maori demonstrate their most exquisite art work. Combs, feathered garments, treasure boxes, cloak pins, greenstone ornaments of several types, including *hei-tiki* ancestral pendants, and weapons have the "personal touch." A well-appointed warrior was not fully dressed without his weapons: a short club thrust into his belt and a long club held in hand. Weapons were always near, mostly for the practical purpose of defence, as a stealthy, sudden attack on an unsuspecting foe was admired. Weapons were essential in the practice of oratory as they were flourished to stress the points of a speech.

Art for the Gods

Religious inspiration in Maori art was based on the prevailing beliefs about gods and ancestral spirits. In pre-Christian times supernatural beings were believed to inhabit natural objects. Rituals and chants were thus necessary to the successful pursuit of any task, including craft work.

People, hand-made things and natural objects were thought to have an inner psychic force called *mana*. This key idea is essential to the understanding of Maori art and behaviour. *Mana* had many shades of meaning, such as prestige, influence, authority, and most significant, psychic power. *Mana's* presence was manifested in efficiency or effectiveness, such as a warrior's success in a battle or a fishhook's fish-catching ability and increased with success or decreased through improper contact or pollution. If a chief or his possessions were touched by a person of lower rank, then there was pollution and *mana* was diminished.

The sexes were kept apart in all craft activities. While men worked the hard materials of wood, bone and stone, women followed crafts using soft materials such as flax strips (as in mat and basket plaiting) or they prepared flax fibres used in making garments and decorative taniko borders. It was believed women were created from the earth by Tane. The first man was a direct spiritual creation of the god Tu. Thus it was that women were "*noa*" – non-sacred – and the male, conversely, a sacred "*tapu*" being. This attitude put females in a position of subservience which precluded them from the high religious practices and those crafts and activities in which high gods and ancestral spirits were directly involved. Women were not allowed to approach men working at their respective crafts. This was the law and severe punishment followed any infringement of this *tapu*.

The workers with the highest status were the chiefs and the priests; their positions were arrived at only after long apprenticeship with training in religious rites.

Art also had peaceful ends. Wooden stickgods (*tiki wananga*), bound with sacred cords and dressed in red feathers were used by priests when communicating with gods and ancestral spirits to protect the welfare of the tribe. Stone crop gods (*taumata atua*) were placed in or near gardens to promote fertility in growing crops.

Remarkable wooden burial chests of *tiki* form, hollowed out and backed with a slab door, were used to contain the bones of the deceased. Maori burial practice, at least for persons of rank, required an initial burial, then

enough to stand vertically. Posts were also erected to mark tribal boundaries and to commemorate momentous events.

Maori Motifs

Maori art can appear as a disordered jumble. However, an understanding of the small number of symbols and motifs used reveals orderliness.

The human form, dominant in most compositions, is generally referred to as a *tiki* and was first created man of Maori mythology. *Tiki* represents ancestors and gods in the sculptural arts, and may be carved in wood, bone, or stone. The nephrite (greenstone) *hei-tiki* is the best known of ornaments. In ceremonial meet-

a recovery of the bones a year or two later when final ceremonial "burial" would take place. The spirit of the deceased was thought to journey to Cape Reinga, at the North Island's northern tip, where it plunged into the sea, en route to the ancient homeland of Hawaiki. Burial chests often have a canoe-like form, some even possess a central keel ridge. These magnificent chests, concealed in caves or hidden places, were found in the Auckland districts and many have been preserved in museums.

Monuments and cenotaphs of various forms were erected in memory of the dead. Some were posts with carved *tiki* while others took the form of canoes buried in the earth deeply

ing-house architecture, ancestral *tiki* were carved on panels supporting the rafters or on other parts of the structure. They were highly stylised with large heads to fill in areas of posts or panels. This design arrangement also served to stress the importance of the head in Maori belief. The head was, along with sexual organs, the highly sacred part of the body.

Sexual organs were often carved large in both male and female figures and both penis and vulva were regarded as centres of potent magic in promoting fertility and protection. Small birth figures were placed between the legs or on the bodies of *tiki* representing descending generations.

The bodies of panel figures were often

placed in the contorted postures of the war dance. The out-thrust tongue was an expression of defiance and of protective magic.

Local styles of carving differ in many respects. The figures of the east coast Bay of Plenty region are square while those of Taranaki and Auckland districts are sinuous.

The general purpose of the Maori *tiki* carver was to provide material objects to serve as the vehicles of gods and ancestral spirits. Some post figures are portraits depicting an individual's tattoo, though most are stylisations of beings not of the mortal world. *Tiki* figures often have slanted, staring eyes, clawed hands with a spur thumb, beaked mouth, and other bird-like features. These bird motifs were superimposed on the basic human

many door lintels. What *manaia* are remains a mystery, although there is a possibility they represent the *tiki's* psychic power. In form, it is a bird-man or lizard-man. Lizards made rare appearances in Maori woodcarving and other sculptural arts. As a symbol, it is of uncertain meaning, though lizards, feared as vehicles of harmful spirits, were often used as guardians.

Whales (*pakake*) and whale-like creatures appeared on the slanting facades of storehouses. The head part terminates at the lower end in large interlocking spirals representing the mouth. Some fish, dogs, and other creatures occurred in carvings, but on the whole they are rare; there was no attempt to depict nature in a naturalistic way.

Marakihau, fascinating mermen monsters

form to create a hybrid – a bird-man – and probably came from the belief that the souls of the dead and the gods used birds as spirit vehicles.

The *manaia,* another major symbol, is a beaked figure rendered in profile with a body that has arms and legs. When it is placed near *tiki* it appears to bite at them about the head and bodies. Sometimes *manaia* form part of the *tiki* themselves and often alternate with *tiki* on

Left, the house of Te Rangihaeata on Mana Island, Cook Strait. **Above**, Maori girl holding a carved gourd. **Right**, portrait of a Maori king (Lindauer paintings).

of the taniwha class, those mythical creatures that lurked in river pools and caves, appeared on panels and as greenstone ornaments. *Marakihau* were probably ancestral spirits that took to the sea and are depicted on the 19th century house panels with sinuous bodies terminating in curled tails. Their heads have horns, large round eyes, and tube tongues, and were occasionally depicted sucking in a fish. *Marakihau* were supposedly able to swallow canoes along with their crews.

Painted patterns can be seen on rafter paintings and are based on a curved stalk and bulb motif called a *koru*. Combinations of *koru* have infinite possibilities: Air New Zealand uses one as the company logo.

Stone, Bone Feathers and Shells

The tools and materials of the Maori craft work were limited to woods, stone, fibres and shells; metal tools did not exist. The principal tools of woodcarvers, *adzes*, were made of stone blades lashed to wooden helves. The blades were of various weights and shapes. A large *adze*, was used in hewing slabs while delicate work required the use of a very small hand-held *adze*. Adzing art was basic to all traditional Maori wood sculpture. Forms were first adzed, then chisels were used to give surface decoration. Greenstone was the most valued blade material. Chisels had either a straight-edged or gourge-type blade which was lashed to a short wooden handle. Stone-

fine-grained rocks for tools, weapons, and ornamental use. The relatively soft yet durable totara and kauri trees, the latter available only in the warm northern parts of the North Islands, were favoured by the carvers. Hardwoods were also abundant. The nephritic jade (*pounamu*) and known today as "greenstone" was valued as a sacred material. Found only in the river beds of the Arahura and Taramakau on the West Coast of South Island, this rare commodity was widely traded. Greenstone is of such a hard texture it cannot be scratched by a steel point. To work it in the days before the diamond cutters of the lapidary was laborious. The worker rubbed away with sandstone cutters to abraid a greenstone piece into the form of a pendant, *hei-tiki*, weapon or some other

pointed rotary drills and various wooden wedges and mallets completed the Maori stone-age tool kit. When Europeans introduced metals, the old tools were cast aside in favour of iron blades with subsequent effects on carving techniques.

The introduction of oil-based paints quickly ousted the old red ochre pigment (*kokowai*), which can be seen today only in traces on older carvings. The later practice of overpainting old carvings with European red paint was unfortunate in that it obliterated much surface patination and often the older ochres resulting in the loss of much polychrome-painted work of the Historic period.

New Zealand offered a remarkable range of

object.

Bone, obtained from whales, small sea mammals, birds, dogs, and humans, was put to use in many ways. Whalebone was especially favoured for weapons while sperm whale teeth made fine ornaments and dog hair decorated weapons and cloaks. The brilliant feathers of New Zealand birds were placed on cloaks in varied patterns.

The iridescent paua shell was widely used as inlay in woodcarving and textile dyes were made from barks. A deep black dye was obtained by soaking fibres in swamp mud.

Flax plants were used by Maori in many ways. Green leaf strips, which served in the quick manufacture of field baskets or platters, could, when scutched, water-soaked, pounded and bleached, produce a strong fibre for making warm garments, cords and ropes. Maori war canoes, houses, and foodstores were assembled using flax cord. Metal nails did not exist and the idea of using pegs as wooden nails, the technique so widely used by Asian craftsmen, was either unknown or unwanted by the Maori artisan.

Communal Meeting Houses

Ornate meeting houses (*whare whakairo*) played a vital role in the 19th century in providing the Maori people places to congregate for social purposes and where the common problems of the tribe could be resolved. The

was added and Western architectural ideas, combined with Maori concepts of building, proceeded into the 20th century, culminating in the modern community halls which, in their general shape, carvings, lattice panelling, and painted rafters, achieve a distinctive Maori style.

Sometimes the house of a senior chief would serve as a meeting house though carvings from these houses were small and lightly decorated as war canoes and storehouses were of more importance. In the 1900s, highly ornamented meeting houses continued to be the focus of Maori social activities.

Often, important Maori houses were named after an ancestor and symbolised the actual person; the ridge pole represented the spine,

ravages of foreign diseases, destruction and loss of lands, wars with traditional enemies, and the fighting with settlers and the British had placed most of the Maori people in a desperate situation. Meeting houses were built in large numbers and were of an ever-growing size. Most of the actual gatherings were in the large open area (*marae*) in front of the principal houses.

These large meeting houses were constructed with the aid of steel tools and milled timbers. In due time, corrugated iron roofing

Left, Maori carver Keri Wilson working on wood.
Above, close-up of a Maori woodcarving.

the rafters were his ribs, and the facade boards, which at times terminated in "fingers," were his outstretched arms. At the gable peak was the face mask. This notion still lives on such that when a tribe member enters a particular house he or she is entering the protective body of the ancestor. Many communal houses are open to the public and a fine example is Tama-te-Kapua at Ohinemutu, Rotorua, erected in 1878.

When travelling through Maori districts such as the Bay of Plenty on the east coast a number of meeting houses can be seen. While they are often on private property visitors are welcome though permission must be sought before entering a house.

This land is a lump with leaven,
a body that has no nerves.
Don't be content to live in
a sort of second-grade heaven
with first-grade butter, fresh air,
and paper in every toilet ...

– A.R.D. Fairburn,
"I'm Older Than You, Please Listen"

Some of New Zealand's great exports
have been its artists. Painter Frances
Hodgkins and writer Katherine Mansfield
were prophets without honour in their own
country. Opera megastar, Kiri te Kanawa, is
a more familiar sight in Milan than in Masterton.

In a country so physically isolated from
the rest of the world and historically culturally tied to the apron strings of England, the
arts have contained a high proportion of
mimicry. It is really only in the 1980s that a
need for a unique cultural identity, one with
its roots in the South Pacific, has begun to
emerge. This is expressed perhaps most
strongly in literature, films and theatre, but is
beginning to be felt in music and several
other arts and crafts as well.

The "Buttocks of a Dead Cow"

The cynic might say that light, landscape
and sheep have preoccupied New Zealand
painters since colonial times. The same
cynic might place the visual arts into three
categories – representational, abstract and
chocolate box.

The sense of public outrage at being presented with anything difficult or challenging
is best illustrated by the "Torso II" affair. In
1963 the Auckland City Gallery director
proposed to spend 950 guineas on a Barbara
Hepworth sculpture. When shown a like-
ness of the proposed acquisition several city
councillors were outraged. "It looks like the
buttocks of a dead cow," said councillor
Tom Pearce, the most vociferous of critics.

**Preceding pages, a potter's workshop. Two of
the country's literary greats: short-story writer
Katherine Mansfield (left) and novelist Janet
Frame (right).**

"I wouldn't give five bob for it," quoted the
Mayor. "Art or a cow's hambone," ques-
tioned a daily newspaper editorial. Letters
raged back and forth and there was standing
room only at a meeting to discuss the use of
ratepayers' money for this particular purpose. The piece was eventually bought for
the gallery by an anonymous donor. A record
1,700 people filed past it in 4 hours when it
was finally unveiled. "It needs the 'Brasso'
on it," was one verdict.

That this incident should be relegated to

the annals of art history is desirable but
similar controversies are never far from the
surface. In 1982, the McDougall Gallery in
Christchurch announced plans to spend
$10,000 on a painting by Colin McCahon,
one of the country's most contentious and
significant local painters. Again there was
civic outrage: "It looks like a school some-
where has lost its blackboard."

McCahon (1919-1987) was used to a high
level of incomprehension when it comes to
his work, perhaps best described as New
Zealand landscape with a Christian theol-
ogy. Living in Auckland in virtual seclusion,
with painting being his communication with

the world, he was considered a messiah by some and a blasphemer by others.

McCahon was never part of any particular art "ism": but his work and teaching (he taught for a while at Elam School of Fine Arts in Auckland) influenced a generation of younger painters including Nigel Brown, Robin White and Claudia Pond Eyley.

A contemporary of McCahon is Gordon Walters, an artist who investigates the relation between a deliberately narrow range of forms, mostly the *koru* or fern bud. The interpretation of this local symbol in a European abstract style which has much in common with Klee or Mondrian gives Walters' work a universal yet distinctively New Zea-

the threat to build an aluminium smelter at Aromoana in the far south and the 1981 Springbok rugby tour provoked a rash of political paintings by hitherto apolitical artists. The response to events is probably strongest from a group of women artists around the country who paint from a feminist perspective. They include Juliet Batten, Carole Shepheard, Di Ffrench and Jacqueline Fahey. Many other artists tend to work in relative isolation being influenced by their surroundings or art "movements" in Europe or the United States.

Len Lye (1901-1980) may yet turn out to be the greatest expatriate artist. He won an international reputation as a pioneer of direct

land flavour.

Tony Fomison is another highly individualistic local painter whose work has a unique power, much of it reflecting the artist's awareness of an identity that is rooted in the South Pacific.

One of New Zealand's most popular and probably most financially successful painters, is Peter McIntyre. His landscapes are unashamedly representational, and cause no irate letters to editors. He identifies what he calls and "art mafia" in Auckland and points out that after all Picasso was a millionaire.

Little of New Zealand's visual art is overtly political although incidents such as

film techniques whereby images are scratched directly on to celluloid, and as a kinetic sculptor. Lye's first "steel motion" compositions were first exhibited in the auditorium of the Museum of Modern Art in New York; they were small versions of work which he planned to build on a grand scale. Before he died he gave his permission for these works to be built posthumously. Several of his works have already been constructed and are housed at the Govett-Brewster gallery in New Plymouth, which specialises in collecting the work of New Zealand sculptors.

A recent development, which has made

artists' work more accessible to a wider public, has been an increase in the production of original prints. Etching and screenprinting are favoured methods. There is also a growing number of galleries specialising in original prints.

Stanley Palmer is a pioneer of innovative techniques such as drypoint printing on bamboo plates. This gives his land and cityscapes a distinctive feel. A prolific printmaker who has enjoyed considerable commercial success is Malcolm Warr. His screen-printed land- and seascapes are now found throughout New Zealand and Australia.

Attention to photography as a creative medium has been fairly recent, although

A Bird, A Hawk, A Bogie and other Stories

"I made my first story on the banks of the Mataura River after a meal of trout and billy tea: 'Once upon a time there was a bird. One day a hawk came out of the sky and ate the bird. The next day a big bogie came out from behind the hill and ate up the hawk for eating up the bird.' The story's not unusual told by a child of three. As I still write stories I'm entitled to study this and judge it the best I've written." So said novelist Janet Frame in a literary magazine, *Landfall*.

Thousands of New Zealanders write stories; there are possibly a hundred good nov-

Brian Brake has a reputation for his work in *National Geographic* magazine and Ans Westra's depictions of Maori subjects along with Marti Friedlander's portraits are widely published. Photoforum, a struggling organisation which publishes and organises exhibitions, has brought into prominence a new generation of talented photographers including Peter Perryer, Robin Morrison, Ann Noble and Gillian Chaplin.

Far left, sculptor Joan Morrell with a bust of poet James K. Baxter. **Left**, the poet Baxter. **Above**, potter Len Castle.

elists and a large number of non-fiction writers, but there is only one Janet Frame – a literary giant, in New Zealand terms, who lives reclusively. Born in 1924, she has published over 20 novels, four collections of stories, a volume of poetry, a children's book and three volumes of her autobiography – *To the Island*, *An Angel at My Table*, and *The Envoy From Mirror City*. A recent work, *The Carpathians* won New Zealand's top book award in 1989. Her books chart mental and physical landscapes with agility and perception. Her love of literature and writing was nurtured as a child when she lived in a poor South Island family.

Many novelists, poets and artists of all kinds have spent some time acquiring OE – overseas experience – to get their country, and a love-hate relationship with it, in perspective. A.R.D. Fairburn (1904-1957) also wrote:

Pine for the needles brown and warm,
think of your nameless native hills,
the seagulls landward blown by storm,
the rabbit that the black dog kills.
                        – To An Expatriate

The sprinkling of poets, some of them aspiring Dylan Thomas types, have on the whole been a colourful lot. James K. Baxter,

Dear Sam I thank you for your letter
And for the poem too, much better
To look at than the dreary words
I day by day excrete like turds.

If the comparison is not too ludicrous, Sam Hunt is to New Zealand poetry, what Kiri te Kanawa is to world opera. Sam, once labelled the Bard of Bottle Creek, would probably appreciate it. Ever cheerful and distinctive in his Foxton straits (his appellation for a type of trouser) Sam recites his poems in bar-rooms, among other places, up and down the country. His slightly tremulous tones have even been heard in New York City.

poet, prophet and teacher wrote in his school notebook: "Born June 29th, 1926, will die when he and Nature see fit." Nature, if not the bard, saw fit rather prematurely in 1972. His poetry expressed social and religious concerns. He was a fanatical convert to Catholicism. In the latter years of his life he left his family to set up a commune at Jerusalem, a small Maori settlement on the Wanganui River. Here he lived as a self-appointed guru, spurning materialism and churning out verse.

He communicated with other poets, sometimes in doggerel like this to contemporary poet, Sam Hunt:

Perhaps the most revolutionary development in local literature has been the writing of a growing number of Maori – including Witi Ihimaera, Patricia Grace and Rowley Habib – expressing in English for the first time what it is like to be Maori in New Zealand.

Music: Hard Times and Exodus

Listening to a New Zealand commercial radio station is little different to the United States or Britain. Struggling local rock bands compete for air time and local venues, most of which are pubs. Some make records and, if they can afford it, videos. Attempts at achieving a distinct local sound are becoming more determined with the music of such bands as "Herbs" and "Diatribe," but with a 40 percent sales tax on records, and supported by such a small population, survival on the New Zealand circuit takes enormous stamina. Most promising musicians take a one-way ticket out.

Tim Finn, former lead singer of a successful group called Split Enz, said in an interview on the television arts programme *Kaleidoscope*: "We got through that New Zealand thing – if it's local it must be scungy – we believed that what we had was good and we could take it to the world." Take it they

Opera is represented by a number of city opera companies which stage regular productions, and engaged both local and international talent.

Experimental music, such as electronic, has largely emanated from the universities where composers such as Douglas Lilburn, John Rimmer, Jack Body and Jenny McLeod have taught.

Whooping it up with Shakespeare

Although professional theatre is just over 20 years old it's hard to imagine that the pioneers didn't whoop it up occasionally with a bit of Shakespeare. You need only tune into

did, to become one ingredient in late-1970s British punk and then to Australia where they now live. The price of success is to live outside New Zealand.

Classical musicians fare little better. If they don't want or can't get a place in the New Zealand Symphony Orchestra, then it's the inevitable OE. The orchestra itself tours constantly with a succession of overseas guest conductors. There are also regional orchestras in the four main centres.

<u>Left</u>, rock singer and former leader of the group Split Enz, Tim Finn. <u>Above</u>, scene from one of Roger Hall's plays.

Parliament on the radio to discover what an acute sense of drama the New Zealander possesses.

Perhaps this explains the success of Roger Hall, whose play *Glide Time* (about the Stores department personnel in a government office) was a smash hit locally and whose *Middle Age Spread* was filmed locally and produced for the London's West End stage with leading British television personalities Richard Briars and Penelope Keith in the lead roles.

Roger Hall would be the first to acknowledge the great debt actors and playwrights in New Zealand owe to Bruce Mason. He was a one-man theatrical band. His source material was largely local and he was one of the first Pakeha writers to sensitively write Maori characters. Mason performed his works *The End Of The Golden Weather* and *The Pohutukawa Tree* many times in theatres and country halls and schools up and down the land thus becoming part of the theatrical experience of thousands of schoolchildren.

In his later years he was a widely respected theatre critic. Before Mason's death in 1982, Roger Hall wrote to him: "It has never ceased to amaze me that in a profession so ego-ridden as the theatre is yours remained not only normal but you also had the gener-

osity continually to be supporting, encouraging, stimulating others ...."

Unfortunately for the theatres not all plays are artistically or financially successful. As they struggle (with some support from the Arts Council) to survive, directors are often forced to put on quickfire success material in order to place bums on seats.

Some of the vibrant theatre happens outside the mainstream as young actors take their contemporary theatre to the streets, factories and schools. Training centres such as the Performing Arts School in Auckland and the New Zealand Drama School in Wellington offer courses in this field.

Film

New Zealand's feature film industry has enjoyed considerable success since the late 1970s, starting with films such as Roger Donaldson's *Sleeping Dogs*, which starred international film and television actor Sam Neill. In the same year, the New Zealand Film Commission began to assist Kiwi filmmakers with finance and advice – and in the last decade more local feature films have been made than in the country's previous film history.

The biggest local box office successes to date have been *Goodbye Pork Pie* and the animated feature *Footrot Flats – the Dog's*

Tale, which put Murray Ball's popular cartoon strip onto celluloid.

Smash Palace was the first local film to sell extensively overseas. It was directed by Roger Donaldson who then went to Hollywood making such movies as *No Way Out* and *Cocktail*.

In the late 1980s the limelight has shifted to Vincent Ward, a young director whose works *Vigil and The Navigator* have been acclaimed at the Cannes Film Festival.

Apart from features there are a number of people making experimental films and documentaries. The most notable of the latter is *Patu*, a look at the huge protest movement against the 1981 Springbok rugby tour of New Zealand. Its director, Merata Mita, is an exception in local film-making on two counts; she's a woman and a Maori. *Patu* has been widely shown in New Zealand and has won acclaim in film festivals in several countries. Mita's first feature film *Mauri* is currently on release.

Pirouettes and Pliés

With the popularity of music videos and general physical fitness, dancing in New Zealand has definitely become "uncissy".

The backbone of dance, however, is still ballet and each week thousands of girls and

tradition to please the conservative and enough experiment to keep them sane, the company's rank are joined by National School dancers and selected other locals.

Other alternatives for young hopefuls are professional contemporary dance groups such as the Southern Ballet Company in Christchurch. Limbs was another company which operated from 1977 until 1989 and which did a great deal to enhance the popularity of modern dance in New Zealand.

Pottery's New Home

Of all the crafts practised to a greater or lesser degree of proficiency, pottery is at the

boys dutifully plod through their pirouettes and pliés and dream of a place at the National School of Ballet or the Royal New Zealand Ballet both based in Wellington.

Despite staying alive for more than 30 years (making it the oldest ballet troupe in Australasia) the Royal New Zealand Ballet has a lean corps of only 26 poorly paid dancers. When they go on tour with their carefully blended programmes of enough

Far left, Maori warrior performing a *haka*. **Left**, Maori carving of Rotorua Whaka. **Above**, St. Paul's Cathedral in Wellington is an artistic achievement in itself.

forefront. Indeed an outsider might conclude that half the nation was up to its elbows in clay. Yet several decades earlier, there was barely a handmade pot in sight. After World War II a stream of immigrants from Britain and Europe brought with them craft traditions from the old world. With its rich clays and strong do-it-yourself ethic, New Zealand was ripe for potting. Today the country is thought to have more potters per capita than any other.

Studio potteries, craft shops and regular exhibitions offer a huge choice of ceramics, from sturdy domestic ware to delicate free-form sculpture.

During the 1950s and 1960s potteries sprang up in town and country. The beauty and relative isolation of places like Nelson and the Coromandel Peninsula suited the alternative lifestyle that pottery offered. Potters, mostly self-taught, made their kiln. dug their clay and swapped glaze recipes. Harry and May Davis of "Crewenna" and Jack and Peggy Laird of "Waimea Potteries" (both in Nelson) are British immigrants who were responsible for training and galvanising the enthusiasm of many of today's top potters. Helen Mason, who now works with young Maori potters in the splendid isolation of Tokomaru Bay, on the east coast of North Island was another pioneer.

In a nation of so many sheep, it's not surprising that spinning, weaving and the fibre arts are very high on the craft profile in the production of knitwear, rugs, wall-hangings and suchlike.

Following developments in pottery, many weavers are moving into spectacular "art" tapestries, some of them multi-dimensional. The works of weavers like Jenny Hunt, John Hadwen, Zena Abbott, and Ian and Yvonne Spalding can be seen in public buildings such as banks and cinemas in several parts of the country.

A lot of modern craftspeople, Maori and Pakeha, carve wood, bone and greenstone. Native timbers are very suitable for furni-

Len Castle of Auckland, with his emphasis on simple forms and clay for clay's sake, was one of the first full-time city potters, Queen Elizabeth II owns a Len Castle pot!

By the late 1970s pottery began to shrug off its solid earthy image. A new generation began to experiment with colour, form and firing methods such as raku, saggar and pit firing. Fibre-insulated kilns replaced smelly diesel ones.

Potters have moved into finer clays and more delicate and decorative shapes – and the advent of two major international craft awards has stimulated considerable interest in the sculptural use of clay.

ture, as well as sculpture. Contemporary jewellery makers use bone and stone to create their own designs or imitate traditional Maori ones.

Glass blowing and stained glass work are reaching high levels of sophistication and a number of stained-glass workers are eager for more architects to use their creations as integral parts of building plans.

The state house, a unique remnant of what was once the world's leading welfare state, provides a modicum of suburban uniformity. This is not to say that uniformity is necessarily desirable but it probably helps to explain the reaction to the "enfant terrible" of New

Zealand architects. Ian Athfield, whose style amounts to a one-man revolution. Athfield built his own house high in Wellington's Khandallah hills. From the Hutt motorway its jutting assortment of white funnels is visible. Inside it's like *Watership Down*.

Athfield has been instrumental in erecting and re-building some of Wellington's more spectacular public buildings. A particular example is the Christian Scientist Church in Willis Street. "To say that it is both intimate and theatrical or that it combines some of the qualities of an Egyptian temple with those of a fabulous white whale ... is still very wide of the mark," wrote Dinah Priestley in the *New Zealand Craft Council* magazine.

with work are gone.

Two noteworthy examples of new civic architecture are the town halls of Christchurch and Wellington, both the work of Christchurch architect Miles Warren. New Zealand is a laboratory for the student of architecture who, with care, can observe every style from Renaissance, Gothic, Victorian and Bauhaus to "nouveau concrete".

There is a growing awareness of the importance of design with the major thrust coming from young art school and polytechnic graduates who, despite the desolate job scene, or perhaps because of it, are setting up their own fashion, furniture and graphic design studios. Manufacturers are finally

Wellington's cityscape is probably the best example of what contemporary architects are doing as hundreds of so-called earthquake-risk buildings have been pulled down – a trend encouraged by former mayor and architect Sir Michael Fowler. The city has witnessed a frenetic burst of architectural one-upmanship and while restoration accompanies construction, many of the buildings which provided the first architects

Left, one of Lindauer's paintings which can be seen in the Auckland City Art Gallery. **Above**, the modern face of the nation's art as seen in *Maheno* by Gordon Walters.

being forced to recognise the importance in competitive world markets of good design and packaging – good news for the many industrial designers graduating from the Design School at Wellington Polytechnic.

There is little actual textile designing though men's and women's fashion design is burgeoning, much of it imitating international trends, a little startlingly original.

As New Zealand and the world enter an increasingly design conscious and environmentally aware era, the scope for our designs and products looks promising. A "Made in New Zealand" label is rapidly becoming a bonus rather than a drawback.

Fawn and furious the river filled its steep course, preventing easy travel. The climbers clambered over a huge boulder and plunged into dense scrub again. Persistent drizzle deepened into drenching rain as the evening light faded. Just on dark, buried in bushes on a high moraine, they found a rock bivvy – a dank cave with sloping bumpy floor. For two hours a wet-wood fire was coaxed to cook a meagre meal, then sleep came slowly. As they retreated next morning a brief clearing cruelly revealed their abandoned goal – high above cloud the col's snow crescent curved into the unclimbed ridge of the mountain.

Another trip. A cave home carved from the snow of a western névé, 2,800 metres (9,200 feet) above the Tasman Sea. On a sun-soaked day a new route climbed on the country's second highest peak. As they wandered down the névé to the cave, sky and sea merged golden in the sunset.

Mountaineering is perhaps this country's most famous outdoor sport and with memories of Edmund Hillary's achievement in being the first to climb the world's highest mountain, this is not surprising. A New Zealander could equal the toughness of a Sherpa because of the sort of trips evoked above. New Zealand mountaineers have few huts and have become accustomed to living high up in rock and snow caves and in tents. Since their weather comes from a wild western sea, sun changing to savage storm with fearsome speed, they are often thwarted in their goals but are swift to succeed on fine days. The rock is mainly loose and treacherous, and fast-moving glaciers and icefalls are split by crevasses and swept by avalanches. Such tough training has been a firm foundation for success on Himalayan heights.

Among the highest peaks there are some climbing huts, and a guiding service, but here too the ice is active, the rock loose, and the weather fickle. The story is told of two climbers who were nearing the summit of Mount Cook, New Zealand's highest peak when a storm broke out without warning. For two weeks they had to huddle in a hole hollowed in

the wall of a crevasse, unable to descend safely in the winds which howled outside. Faced with such ferocity, climbers know why Tawhiri-matea (Maori god of winds) is regarded as the most hostile of the gods.

In winter, the mountains are a playground for skiers as well as climbers. At commercial and club fields, in North Island and South, there are facilities familiar to skiers in Europe and North America. Some club fields have a distinctive New Zealand style. Long ropes on pulleys, driven by converted tractor engines, pull people up ungroomed sloped. Club huts are lively social centres for members ranging in age from seven to 70. Some fields can be reached only by walking an hour or more, with skis and food on one's back or shoulder. Devotees declare these fields are friendlier, and break fewer bones, than those where you can step from car seat to ski.

Ski-mountaineering can be more rugged still. Even in areas with huts, food, fuel and sleeping gear have to be taken in, and elsewhere tents are also necessary. This is hard work on foot on skis, but the rewards are considerable – scintillating descents through criss-crossed crevasses and eerie ice cliffs, with high peaks crowding the sky. And in the central alps, and from some commercial ski fields, helicopters and ski planes provide easier access to mountain skiing. Mountain winters also service skaters as small lakes freeze to form natural rinks.

Into the Realm of Tane

Winter and summer mountain valleys and passes are the domain of trampers and bush-walkers and trips vary greatly in difficulty. A proposed national walkway from one end of the country to the other, with comfortable huts easy distances apart, is in an early stage of development concentrating on areas close to urban centres. National and Forest Parks provide tracks and huts spanning a middle range. Wilderness areas are being preserved, with neither huts nor tracks, humans venture into untamed nature dependent on their own wits and resources.

A trans-alpine crossing in the South Island is the most dramatic tramp. From the east, in the rain shadow of the ranges, the mountains are approached through wide and spacious shingle and tussock valleys. Once over the

Preceding pages, kayak briefing at the Outward Bound School on Marlborough Sound. **Left**, steep ascent: rock climbers Graham Dingle (top) and Graham Mourie (bottom).

Main Divide, however, the track drops suddenly into deep-cut gorges and dense forests. Sombre and mysterious in the rain, in sunlight these forests dance with shifting shades of green and yellow, and always are alive with the songs and swift movements of birds. The trekker is immersed in the realm of beneficent Tane, the Maori god of forests.

Having evolved in isolation, many of Tane's plants and birds are unique to New Zealand and are the central attraction for other groups of forest visitors. Patient, birdwatchers drift silently through, sensitive to complex interactions of species, and active, along with many others, in attempts to preserve native forests from further felling for timber. Native forests are threatened also by introduced game animals.

highly manoeuvreable and needs only a few centimetres of water when planing at speed making it ideal for shallow or rocky rivers, and rapids.

Fishing is the other major river activity. In past days eels and native fish were an important source of Maori food, harvested with a variety of nets and traps. Europeans brought brown and rainbow trout in the 19th century, stocking rivers and lakes. They acclimatised well, and frequently trout of 3 kg (7 lbs) or more are caught with rod and fly. During the season salmon run in many rivers too.

Some of this river sport, however, is under threat. Hydro-electric dams have already created chains of lakes, where once wild waters ran. In the past New Zealanders have tended to

mals. Prior to European settlement there were no browsing animals, but now thar, chamois, wild pigs and goats can all be found in New Zealand's forests and mountains.

From New Zealand's mountains swift rivers race down rapids and carve deep gorges – ideal for river running. Expert canoeists shoot arrow-like through wild water, and rubber dinghy enthusiasts crash down a turmoil of rocks and white waves. Commercial rafting companies are now making some of these thrills available to a wider range of people.

Another sort of craft, a New Zealand invention, carries people up these rivers. The jet boat is driven by a pump which sucks water in and shoots it astern in a deflectable plume. It is

think that they had plenty of wild country, but many are anxious now to tilt the balance towards preservation before rather than after discovering that the country's outdoor resources are finite.

Sailing is the premier sea sport. Every weekend, and in the leisurely evening light of summertime, thousands waft out with the wind. Some sail small centre-board boats on estuaries or harbours; the keels of others cleave deeper waters out from the coast. Some sail just for fun, others compete in fierce-fought races which have thrown up an astonishing number of international winners. As with mountaineering the island climate's wayward weather, changing rapidly from calm to chaos, adds a distinctive and dangerous New Zealand note.

Power boats are also popular for family recreation and picnics, and for racing. Water-skiers and wind-surfers have multiplied in recent years and some of the more popular stretches of water are close to becoming over-crowded. Board surfing is also gaining in popularity. As the prevailing weather is westerly the Tasman Sea has the biggest swells. East coast waves are generally smaller, but the funnelling effect of bays and points gives good breaks at select spots. The surf doesn't match that of the world's main surfing centres; New Zealanders can only envy Bali's perfect tubes or Hawaii's walls of water.

In earlier times the sea was more than a

recreation area. For traditional Maori society it was the realm of Tangoroa, god of the sea, and the vital source of *kai moana* (sea food). To this day it retains much of its cultural and spiritual significance for Maori, and some of its economic importance too – Maori predominate amongst those who fish and gather shell-fish for food in a non-commercial way. For them and for others, however, sea-fishing is also recreational. From wharves and sea walls

and boats young and old hopefully hang hooks, others drag nets through rich waters of estuaries, or fare out to sea to battle with deep-water fish.

Some go further. Snorkelling and scuba-diving is popular. Though much coastal water is murky there are some superb diving areas. At the Poor Knights Islands, north of Auckland, cliffs plunge sheer beneath the sea for hundreds of metres. And in the fiords of south Westland the water is opaque on the surface but very clear below. A rewarding sight is a black coral, normally only found far down, but growing here at moderate depths.

Sky High

Going up rather than under, New Zealanders take to the air for recreation as well. The most dramatic powered flights lift people from air-strip to mountain in moments – rock cliffs and teetering ice outcrops seemingly at the wing-tip. Gliders, and even hang-gliders, fly amongst mountains too, whispering by valley walls and along ridges. Indeed, gliding is another New Zealand speciality. Many ranges rear at right angles to strong north-west winds creating in their lee towering wind waves which have lifted New Zealand glider pilots to world records.

New Zealanders enjoy outdoor living in more relaxed ways. Camping is almost a national way of life during summer holidays. The densest concentration are in well-appointed camping grounds at popular beaches, rivers and lakes. Often groups of families return again and again to the same place, creating for two weeks each year a canvas community possibly more stable and significant to them than that of their shifting urban lives. Others seek more secluded spots, assisted by New Zealand law which retains river beds and lake and sea-shores in public ownership. On occasions storms and floods assail these tent dwellers though most people endure this cheerfully as an inevitable part of the contrast they seek to their normal life-style. In good weather they revel in freedom and informality.

Family camping holidays and tramping trips introduce many New Zealanders to outdoor life at an impressionable age, allowing them to grow up with the ability to gain deep pleasure from simple and relatively inexpensive pursuits. They take for granted, perhaps, the ease with which they can do so. Sometimes it takes an overseas visitor, used to dense populations, crowded beaches and polluted rivers, to remind them of their good fortune.

Left, yachts in a racing competition lend colour and excitement to Auckland Harbour. **Above**, two big ones that didn't get away at the Bay of Islands Swordfish Club.

One of New Zealand's favourite spectator sport is rugby football, an odd mixture of skill, hard running, and the sort of violence that might earn an "X" rating for a feature movie.

The game developed in the public schools of Britain, possibly as a means for large boys to physically damage smaller boys without being accused of bullying. Why it took such a stranglehold on New Zealand is rather difficult to tell. Perhaps it is the fact that men of all sizes and abilities can play rugby. In the national team, known as the All Blacks, who wear ominous black jerseys and shorts, one star may be a man as small as a soccer midfielder and another hero a giant who would not look out of place as a linebacker in an American football squad.

The rules are complicated, and change every year. Top-class referees admit they are unable to referee to the letter of the law because if they did there would be no actual play in a match. At its best the game is thrilling even to the uninitiated. Because the players do not wear padding they move faster, and hit each other harder, than American football players. The best runners are almost balletic in their grace; the toughest players are as fierce as prizefighters.

For atmosphere the best rugby matches are internationals, played in New Zealand at any time between June and September. Club and provincial rugby starts earlier, in April, but also finishes in September.

Eden Park

New Zealand's best ground is Eden Park in Auckland. With a crowd capacity of just 47,000, it is relatively modern, and for test matches all seats are numbered and guaranteed to ticket holders. There is a catch. A lot more than 47,000 New Zealanders want to see test matches in Auckland so seats are extremely difficult to buy. There are no large-scale ticket touts or scalpers in New Zealand, but earnest enough enquiries will usually turn up somebody who can produce one, or even two tickets. If all else fails try visiting the hotel of the

Preceding pages, the New Zealand All Blacks and the French team locked in a tussle. Left, perfecting the skills for a winning combination, perhaps.

touring international team, and ask anyone in a blazer with a broken nose if they have a ticket to spare. Touring sides are allocated tickets for internationals and usually sell them at the hotel to add to team funds.

The other international venues for rugby are Athletic Park in Wellington, Lancaster Park in Christchurch and Carisbrook in Dunedin. The main stand at Athletic Park, which has all the grey concrete charm of a public lavatory, is not popular, but thrillseekers might enjoy the Millard Stand, which is a spindly looking structure that shakes in the Wellington winds. At Lancaster Park there are large terraces where everybody stands. Spectators at Lancaster Park are famous for being bitterly one-eyed so it's wise not to cheer until you're sure you're encouraging the same side your neighbours support.

In Dunedin at Carisbrook there is usually room on the terraces, and even a free view from a railway track that runs above the ground, though in rugby's winter season the winds from the south usually carry more than a hint of sleet and snow, which is probably the reason the locals prefer to stay indoors and watch the game on television.

If there are no test matches on during a winter visit to New Zealand, the visitor could consider watching a club match. On most club grounds there are clubrooms, and a newcomer showing some interest will usually be welcomed to stay for a drink.

Speedy Balls and Streakers

The atmosphere of a football game can also be found at one-day cricket tests, played, in Auckland and Christchurch, at the same grounds used for rugby. Cricket is a game of mystery when played over several days, but one-day cricket, perfected for Australian television, strips away the subtleties. What is left is a contest in which men like New Zealand's Richard Hadlee hurl down a hard, leather-covered ball at speeds approaching 160 kmh (100 mph) at batsmen who must hit it as hard as possible, as often as possible. One-day cricket has taken such a hold that grounds once a quarter full now creak at the seams with spectators who merrily bring along their packs of beer.

There is nothing genteel about the spectacle. Comments from the crowd are sometimes witty, more often scatological, and naked streakers, male and female, are hauled away by police from most games. A Munich beer hall in a southern summer is the best way to describe the ambience.

Serious cricket followers will find the highest quality matches in February and March when overseas teams, having visited Australia, round off their tour with matches in New Zealand.

Two of the best chances to see New Zealanders at play en masse both occur in Auckland. On the last Monday of every January, the Auckland Anniversary regatta for yachts is held, with more than 1,000 entries making it the biggest one-day yachting event in the world. Auckland harbour, an attractive, safe

fun run in the world. Started in 1974 in a modest way with a couple of thousand people jogging from the Town Hall around the harbourside to St. Heliers, the run has indeed become one of the biggest gatherings of New Zealanders. Walk the course, or jog it, and nobody will object if you have no official entry form. Or just stand on the edge of the road and watch the population of a reasonable-sized town shuffle past you. If you do make it to St. Heliers take the time to wander among the dozens of tents set up near the finish. Everybody will be in a fiesta mood, cooking barbecue food, and sharing cold drinks. You will never see New Zealanders looking happier in a crowd.

Road running has been growing in popular-

sailing venue is almost covered in boats, from little boys and girls in one-person P-class yachts to the A-class keelers, many of them previously raced in deep water classics. The whole magnificent sight can be viewed from the shore, probably best from Mount Victoria or North Head in the suburb of Devonport, or from ferry boats that cruise from the terminal in downtown Auckland.

As the Town Jogs By

On a Saturday in early March the waterfront drive in Auckland is covered for 11 km (7 miles) by more than 70,000 runners in the annual round Round the Bays run – the biggest

ity in New Zealand ever since a tough little milkman called Arthur Lydiard produced two Olympic champions, Peter Snell and Murray Halberg, in 1960. Their training background involved running 160 km (100 miles) a week. The line of great New Zealand runners has continued through to 1976 Olympic gold medal winner John Walker and 1983 New York marathon champion Rod Dixon.

New Zealand's athletics champions are on show in January, February and March when the national track and field championships, international track meetings and major marathons are held.

Internationally, New Zealand rowing has enjoyed its share of success. In the last decade, world championships and Olympic gold medals have gone to New Zealand's crews. The national championships are held late in February, and the best venues are Lake Karapiro near Hamilton, and Lake Ruataniwha in the Mackenzie Basin.

Hot Favourites

The major women's sport in New Zealand is netball, a game similar in some ways to basketball, but played outdoors in winter with the players barred from running with the ball. The country's national team consistently ranks with the best in the world, and visits from Australia and England are frequent. Tests are usually played between May and June, and

while the sport does not flow as well as basketball, the speed of scoring makes it constantly interesting.

Basketball here revolves around a national league played during the winter. American imports have raised the standard of the sport, and at many of the stadiums in Auckland, Hamilton, Napier, Wellington, Nelson, Christchurch and Dunedin capacity crowds are common.

Boxing and professional wrestling both

Left, warming up with a game on the green. Above, a competitive skier on the slopes of Mount Hutt.

have followings, but in the case of boxing it is difficult for the world's best to fight here, with a limited population cutting purses. The biggest fights are held outdoors in the summer but are rare enough for daily newspapers to cover the build-ups for a week before the bout. Wrestling events undoubtedly attract the same hysterical audience it does throughout the world.

The other winter sports involving major international competition are soccer, rugby league and hockey. Hockey in New Zealand had a moment of true glory in 1976 when the national team won a gold medal at the Montreal Olympics. Unfortunately the sport has not really captured the imagination of the New Zealand public and despite visits from sides as skilled and highly rated as the Indians and the Australians there will always be room for enthusiastic spectators at hockey tests, played in the major cities of Auckland, Wellington and Christchurch.

Other Diversions

Soccer jumped in public esteem when the New Zealand side went to the World Cup in Spain in 1982, and may eventually overtake rugby as the main winter sport. In the national league, games are played on Sunday throughout the country. Internationals are mostly played at Auckland's Mount Smart Stadium, which is a magnificent arena carved from volcanic rock.

Rugby league, a streamlined version of rugby union, has its headquarters at Auckland's Carlaw Park, near the city centre. Club matches are played regularly on Saturday and Sunday through the winter, but the most exciting matches are those played against the internationals, especially those against Australia. Many of the best New Zealand players now live in Sydney and play for Australian clubs, but they still return to Auckland to represent New Zealand. The New Zealand-Australia clashes are both exciting, and, often, blood matches.

Gamblers will have to rely on private wagers and horse racing for their enjoyment. There are no legal private bookmakers in New Zealand, but betting on horses is relatively easy. For this, government betting shops, known locally as the TAB (short for Totaliser Agency Board), are located in even the smallest towns. There is horse racing throughout the year and all daily papers carry a special racing section, so nobody should have to go to the races uninformed.

Travel New Zealand by road and one feature, generally glimpsed through mature trees, seems to recur on the outskirts of every city, township and village: a sudden expanse of green sward encircled by a mile or more of white railing, with a grandstand (of varying size and ostentation) lifting skywards.

In the neighbouring countryside, too, the sheep and cattle farms are likely to have given way to railed paddocks grazed by sleek horses. Stable blocks in the background look hardly less comfortable than the human habitations. If the impression is of a horse-mad, racing-oriented country, it is no illusion.

Tiny New Zealand boasts more horses and racecourses per capita than any other country in the world. New Zealand, with a population around 3.3 million, has 88 racing clubs using 59 racecourses. Trotting is now officially known as harness racing which has 65 clubs using 34 tracks. Racing has 93 clubs on 57 courses. The 1989/90 search racing had 349 meetings; harness racing 233; and 98 greyhound meetings.

Approximately, 6,600 thoroughbreds race each year on the courses which dot the countryside from Ruakaka (near Whangarei) in the north to Invercargill in the south. Each year some 2,300 go overseas, mainly to Australia but also to markets in the United States, South Africa, Britain and several Asian countries.

New Zealand's thoroughbred population, climbing steadily, produced a crop of nearly 7,000 live foals in the spring of 1989, placing New Zealand fourth in the breeding world behind the United States, Japan and Australia and ahead of such traditional breeding grounds as England, Ireland and France. Added to that total, already extraordinary enough on a per capita basis are some 5,000 standard-bred foals from 8,000 mares served.

New Zealand with its temperate climate, large tracts of limestone country and plentiful pasture, has proved an ideal thoroughbred nursery since the earliest days of European settlement. Australia had some 30 years head-start on New Zealand in thoroughbred breeding and was the source of most early thoroughbred imports to this country. But Henry Redwood, dubbed "Father of the New Zealand Turf," made the first raid on the Australian

Left, eyeing on the best bet at the New Plymouth Racetrack.

racing scene in 1858, only 18 years after the first thoroughbred arrived in New Zealand. Mr Redwood's team of three – Zingara, Zoe and Chevalier – covered themselves in glory. It was a sign of things to come, in generations then long unborn.

Over the next 125 years, New Zealand gallopers would prove time and again that, in staying (long-distance) events in particular, they were generally superior to their trans-Tasman cousins. Kiwi, the 1983 Melbourne Cup winner with a sensational last-to-first burst, was only one of a long line of New Zealand-bred gallopers to win Australia's glamour staying race. And it is significant that the three racehorses Australians would name as indisputable champions of their era – Carbine, Phar Lap and Tulloch – were all New Zealand-bred.

The selection and replenishing of breeding stock from the long-established European nurseries hardly accounted for the disproportionate dominance New Zealand thoroughbreds assumed in southern-hemisphere racing. In wealthier Australia, breeders had always had access to more fashionable bloodlines and better racing performance, just as their clubs had always put on stake money which dwarfed the purses available for feature races in New Zealand. By comparison, New Zealand breeders traditionally shopped bargain-basement when looking for stallions from Europe or, in later years, the United States.

Probably the key to New Zealand's success lay in its climatic advantages, its ideal conditions for rearing young horses with strong bones, sound legs and good constitutions. Carbine and Phar Lap, those two great New Zealand-breds, carried the fame of their homeland beyond the southern hemisphere.

Carbine, foaled at Sylvia Park, Auckland in 1884, won 33 of his 43 starts in New Zealand and Australia. The only time he was unplaced was when he split a hoof and had to be pulled up. His record-breaking run to win the 1890 Melbourne Cup under 66 kg (more than 10 stone) must still rank as one of the world's great handicap performances.

Carbine went to stud in Australia and his impact was so great that he was bought for stud duties in England. There he founded a triple Derby-winning dynasty; his son Spearmint, grandson Spion Kop and great-grandson Felsted all won the English Derby in then record times. Through that male dynasty the blood of New Zealand-bred Carbine is stamped in the pedigrees of top thoroughbreds worldwide.

Phar Lap, such a legend in his time that a film of his life packed "Down Under" theatres 50 years later, was bought cheaply as a yearling in New Zealand. He proved virtually invincible in Australia, where his wins included the 1930 Melbourne Cup, but died tragically after winning the Agua Caliente Handicap in Mexico.

In the 1960s, horses like Cadiz and Daryl's Joy began to bring New Zealand-bred horses into prominence in the United States. But it was not until the mid-1970s, when Balmerino undertook a remarkable world odyssey, that the English realised New Zealand's best

If Balmerino was the first thoroughbred since Phar Lap to show conclusively that little New Zealand could produce racehorses of world class, New Zealand's standardbreds had been doing just that for several decades. Galloping greats of the 1980s include Bonecrusher and McGinty and the New Zealand-bred Beau Zam raced in Australia.

The trotter Vodka, taken to the USA as a nine-year-old in 1956 by veteran racing man Jack Shaw, won nine races there despite his age and became the first "Down Under" standardbred to win on American soil. Fine trotters Ordeal, Durban Chief and Annual Report followed Vodka, with comparable success. Caduceus, "the Mighty Atom," paved the way for New Zealand pacers; though a 10-year-old

horses could measure up to theirs. Globetrotting Balmerino had already proved himself the best galloper in New Zealand and Australia when, in 1977, he made an attempt on the most prestigious horse race in France, the *Prix de l'Arc de Triomphe*. On the way he won in the United States and England (the Valdoe Stakes at Goodwood) and he was a gallant second in the Arc behind fine English three-year-old Alleged. For good measure he then journeyed to Italy and finished first (subsequently relegated to second) in a valuable race there. Between April and October that year, Balmerino had raced and won in New Zealand, Australia, the United States, England and Italy and almost won the most important race in France!

when he left for America, he won seven races there. Caduceus was followed by other top New Zealand pacers during the 1960s like False Step, Arania, Robin Dundee and Orbiter, who all performed with distinction in America. Young Quinn also scorched a great reputation in the United States during the 1970s. The fastest New Zealand horses racing in the United States in the 1980s included Ashley Knight and Remarkable.

However, all were overshadowed by Cardigan Bay, already proven a champion several times over in his homeland and Australia when he was taken to the United States as an eight-year-old in 1964. He beat the best the Americans could throw at him and in 1968 became the first horse in harness racing history to win $1 million in prize money.

Racing and trotting clubs in New Zealand have developed on strictly non-proprietary lines. Bookmakers were barred from courses in 1910 and outlawed by Parliament in 1924. All betting on the course is through the totalisator; off-course betting (except for the illegal bookmakers, who still flourish) is through the Totalisator Agency Board, which has offices in every township and city suburb.

New Zealand was a pioneer in the introduction of mechanically operated starting gates for gallopers and was early in the fields of photo-finishes, race-filming (to aid the control of interference and rough or foul riding) and drug detection. Its major race-courses and

from smaller course-betting-only clubs which also use the course. The major meetings are the Auckland Cup carnival, held during the Christmas-New Year holiday period, and the Great Northern meeting at the beginning of June. This winter carnival features the Great Northern Steeplechase, one of the toughest tests of stamina anywhere, encompassing 6,400 metres, 25 fences and three climbs of Ellerslie's famous hill.

Moving south through the North Island, the major racing tracks are Te Rapa (just outside Hamilton), Awapuni (Palmerston North) and Trentham (Wellington). The Wellington Racing Club holds 17 meetings at Trentham, the feature carnival being the Wellington Cup meeting in the second half of January.

their amenities are, like the racehorses it produces, of world standard.

Following the population and money, the heart of racing has been in Auckland since early in the 20th century. Auckland boasts of two galloping courses, at Ellerslie (the show case of New Zealand racing) and Avondale. The trotting track is Alexandra Park, home to three full-scale trotting clubs which together hold nearly 40 floodlit night meetings.

Racing is held at Ellerslie on 27 days, apart

Left and above, New Zealand thoroughbreds display world-class form in racing and trotting (harness racing).

The South Island may have long since lost its early dominance in racing but the Canterbury Jockey Club still holds two major carnivals at Riccarton, in Christchurch. These are the Grand National meeting in the first week of August and the New Zealand Cup carnival in November. This carnival spans a fortnight of galloping and harness racing, with a celebration of all things equine during that time. It remains the major carnival on the national racing calendar.

Canterbury remains a stronghold of trotting, too, and the New Zealand Trotting Cup carnival at Addington, which coincides with the Christchurch galloping meeting in November, is the highlight of the year's trotting calendar.

A visitor isn't in New Zealand for long before he is told that there are more sheep in the country than people. It is right. There are millions more. At the last count there were over 60 million. Compare that with a population of just over 3.3 million and you'll have learned something about the way New Zealand's agriculture developed and prospered.

Since the refrigerated vessel, the *Dunedin*, sailed for Britain in 1882 loaded with 4,908 frozen sheep carcasses, meat exports have been New Zealand's economic mainstay. For years before that, many fortunes had been made from wool.

Through shaky times since then, meat and wool have been the country's prime international marketing commodities. Sheep farms are spread throughout the country: in the North Island in the Waikato, Poverty Bay, Hawke's Bay and Manawatu; and in the South Island in Marlborough, Canterbury and Southland. They are the best areas – with help from the tonnes of fertilisers farmers apply.

Sheepfarming is essentially a simple business. It's all about converting grass into meat and wool, via a docile and easily managed animal. But the quest for efficiency and profitability has made it a sophisticated game. Breeds have been developed for a variety of features to suit climate, topography and markets. The killing and processing industries are giant concerns, adapting technologies and developing new cuts and products to remain profitable.

Sheep flocks of 2,000 are common; New Zealand's sheepfarmers are shepherds on a grand scale. In recent years, many have started to gear themselves up with microcomputers to help them manage their enterprises more productively.

Gentlemen's Business

Large-scale wool growing got off the ground in the 1850s. It was in the hands of gentlemen from Victorian England who became the closest thing to the country's instant aristocracy. They moved in, claimed their massive chunks of land, cleared them, and set the sheep out to grow wool. The first centre was in the Wairarapa, a fertile valley in some gentle hill country in the south of the North Island. Land could be bought or leased for peppercorn prices, and wool prices, errant though they were with booms and busts, could amass tidy family fortunes.

Sheepfarming soon spread, to Marlborough and south to the plains and hills of Canterbury. The "runs," as they were called, were vast, covering many thousands of acres. The most famous runholder of them all was Samuel Butler, author of *Erewhon*. In 1860 the famed author came to New Zealand and took up a run called Mesopotamia in the foothills of Canterbury's Southern Alps.

Rough and ready Australians got in on the South Island's sheep boom. The sheep themselves had come via Australia. They were Merinos, a tough breed with fine wool and stringy meat, and perfectly suited for grazing the rocky, tussock-covered slopes of high country runs. To help them out, runholders regularly set fire to the hillsides, encouraging new growths of edible young tussocks. The practice added to New Zealand's high erosion problems.

The coming of the frozen meat export industry changed everything. It also solved a massive problem. On one side of the world, New Zealand sheep were producing abundant wool but their meat was next to worthless. There was practically no way the meat could be shipped to the other side of the world in whole, edible form.

Meanwhile, on the other side of the world, England was busying itself with the Industrial Revolution. More and more people were living in cities, and England didn't have the land to support them. Refrigerated shipping was an idea whose time had come.

New breeds of sheep with better meat than the Merino were imported and developed. The classic breed was the Romney – solid, hardy and a great producer of fat lambs. By the 1920s it outnumbered all other breeds in New Zealand combined. Its wool was strong and coarse, totally different from the fine Merino's. So an innovation that had been introduced for its meat changed the face of New Zealand's wool production. Strong, resilient wool suitable for carpets became the country's major export.

Locally produced breeds have brought more adaptations. Sheep have been selected for their wool type, their meat (for markets that now demand lean lambs) and for their "lambing percentage" – the number of lambs a flock can be relied upon to produce.

Hard Times

New Zealand relies so heavily on its sheep for export dollars that disease is guarded against with near-neurotic urgency. Visitors are sprayed on arrival with aerosols before they leave their aircraft since a disease which threatened the country's sheep flock could debilitate its exports. Quarantine regulations are among the strictest in the world.

Even the best quarantine can't keep international developments out of the country. And two of them hit the sheep industry harder than anything else in its 100-year history: Britain's entry into the European Economic Community and the trend away from red meats in some Western markets. Both hit New Zealand in the

early 1970s. And though the writing had been on the wall for a long time before, the industry has had a hard time coming to grips with them.

Britain, in a traditional agreement between the "Home Country" and its erstwhile colony, had always been the prime market for New Zealand's lamb and mutton. When it threw in its lot with the European community the old tie was broken. Access to the market became limited and trade became subject to much

Preceding pages, sea of sheep: the flock on Mount Possession in the Ashburton Gorge totals nearly 11,000. **Above,** the man shears 300-350 sheep a day.

tougher regulations. Politically that was a much tougher nut to crack than the feat of shipping frozen mutton across the world in a creaky vessel had been a century before. New Zealand had to find new markets for its meat. It has, in Japan, Canada, the United States, Russia and Iran, found others. New markets have meant new marketing skills, and some tradition-bound meat exporting companies have been accused of failing to adapt.

The Middle East demands lambs slaughtered according to Muslim religious practices, so most meat plants have set up *halal* killing chains which face towards Mecca. Muslim slaughtermen recite a prayer over each lamb before the ritual killing. The companies' attitude is: "if it gets a sale, we'll do it."

Economists call it a downturn in the world red-meat trade. Poultry, pork and fast foods are what the world wants. The traditional roast of lamb is less attractive in these cholesterol and cost-conscious days.

More aggressive marketing of New Zealand's meat has also tried to counter the trend since the mid-1970s. The development of the chilled meat trade is also showing considerable promise, getting meat into supermarkets in prime condition. The industry has also tried to give the consumer what he wants: oriental style slices for Japan, kebabs for Greece, or tidy boneless packaged cuts for North American supermarkets.

Diversification is a continual process. Food fashions are always changing and farmers must meet these, while attempting to keep their activities profitable. World demand has been strong, commodity prices have been high, but the benefits have not been enjoyed by all New Zealand farmers. Some have been faced with devastating droughts and since the Labour Government began restructuring the rural sector in 1984, many have faced a debt crisis. All subsidies were swiftly removed, land values fell, and returns dropped. There is now a cautious return of optimism, however, with the healthy demand for agricultural products – particularly in the dairy, wool and meat industries.

New Zealand's farmers, with generations of free-enterprise individualism behind them, have taken the subsidies begrudgingly. Many have decided that turning grass into meat and wool just isn't worthwhile anymore. Those with the right land have turned to horticultural saviours such as kiwifruit, berries and even grapes.

Other farmers are holding on, believing that they can "farm their way out of the bad times."

Antarctica is the coldest, windiest and most remote continent on Planet Earth, an environment utterly inimical to people. It has teased our curiosity for centuries and its short history is peopled by heroes. It was the last challenge explorers overcame before they turned their attention to the stars.

Those who have been there report awesome encounters with the raw forces of the weather, but also times of ineffable, luminous peace and beauty. Technological advances have made Antarctic visits for tourists possible in recent years and many have gone there in the summer

step off his column into a boat ...."

But amazingly there are oases in Antarctica – the "dry valleys" – opposite Ross Island near McMurdo Sound, as well as other ice-free areas, and some "hot-lakes" beneath the ice-cap. These oases are under intense study by scientists.

In Search of a Continent

The exploration of Antarctica has close associations with New Zealand. The existence of a great southern continent had been mooted

months, but now and then the southern continent extracts its revenge for the invasion of its privacy. Antarctic scenic flights, a growing business in the 1970s, came to an abrupt end with the Erebus aviation disaster there in 1979.

Antarctica is the last great wilderness, with close to 90 percent of the world's ice sprawling over an area larger than the United States, and packed up to an average height of 2,000 metres (6,550 feet). If the ice melted the continent would be about three-quarters of its present size and much less mountainous than now. In addition, the rest of the world would have a problem – sea level would rise high enough to cover all the ocean's low-lying littorals. As one writer has put it: "Nelson would be able to

for hundreds of years before the Dutch explorer, Abel Janszoon Tasman, was sent from Java in the Dutch East Indies to find if there was a sea passage eastwards across the southern ocean to South America. When Tasman arrived off the west coast of New Zealand in 1643 (the first European known to sight New Zealand) he believed it might be the western edge of a continent that stretched across to South America. Accordingly he called it Staten Landt, the name then for South America. A year later, when it was decided there was no huge nation across the South Pacific, the name was changed to Zeelandia Nova, and later, of course, New Zealand.

The next European visitor to New Zealand,

Captain James Cook, also showed an interest in a possible southern land mass. In one of the most calculatedly daring voyages ever made, Cook sailed along the 60 degrees latitude and then penetrated as far as 71 degrees 10 minutes south without sighting the legendary continent. Cook was adulated by his men but he stayed south so long his crew was on the verge of mutiny by the time he headed north again. That first known sighting came 50 years later when the Russian navigator von Bellinghausen sailed completely round the world between 60 and 65 degrees south, dipping to 69 degrees on two occasions thus becoming the first man to see land inside the Antarctic Circle.

James Clark Ross in 1840 discovered that

for mounting its own expeditions, New Zealanders took part in the explorations by Englishmen Robert Falcon Scott and Ernest Shackleton between 1900 and 1917, and Australian Sir Douglas Mawson during the years before World War I. Scott and all the men in his party which drove overland for the South Pole, died on their return journey having learnt on their arrival at the Pole that the Norwegians under Amundsden had beaten them to it.

In 1923, the territory south of latitude 60 degrees south and between longitudes 160 degrees east and 150 degrees west was claimed by the British Government and placed under the administration of the Governor-General of New Zealand as the "Ross-Dependency."

Between 1929 and 1931 a British-Austra-

area of Antarctica south of New Zealand which has been within the country's sphere of interest throughout this century. In fact, it is believed that the first person to step ashore on Antarctica was New Zealander Alexander von Tunzelmann, the 17-year-old nephew of a pioneer settler and explorer of Central Otago, at Cape Adare, in January 1895. Exploration on the land began soon afterwards and although New Zealand showed no enthusiasm

Preceding pages, another time, another place – Antarctica the southern continent. Left, Scott's expedition began from the *Discovery*. Above, unchanging polar transport.

lian-New Zealand Antarctic-Research Expedition focused interest on the continent as did the exploration from the air about the same time by the United States Navy Admiral Byrd. In 1933 the New Zealand Antarctic Society was formed but it was not for another 15 years that the first New Zealand onshore base was established, near Cape Adare.

The New Zealand base was first established during the International Geophysical Year in 1957 when Everest conqueror Sir Edmund Hillary led a group of five fellow countrymen on an overland dash by tractor to the South Pole. He was to have acted solely as a support for Britain's transpolar expedition led by Sir Vyvian Fuchs, laying down supply bases on the New Zealand side of Antarctica for Fuchs to use as he made the journey from the Pole across to the side below New Zealand. Hillary and his small group made such excellent progress and got so far ahead of schedule they decided to push for the Pole themselves, becoming the first to make it overland since Scott 45 years before.

Since 1958, parties from New Zealand have wintered over, exploring and trapping huge areas, intensively researching the geology of the region and generally carrying out work assigned by the Antarctic Division of the Department of Scientific and Industrial Research. New Zealand has always operated in close association in the Antarctic with the United States Navy which has its own base at

McMurdo Sound. In 1964, when a fire destroyed most of the equipment at the combined NZ-US base at Cape Hallett, New Zealand erected a new base of her own (named Scott Base after Captain Scott), at McMurdo Sound close to a new American base.

Care of Resources

Five years earlier, the Antarctic Treaty designed to "ensure the use of Antarctica for peaceful purposes only and the continuance of international harmony" had been signed by 12 nations – New Zealand, the United States, Australia, Britain, Belgium, Chile, France, Japan, Norway, South Africa, Russia and

Argentina. Poland also became a signatory in 1977. All these Antarctic Treaty signatories have signed a convention since 1980 for the protection and proper exploitation of Antarctic marine living resources. This culminated in a Convention on the Regulation of Antarctic Mineral Resource Activities (CRAMRA) in Wellington in 1988. But the final fate of this Convention was placed in doubt the following year when France and Australia – both claimant nations to Antarctica – announced they would not ratify it. They want the area to become a wilderness park instead.

The economic exploitation of Antarctica began with the hunting of whales and seals in the sub-Antarctic islands and surrounding seas south of the Pacific Ocean at the close of the 18th century. The stocks were so depleted that there is little prospect of them ever recovering sufficiently to make them an economic proposition again. However, a number of Russian and Japanese scientists are investigating the krill which are plentiful in the Antarctic waters and could well become a major protein resource in the future.

There has been much discussion also about mineral resources on the Antarctic mainland and it is thought probable that mineral bearing rocks of the sort prevalent in Australia and South Africa are common throughout the southern continent. It is known that there are huge deposits of sub-bituminous coal and large deposits of low-grade iron ore. CRAMRA was an attempt to impose the strictest rules on any possible exploitation activities. This response has now combined with growing environmental awareness to put pressure on the Treaty partners to consider some total protection regime.

Tourism interest continues with some ocean cruise companies making summer visits to the Antarctic Circle, mostly on the South American side of the continent. It is possible that as the horror of the Erebus aviation disaster recedes, there will be a renewal of interest in sightseeing flights from New Zealand, especially if satisfactory air traffic control services are made available on the Antarctic land mass, and possibly even adequate facilities for landing at McMurdo Sound. However, tougher protection of this special place may have to include stringent controls on tourism, which is regarded as one of its biggest threats.

TRAVEL TIPS

GETTING THERE

BY AIR

New Zealand—as an island nation and one of the most isolated countries in the world—is now almost entirely dependent on air travel. Of the 763,000 tourists who visit each year, more than 99 per cent arrive on services provided by 12 international airlines. The remaining few arrive by cruise ships which occasionally call at Auckland or Wellington.

The main gateway is the Auckland International Airport at Mangere, 15 miles south of the city's downtown area, bus and taxi transfers are available.

There is a fine international airport at Harewood, quite close to Christchurch, the main South Island city, and Air New Zealand and Qantas use this as a gateway mainly for visitors coming from Australia.

The airport at Wellington, the capital city, has a restricted access for most wide-bodied aircraft types because of runway length.

The carriers link Auckland with direct flights to the Pacific Islands, the major Australian cities, and through Southeast Asia and North America to Europe. Again because of the isolation, flights linking New Zealand with countries other than Australia and the Pacific Islands tend to be long-haul and passengers arriving are advised to provide themselves with time to rest during the first day or two of their stay.

BY SEA

Most of the shipping lines which operate cruises in the South Pacific originate their services from Sydney and fly passengers to and from New Zealand, but P & O Line, Sitmar, Royal Viking Line, Blue Funnel Line and the Russian national line make calls at Auckland on occasions during the year. Some cargo vessels take small groups of passengers. But there are now no regular passenger services linking New Zealand with other countries on a scheduled basis.

TRAVEL ESSENTIALS

VISAS & PASSPORTS

Immigration regulations stipulate that tourists arriving in New Zealand should be in possession of valid entry documentation; should hold fully paid onward travel tickets and have sufficient funds to maintain themselves during their stay; and should be in good health.

Provided they do not intend to take jobs of any sort for payment, citizens of the following countries will be granted entry permits for *up to six months* without previously obtaining visas: the United Kingdom (and those Colonies whose passports enable their holders to enter the UK for permanent residence), the Republic of Ireland, Canada, Belgium, Denmark, Liechtenstein, Luxembourg, Monaco, the Netherlands, Norway, Sweden, Switzerland; and those citizens of France normally resident in Metropolitan France.

Entry permits without visas for stays up to three months will be granted to citizens of the Federal Republic of Germany, Finland, Iceland and also Malta.

The same conditions apply to the citizens of the following countries for stays of *up to 30 days*: The United States (excluding American Samoa), Japan and residents of French Tahiti and French New Caledonia.

Citizens of all other countries require visas issued in advance of arrival in New Zealand.

Special conditions apply to Australian citizens who may enter New Zealand for any length of stay without prior permission and without documentation. This applies also to citizens of other British Commonwealth countries and the Republic of Ireland who have been granted permanent residency in Australia—but only when they travel to New Zealand direct from Australia.

No entry authority is required for anyone "in transit"—that is, anyone booked to leave the country on the ship or aircraft by which he or she arrived; or who is booked onward using the first available transportation for the next destination, provided the stay here is not more than 48 hours.

MONEY MATTERS

There is no restriction on the amount of domestic or foreign currency (or traveller's cheques expressed in New Zealand currency) a visitor may bring into New Zealand.

A visitor may also take out without limitation any unused funds from those he brought in. Currency conversion facilities are available at Auckland International Airport.

The New Zealand dollar, divided into 100 cents, is the unit of currency. The country adopted decimal currency in 1967 after having previously followed the British system of pounds, shillings and pence. The value of the New Zealand dollar in relation to Sterling and the American dollars varies from week to week.

HEALTH & OTHER RESTRICTIONS

All persons entering New Zealand are required to complete passenger declaration forms on arrival and departure.

Medical treatment is usually not available free to visitors so health insurance for incoming tourists is recommended.

The following classes of people are prohibited by law from entering regardless of their country of origin, either as tourists or settlers:

• Those suffering from tuberculosis, syphilis, leprosy or any mental disorders.

• Those convicted of an offence which drew a sentence of imprisonment for more than one year.

• Those who have previously been deported from New Zealand.

QUARANTINE

Because New Zealand relies heavily on agricultural and horticultural trade with the rest of the world, it has stringent regulations governing the import of animals, and the import of vegetable and animal matter. Visitors planning to bring in any material of this sort should make detailed inquiries at New Zealand Government offices overseas before proceeding.

GETTING ACQUAINTED

GOVERNMENT & ECONOMY

New Zealand is a centralised democracy with a Western-style economy. Parliament and the government bureaucracy are based in Wellington, the capital city. Society is generally relaxed and friendly.

TIME ZONES

There is one time zone throughout the country—12 hours in advance of Greenwich Mean Time (GMT).

From late October until the end the first week in March, time is advanced one hour to give extended daytime through the summer. (Time in the remote Chatham Islands is 45 minutes ahead of New Zealand Standard Time.) Travellers from the Western Hemisphere, moving west into New Zealand lose a full day crossing the International Dateline, and regain a full day returning eastwards from New Zealand. Because the country is so advanced in time, being close to the International Dateline, it is one of the very first nations in the world to welcome each day (preceded only by Fiji and some other small Pacific Islands).

New Zealand is 12 hours ahead of Greenwich Mean Time. During standard Time periods, when it is noon (Monday) in New Zealand it is:-

12 a.m. in London (Monday)
1 a.m. in Bonn, Madrid, Paris and Rome (Monday)
3 a.m. in Athens (Monday)
4 a.m. in Moscow (Monday)

5:30 a.m. in Bombay (Monday)
7 a.m. in Bangkok (Monday)
8 a.m. in Singapore and Hong Kong (Monday)
9 a.m. in Tokyo (Monday)
10 a.m. in Sydney (Monday)
2 p.m. in Honolulu (Sunday)
4 p.m. in Los Angeles (Sunday)
7 p.m. in New York and Montreal (Sunday)
9 p.m. in Rio de Janeiro (Sunday)

CLIMATE

New Zealand has three main islands—the North Island, the South Island and Stewart Island—running roughly from north to south over 1,600 kilometres, between 34 and 47 degrees south.

The climate is generally temperate with rainfall spread fairly evenly through the year. The summer season from December through March is the most settled and the best for holidaying. New Zealanders traditionally take their main family holiday break at Christmas and through January; so visitors are advised to make sure of advance bookings for accommodation and domestic transport over this period because of the pressure on facilities.

Winds can be strong at any time of the year, especially round Cook Strait. But summer days are generally warm and pleasant in most regions.

Winters can be cold in the central and southern North Island and coastal districts of the South Island, and winter conditions can be severe in central regions of the South Island.

WHAT TO BRING/WHAT TO WEAR

For summer visits, you are advised to bring sweaters or wind-breakers for the cooler evenings or brisk days, specially for those regions south of the top half of the North Island.

Medium thick clothing with a raincoat or umbrella is adequate for most regions most of the year, but in midwinter in the tourist areas of Rotorua-Taupo and Queenstown, winter clothing and shoes are essential.

New Zealand is noted for the brilliance of its light. This can lead to sever sunburn on days when temperatures may be deceptively low. You should remember to bring along sunscreen lotions.

TIPPING

Tipping is not the norm in New Zealand. In some restaurants and hotels tipping is appreciated for courteous and efficient service. Tipping has become more prevalent in "tourist" areas but is still not considered obligatory.

BUSINESS HOURS

Shops open for business from 9 a.m. and shut most nights at 5:30 p.m. There is at least one late night a week in each town and in the major cities such as Auckland, various areas have the late night at different times of the week. Many shops now open on Saturday mornings, and in areas serving tourists, business hours are generally longer. Trading banks are open 9:30 a.m. to 4:30 p.m.

EMERGENCIES

In an emergency dial 111 for ambulance, police or fire. Call boxes take one 20 cent coin for local calls of any length.

PUBLIC HOLIDAYS

National public holidays are:
New Year's Day, January 1
Waitangi Day, February 6
Good Friday/Easter Monday
Anzac Day, April 25
Queen's Birthday, "Monday-ised" during the first week in June
Labour Day, "Monday-ised" during the last week in October
Christmas Day, December 25th
Boxing Day, December 26th.

In addition, each provincial region has a holiday to celebrate the provincial anniversary. The dates are:
Wellington—January 22
Northland and Auckland—January 29
Nelson—February 1
Otago and Southland—March 23
Taranaki—March 31
Hawke's Bay—October 20
Marlborough—November 1
Canterbury—December 1
Westland—December 1
If the day falls on a Saturday or Sunday then the following Monday is taken.

COMMUNICATIONS

MEDIA

There is a high level of literacy in New Zealand. Most communities have a library, and sales of books, magazines and newspapers on a per capita basis are unparalleled anywhere in the world. *The New Zealand Herald*, the Auckland morning daily, sells better than one copy for every four people in Greater Auckland, a figure that is regarded as well past saturation for any other city in the world. Almost every large town has its newspaper and community newspapers abound in towns, provincial cities and in the suburbs of major cities.

The high level of book sales has seen all the major British publishing houses set up distribution organisations in New Zealand. Several companies publish local work. The industry is supported by fine bookshops and excellent libraries.

The two national television networks are both owned by the Government though administered by a nominally independent state corporation. There are plans for a third network to be licensed.

GETTING AROUND

DOMESTIC TRAVEL

By Air: Air New Zealand is the primary domestic carrier. It uses Boeing 737 jets and F27 Friendship turbo-prop aircraft on a wide ranging network. Mount Cook Airlines operate mainly from cities to resort areas, using mainly Hawker Siddley 748 turbo-prop aircraft. Ansett New Zealand fly between the main cities and to resort areas, mostly using Boeing 737 jets and Dash 8s. Other airlines also operate between provincial centres.

By Sea: Several passenger and vehicular ferries daily link the North and South Islands each way, between Wellington and Pidon. It is a three-hour journey between the two islands.

By Rail: New Zealand Railways and several private companies operate modern coach services throughout the country on main routes. Comfortable passenger train services are also available on the main trunk lines between Auckland and Wellington in the North Island and between Christchurch and Invercargill in the South Island. The most popular services for tourists are the Silver Fern service in the North Island (both ways each day), and the Southerner express train in the South Island (both ways each day). Meals and refreshments are available on each, and a commentary is given on the Silver Fern. The scenery on both services is magnificent.

Commuter and/or train services are available in each of the four main centres, but in Wellington, the train service to northern suburbs and satellite cities reach reasonable levels of regularity and efficiency.

By Road: All towns and cities have 24-hour taxicab services.

Modern motor coaches operate on scheduled services throughout the country. It is wise to reserve seats in advance, especially during the summer months.

PRIVATE TRANSPORT

Chauffeur-driven services are readily available as are hire cars over a wide range of vehicle types. Driving is on the left-hand side of the road. Main road surfaces are good and conditions are usually comfortable, the main problem being wet road surfaces after heavy showers. Roads are well signposted by the Automobile Association.

Hirers of cars must be 21 years old, must hold a current New Zealand or International driver's licence, or one issued in any of the 1949 convention countries (128 members) or the German Federal Republic or Switzerland. Third party insurance is compulsory.

There are excellent camping grounds in all towns and cities throughout the country and caravans and trailers may be hired. Many camping grounds have excellent cabins as well as camping sites (see under accommodation). Petrol is expensive (around NZ71 cents a litre). Compressed natural gas and liquid petroleum gas are cheaper and many vehicles are now fitted for these alternative fuels.

A comprehensive range of services for motorists is available from the Automobile Association, and reciprocal membership arrangements may be available for those holding membership of foreign motoring organisations.

WHERE TO STAY

HOTELS & MOTELS

Hotels of an international standard are available in the major cities, in most provincial cities, and in all the resort areas frequented by international tourists. In smaller cities and towns, more modest accommodation in hotels is often relaxed and enjoyable for visitors on holiday.

Small motels have proliferated throughout the country and are almost always clean and comfortable with facilities ideal for family holidays. Almost every small town has a camping ground, with well-serviced camping lots and (usually) with cabins.

There is no national system of grading hotels and motels and standards do vary, but the location of the accommodation and the tariff will give a reliable indication. Travel agents are good sources of information on this subject and will be able to give details of concessions generally available for children. (A guide is: children under two years of age, free; two to four, quarter of tariff; five to nine, half tariff; ten years and over, full tariff.)

Some popular hotels and motels in the four main cities and in some of the many popular resort areas are as listed below, complete with telephone numbers and addresses. New Zealand now has a goods and services tax (GST) of 12½ percent tax added to many goods and services.

All prices in this list do not include GST unless otherwise indicated.

AUCKLAND

Airport Lodge Motel, 294 Kirbride Road, Mangere; tel: 275-8192; 12 flats (max. occ. 4), $72, $10 per extra person. Situated close to airport, courtesy phone and coach. 18 km from city.

THC Auckland Airport Hotel, corner of Ascot and Kirkbride Roads, Mangere; tel: 275-7029; 160 rooms, including 6 paraplegic rooms, 5 executive rooms (max. occ. 4), single or twin $149, $15 per extra. Gymnasium, sauna, outdoor swimming pool; 1.5 km from airport, 17 km from city.

Auckland Airport Travel Lodge, corner of Ascot and Kirkbride Roads, Mangere; tel: 275-1059; 248 rooms and suites; single or twin $165, additionals $15 per adult, $2 per extra child; suites range from $175-$435. Gymnasium, spa, sauna, pool, children's play area. 5 km from airport—courtesy coach. 17 km from city.

Best Western Barrycourt Motel, 10-20 Gladstone Road, Parnell; tel: 303-3789; motel—single or twin $90, additionals $15 per adult, $10 per child; motor inn—single or twin $92, double bed $104. Licensed restaurant, bar, spa.

Garden Inn, 10 Tidal Road; tel: 275-0194; 62 rooms; single $70, double $76. Pool, restaurant, bar. Near airport.

Gold Star Motor Lodge, 255 Kirkbride Road, Mangere; tel: 275-8199; 20 units, single $81, double or twin $85 (inclusive of GST), additionals $10. Pool, spa. Shuttle to airport and nearby restaurants.

Hyatt Kingsgate Auckland, corner of Waterloo Quadrant and Princes Street; tel: 366-1234; 275 rooms, single/twin/double

It may look relaxed, but will you be able to stand the excitement?

For the world-weary traveller, one adventure remains.

Huka Lodge. At the very heart of the North Island's central high country.

Only minutes north of Lake Taupo, the Lodge stands on the banks of the Waikato River. Although part of angling folklore, a renaissance has recently taken place and a new chapter in its history is being written.

A series of beautiful, utterly private guest lodges have just been built.

Each has been carefully placed in native bush only casting distance from the river bank.

Without losing touch with all that has gone before, the Lodge is fast becoming known as the best of its kind in the world.

We have been honoured with a prestigious Relais & Chateaux listing. Worldwide, less than 350 hotels and restaurants are entitled to use their Fleur de Lis.

Once our guest, you may wish to venture forth with a guide to flyfish Taupo's famous rainbow trout streams.

A launch trip to the lake's beautiful and remote Western Bay can be arranged.

For the more adventurous, a helicopter will lift you into nearby mountains to stalk deer in beech and tussock or trophy trout in tumbling rivers.

Skiing? An hour away are some of the longest and most open slopes in the southern hemisphere.

Golf: Play on any one of five courses on a par with the best in the world.

Play tennis on our own Astrograss court.

In the evening, drinks are poured during the hour prior to dinner.

The chef, who begins his preparation at 11.00AM, will carefully explain his menu. Most of the six courses will feature local fish and game: Feral venison, wild boar or fresh trout.

Dessert, he will tell you, will be light on the palate and may favour fresh fruits. The Lodge's wine list is truly eclectic. International wines have been bought in their place of origin and our New Zealand list is one of the best in the country.

When the last liqueur has been poured, you will return to your lodge to sink into beds that can only be described as wickedly comfortable.

Next morning, after you've awoken to the toll of bellbirds, breakfast will be another delight. Venison sausages, home-cured bacon, free-range eggs, wholemeal toast and oranges freshly juiced in front of you.

When the time comes to leave the Lodge, you will be invited to make an entry in the Visitors' Book.

Leaf through its pages and you will find names of the rich and famous.

Who, just like you, found the excitement of Huka Lodge quite unbearable.

So much so, that many of the names appear twice.

HUKA LODGE

On the Huka Falls Road, Taupo, New Zealand, Telephone (074) 85-791. Telex 63229 'HUKA'. Fax (074) 80-427. Relais & Châteaux.

THE PROBLEMS OF A

HEAVY TRAFFIC.

You'll come across massive Thai jumbos at work and play in their natural habitat. In Thailand, elephants are part of everyday rural life.

FALLING MASONRY.

A visit to the ruined cities of Sukhothai or Ayutthaya will remind you of the country's long and event-filled history.

EYESTRAIN.

A problem everyone seems to enjoy. The beauty of our exotic land is only matched by the beauty and gentle nature of the Thai people.

GETTING LOST.

From the palm-fringed beaches of Phuket to the highlands of Chiang Mai there are numerous places to get away from it all.

OLIDAY IN THAILAND.

GETTING TRAPPED.

In bunkers mostly. The fairways, superb club houses and helpful caddies make a golf trap for players of all standards.

HIGH DRAMA.

A performance of the 'Khon' drama, with gods and demons acting out a never-ending battle between good and evil, should not be missed.

EXCESS BAGGAGE.

Thai food is so delicious you'll want to eat more and more of it. Of course, on Thai there's no charge for extra kilos in this area.

MISSING YOUR FLIGHT.

In Thailand, this isn't a problem. Talk to us or your local travel agent about Royal Orchid Holidays in Thailand.

Thai
We reach for the sky.

New Zealand's mild climate means you can enjoy the warm hospitality of a farm stay all year round.

Adventurous types can join in farm activities and share the hosts' hobbies and sports. Or simply relax and experience a totally different lifestyle.

YOU'LL LOVE THE WAY OF LIFE IN NEW ZEALAND

"I could live here forever.
Beautiful scenery.
Fresh clean air.

Friendly people..."

"Ahh... this is the life."

YOUR TRIP TO NEW ZEALAND STARTS HERE
PLEASE RUSH ME A FREE COPY OF THE
1989 COLOURFUL NEW ZEALAND BOOK AND
NEW ZEALAND OUTDOOR ACTION HOLIDAYS

NAME

ADDRESS

SEX/AGE

OCCUPATION

1990
New Zealand's Year

New Zealand Tourism
OFFICE
Te Tari Tapoi O Aotearoa

P.O BOX 678, ORCHARD POINT POST OFFICE. SINGAPORE 9123

$210, additionals $33. Restaurants, night-club, bars, 1 km from city.

Mon Desir Hotel, 144 Hurstmere Road, Takapuna; tel: 495-139; 37 serviced units, single $115.50, twin $121; four suites $140-$165 (inclusive of GST). Restaurant, pool, sauna. 10 km from city. On Takapuna beach.

Park Royal Auckland, corner of Queen and Custom Streets; tel: 778-920; 188 rooms; single/double/twin $225; studio suite $295, luxury suite $450. Licensed restaurants, bars. Mid-city.

Quality Inn, 150 Anzac Avenue; tel: 798-509; 110 rooms; single/double/twin $170, additionals $11; suites $225. Restaurant, bar, sauna, central location.

Rose Park Quality Inn, 100 Gladstone Road, Parnell; tel: 773-619; 116 rooms (max. occ. 4); single/double $165, additionals $12. Four 2-bedroom villas (max. occ. 6), $330. 2 km from city.

Sheraton Auckland, 83 Symonds Street; tel: 795-132; 407 rooms; single/double/twin $220-$290. Towers $385 includes breakfast, butler, cocktails. Suites $605. Gymnasium, indoor swimming pool, spa, restaurants, bars. Downtown.

Travelodge, 96-100 Quay Street; tel: 770 349; 189 rooms; single/double/twin $190, additionals $15, suites $350. Restaurants, bar. Mid-city.

Windsor Park Hotel, 550 East Coast Bay Road, Mairangi Bay; tel: 478-5126; single or double $75, twin $88, triple $109 (max. occ. 3). 14 km from city.

GENERAL

Freeman's Travellers' Hotel (bed and breakfast), 65 Wellington Street, Freeman's Bay; tel: 765-046; triple $60, double/twin $50, single $35—includes breakfast and GST.

Georgia Hostel (for backpackers), 189 Park Road, corner of Carlton Gore Road, Grafton; tel: 399-560.

Ivanhoe Lodge (private youth hostel), 14 Shirley Road, Grey Lynn; tel: 862-800.

North Shore Caravan Park (cabins and motels), 52 Northcote Road, Takapuna; tel: 419-1320.

Plumley House (for backpackers), 515 Remuera Road; tel: 520-4044; bunkroom $13, twin $15, single room $17.

CHRISTCHURCH

(All prices include 12.5 percent GST)

Airport Lodge Motel, 105 Roydvale Avenue, Burnside; tel: (03) 585-119; fax: (03) 583-654; 24 motel flats (max. occ. 6); single $63-72, double $76-84. Each additional adult $16; child under 12 yrs, $12.50. 8 km from city centre and 2.5 km from airport.

Airport Gateway Motor Lodge, 45 Roydvale Avenue, Burnside; tel: (03) 587-093; fax: (03) 583-654; 30 motel suites, (max. occ. 5); single $72-80, double $80-88. Each additional adult, $17; child under 12, $13.50. 1.5 km from airport; 8 km from city centre.

Ashleigh Court Motel, 47 Matai Street, West Riccarton; tel: (03) 481-888; fax: (03) 482-973; 10 motel flats (max. occ. 5) single/double $76. Each additional adult $15; child under 12 yrs $12. Situated 1 km from city centre.

Autolodge Motor Inn, 72 Papanui Road, St. Albans; tel: 556-109; fax: (03) 553-543; 74 rooms; $129.40 single or double, children free. Central location.

Belmont Luxury Motel, 168 Bealey Avenue, Christchurch; tel: 794-037; fax: (03) 669-194; 17 motel flats; single $77, double $80, additional adult $13. Continental breakfast available. Situated 1 km from city centre.

Christchurch Airport Travelodge, Memorial Avenue, Harewood; tel: 583-139; fax: (03) 583-029; 155 rooms; 2 family rooms, $132.75 single or double. Deluxe $157.50. 3 suites, single or double $303.75, child under 19 yrs if sharing with adult $2.25. Situated 10 km from city centre. Closest hotel to airport.

Commodore Motor Inn, 447 Memorial Avenue, Burnside; tel: (03) 588-129; fax: (03) 582-231; 105 rooms; $123.75 (standard); $140.63 (deluxe).

DB Redwood Court, 340 Main North Road, Redwood; tel: (03) 529-165; fax: (03) 522-559; 27 twins, 1 suite, from $54 to $74. Breakfast available. About 14 km from city centre.

George Hotel, 50 Park Terrace, opposite North Hagley Park; tel: (03) 794-560; fax: (03) 666-747; 53 serviced units (including 4 suites) $185.63 single, twin or triple. Walk-in and weekend rates available. Situated 1 km from city centre.

Latimer Motor Lodge, Latimer Square, Central City; tel: (03) 796-760; fax: (03) 660-133; 51 rooms; single $128.25, double $135. Each additional adult $11.25; children under 12 free.

Noahs Hotel, corner of Worcester Street and Oxford Terrace, Central City; tel: (03) 794-700; fax: (03) 795-357; 203 twin/double rooms; $175 standard; additional beds, $15; 5 suites available from $450 for 2 persons.

Pacific Park Hotel, 263 Bealey Avenue, Christchurch; tel: (03) 798-660; fax: (03) 669-973; 66 rooms, 10 serviced units (max. occ. 3); $100.13 (standard); $140.63 (suite).

Pavillions Motor Lodge, 42 Papanui Road, St. Albans; tel: (03) 555-633; fax: (03) 553-554; 70 rooms, from $90 to $163; children under 12 free. 1.5 km from city centre, 15 km to airport.

Quality Inn Chateau Hotel, 187-189 Deans Avenue, opposite Park; tel: 488-999; fax: (03) 488-990; 162 twin/double rooms; single $123; each additional adult $11.82. Situated 4 km from city centre.

Russley Hotel, Roydvale Avenue, Burnside; tel: (03) 588-2289; fax: (03) 583-953; 29 single $113, 18 twin, 7 double $124.

4 twin suites $146, children free. Situated 2 km from airport.

Vacation Inn, 776 Colombo Street (central city); tel: (02) 795-880; fax: (03) 654-806; 85 twin/double rooms, $112.50; five suites $196.95; children free. Weekend rates available.

DUNEDIN

Abby Lodge Motels, 900 Cumberland Street and 689 Castle Street; tel: 775-380; single $82, double $95, additional adult $20.50, additional child $16.60. Serviced units, single/double from $123. Waterbed suites $154. 1.5 km from city centre.

Adrian Motel, 101 Queens Drive; tel: 52-009; 17 units (max. occ. 6), double $70. Each additional adult $12. 4 km from city and near beach.

Cherry Court Lodge, 678 George Street; tel: 777-983; 50 units (max. occ. 4), double $90. Each additional adult $12, child $8.

Leisure Lodge, Duke Street; tel: 775-360; 76 units (max. occ. 3), single $90, double $102, each additional adult $12. One motel suite $165.

Pacific Park Motor Inn, 21-24 Wallace Street, Roslyn; tel: 773-374; motel flats—single $112.50, double $128, triple $145. Serviced units (max. occ. 3), $100 per unit. Situated close to Moana Pool.

Quality Inn, 10 Smith Street; tel: 776-784; $126 per room, corporate rate $101. City centre.

Shoreline Motor Hotel, 47 Timaru Street; tel: 55-195; 36 rooms (max. occ. 3), $70 per room. 3 km from city

Southern Cross Hotel, corner of High and Princes Streets; tel: 770-752; 71 twin/double rooms $124, 30 deluxe rooms $144, 7 suites $225. City centre.

Wains Hotel, 310-314 Princes Street; tel: 779-283; suites $85, double/twin rooms $75, singles $60, family rooms $96. City centre.

FOX GLACIER

Alpine View and Motor Park, Kerrs Road; tel: 821; 37 rooms (max. occ. 6); single/double $55.

Golden Glacier Motor Inn, tel: 847; 51 rooms (max. occ. 4); single/double $66.

FRANZ JOSEF GLACIER

Motel Franz Josef, Highway 6; tel: 742; 8 motel flats (max. occ. 6); single/double $60.50.

THC Franz Josef, tel: 719; 47 rooms (max. occ. 3); single/double $88.

HAMMER SPRINGS

Hanmer Resort Motel, 4 Chaltenham Street; tel: (0515) 7362; 16 motel flats (max. occ. 6); studios single/double $72, $12 for additional adult; 4 doubles $78, 2 persons suites $90-$95 with waterbed; $10 for child under 12.

Spa Motel, 4 Harrogate Street; tel: (0515) 7129; 30 motel flats; executive suites $90 single; standard units $30 single; $15 each additional person; $11 for child under 12 years.

MARLBOROUGH SOUNDS

The Portage Hotel, Kenepuru Road; tel: (057) 34-309; 38 rooms (max. occ. 4); single $80, double $89.

Punga Cove Holiday Resort, Endeavour Inlet, Queen Charlotte Sound; tel: (057) 34-561; 8 rooms (max. occ. 8), $18 per person.

Raetihi Lodge, Kenepuru Sound; tel: (057) 34-300; 18 rooms (max. occ. 2); single/double $70.

MOUNT COOK

THC Mount Cook—The Hermitage
809 Mt. Cook; tel: 05621; 104 rooms. Premium $208.15, suites $281.25

THC Mount Cook—Glencoe Lodge, 809 Mt. Cook; tel: 05621; 57 rooms; single

$157.50, double $168.75 (both rates include breakfast).

THC Mount Cook Chalets, 809 Mount Cook; tel: 05621; 20 self-contained chalets (max. occ. 4), single/double $84.40; each additional adult $16.90; child under 14 years free.

MOUNT HUTT

Mount Hutt Lodge, Zig Zag Road, Rakaia Gorge, Glenroy; tel: (0516) 66-898; 6 fully contained hotel units with kitchen, 4 doubles for 3 persons with spa bath, 4 twin rooms for 2 persons. Peak season rate (June to September) $100—2 persons, $10 for each additional adult; child under 5 free. 10 km from toll gate. Closest accommodation to the ski field.

Methven Aorangi Lodge, 38 Spaxton Street, Methven; tel: (053) 28-482; 9 double/twin rooms (max. occ. 2) $30 per person. Child under 12 yrs $15. Half hour drive to ski field car park.

Centrepoint Resort Hotel, Rakaia Gorge Road, Methven; tel: (053) 28–724 or (053) 28–725; 45 luxury suites (max. occ. 5). Peak season rate (June-September) $128-double/twin/triple. Off-peak season rate $112.50.

PAIHIA

Autolodge Motor Inn, Marsden Road; tel: 27 416; 76 rooms (max. occ. 3); single/double $105-$110.

Bayswater Inn, 40 Marsden Road; tel: 27-444; 7 rooms (max. occ. 6); single/double $66.

Aloha Motel, 32-36 Seaview Road; tel: 27-540; 15 rooms (max. occ. 9); single/double $50.

QUEENSTOWN

Ambassador Motor Lodge, Man Street; tel: (0294) 442-8593; 16 units, studio to family; $81-$146.25; each extra adult $13.50; children under 3 years free.

Blue Peaks Lodge, Stanley Street; tel: (0294) 442-9224, fax: (0293) 442-7544; 60 units, studio to family; $60.75-$94.50; each extra adult $11.25; children under 5 free.

Garden Court, Frankton Road; tel: (0294) 442-9713, fax: (0294) 442-6468; 11 units, 2 bedrooms; $90 double, $13.50 extra adult.

Holiday Inn, Sainsbury Road, Fernhill; tel: (0294) 442-6600, fax: (0294) 442-7354; 150 rooms, twin $112.50-$171; each extra adult $32.50; children up to 10 sharing with parents free (max. 2).

Lofts Villas, Shotover Street; tel: (0294) 442-391, fax: (0294) 7396; 24 apartments, studio to 3 bedrooms. $123.75-$247.50 up to 6 adults.

Nugget Point , Arthur's Point; tel: (0294) 442-7273; fax: (0294) 442-7308; 35 one- and two-bedroom apartments, $219.40 up to 4 persons.

Parkroyal, Beach Street; tel: (0294) 442-7800; fax: (0294) 442-8895; 139 rooms, doubles to suites, from $230.60; children under 15 sharing with parents free.

THC Hotel, Marine Parade; tel: (0294) 442-7750; fax: (0294) 442-7469; 150 rooms, $208.15; extra adult $16.90; children 15 yrs and under sharing with parents free (max. 2).

The Lodges, Lake Esplanade; tel: (0294) 442-7552; fax: (0294) 442-6401; 15 3-bedroom apartments; $147.50 for 2, $11.25 extra adult; children under 12 free.

ROTORUA

Best Western Thermal Gardens Motel, 88 Ranolf Street; tel: (073) 479-499; fax: (073) 794-498; 12 units, $55 single, $75 double; each additional adult $10. Breakfast available. Some units with private pools. 30-foot heated outdoor pool. Wheelchair access to some units. Close to city.

Cleveland Motel, 113 Lake Road; tel: (073) 482-041; fax: (073) 478-059; 30 units. Single from $60, double from $70. Special children's rates. Breakfast available. Private indoor mineral pools. Fresh water heated swimming pool.

Four Canoes Inn, 273 Fenton Street; tel: (073) 489-184; fax: (073) 486-184; hotel and motel facilities: single, hotel $67; 1 person, motel $45; double, hotel $78; double, motel $45; additional adults hotel $11, motel $9. First child under 12 free, second onward adult rate. Suite, double $160. Licensed restaurant. Heated outdoor pool. Private pools available. Situated opposite racecourse.

Geyserland Resort, Fenton Street, Whakarewarewa; tel: (073) 482-039; fax: (073) 482-033; superior rooms, double $126.50; single $115.50. Standard rooms, double $104.50, single $93.50; children under 12 free. Fully licensed. Conference facilities. Hangi and Maori concert available. Heated outdoor pool and spa. Overlooks thermal reserve.

Grand Establishment, Hinemoa Street; tel: (073) 482-089; fax: (073) 463-219; 5 singles, 35 twins; single $61.90, double $67.50; each additional adult $12. Children under 12 free. Cobb & Co. restaurant attached. In city centre.

Hyatt Kingstage Hotel, Eruera Street; tel: (073) 477-677; fax: (073) 481-234; 229 rooms; superior room $150; deluxe room $175; suite $380; regency club $215; room with private spa $225; room with private spa and Regency Club access $285; family package $79. Corporate rates negotiable. No charge for two children under 18 occupying same rooms with parents. All rates exclusive of GST. Outdoor heated pool. Full fitness centre facilities including two communal spas. Conference rooms available. Wheelchair access. 2 blocks from city centre.

Manary Lodge & Conference Centre, 77 Robinson Avenue, Holdens Bay; tel: (073) 456-792; fax: (073) 459-339; 20 studio units (sleep 2) $66. 10 family rooms (sleep 4) $88. Licensed restaurant. Full conference facilities. Outdoor pool and spa. Trout stream borders 2½ acres park-like grounds. Close to lake. 7 km from city.

Muriaroha Lodge, 411 Old Taupo Road; tel: (073) 461-220; fax: (073) 461-338; 5 units in garden setting. Low season, single $170 per night for ensuite, $190 garden suite. High season single $210 per night ensuite, $300 per night garden suite. Dinners and breakfast served. Limited conference facilities. Thermal pool and two spa pools. 4.5 km from city centre.

Puhi Nui Motel, 16 Sala Street; tel: (073) 484-182; fax: (073) 476-595; 40 motel flats (max. occ. 5) each with private plunge pool attached; single $76, double $82; each additional person $6. GST not included. Breakfast available. Outdoor pool and spa. Close to Whakarewarewa.

Sheraton Hotel, corner of Fenton and Sala Streets; tel: (072) 487-139; fax: (073) 488-378; standard rate $155, executive floor $175, deluxe floor $195. Suites range from $300. Presidential suite $550. All rates exclusive of GST. Heated outdoor pool and spa. Four indoor heated spa. Sauna. Night Hangis and Maori concert. Full conference facilities.

Solitaire Lodge, Ronald Road, Lake Tarawera; tel: (073) 28-208; fax: (073) 28-445; 10 units, 20 guests. 1 person $300 per day (units twin occupancy), or single $400 per day. $900 for Solitaire suite single, double or twin. Tariff includes all meals. Fishing guides available. Sweeping views of lake and mountain from native bush setting. 20 km from Rotorua.

THC Rotorua, Tryon Street; tel: (073) 481-189; fax: (073) 471-620; 124 rooms. Standard room $90, premier room $120, suite $250. Rates GST exclusive. 2 children in room with parents no extra charge. Outdoor pool. Full conference facilities. Hangi and Maori concert every evening. 3 km south east post office.

THC Rotorua Villas, Tryon Street; tel: (073) 482-189; fax: (073) 471-620; 39 units. 10 apartments $135. 29 studios $120. Outdoor pool and three spas. Situated across road from THC Rotorua. Guests have full access to all hotel facilities. Close to Whakarewarewa.

Travelodge, 6 Eruera Street; tel: (073) 481-174. Fax: (073) 46-238; 200 rooms. Single/twin/double $132, plus GST. Conference facilities. Hangi and Maori concert nightly. Outdoor heated pool and three private spas. Situated on lake shore and close to city centre.

Wylie Court Motor Lodge, Fenton Street; tel: (073) 477-879; fax: (073) 461-494; 4 family units (sleep 6), 21 mezzanine suits (4 with waterbeds). All with private plunge or spa pools. Tariff $93 double. $12.50 each extra person. Children 5 yrs and under free. Conference facilities. Outdoor swimming pool. Wheelchair access to some units. Walking distance to Whakarewarewa and city.

RUSSELL

Dikes Lodge, Waterfront, Russell, tel: 37-899; 12 rooms (max. occ. 6); single/twin $92

Duke of Marlborough, The Strand; tel: 37-829; 29 rooms (max. occ. 3); single/twin $55.

Mako Motel, Wellington Street; tel: 37-770; 7 rooms (max. occ. 5); single/twin $66.

TE ANAU

Aden Motel, 59 Quintin Drive; tel: 7748; 12 rooms (max. occ. 3), $55.

Fiordland Motor Lodge, Highway 94; tel: 7511; 126 rooms (max. occ. 3); single/double $76.

Lakeside Motel, 36 Te Anau Terrace; tel: 7435; 9 rooms (max. occ. 8); single/double $60.50.

Te Anau Downs Motor Inn, Te Anau-Milford Sound Highway, Te Anau; tel: 7811; 68 rooms (max. occ. 6), single $68, double $81.

THC Te Anau, tel: 7411; 112 rooms (max. occ. 5), single/double $203.50.

Matai Travel Lodge, corner of Mokonu and Matai Streets; tel: 7360; 7 rooms (max. occ. 3), single $49.50, double $58.

WAIRAKEI

THC Wairakei, tel: (074) 48-021; 90 rooms (max. occ. 3); single/double $71.50.

WAITANGI

THC Waitangi, tel: (0885) 27-411; 145 rooms (max. occ. 3); single/double $215

WAITOMO CAVES

THC Waitomo, tel: 88-227 Te Kuiti; 30 rooms; single $38, double $45; additional adults $17; children under 10 free.

WELLINGTON

(Tariffs do not include GST)

LICENSED HOTELS & MOTOR INNS

The Tas Hotel, corner of Willis and Dixon Streets; tel: 851-304; twin $121 weekdays, $82.50 weekends, mid city.

James Cook Hotel, The Terrace; tel: 725-865; twin/double $195, premium double $215, mid city.

Park Royal Hotel, 360 Oriental Parade; tel: 859-949; twin $207, limousine service, 2 km from city centre.

Sharella Motor Inn, 20 Glenmore Street; tel: 723-828; twin $110 or $125.

St. George Hotel, corner of Willis and Boulcott Streets; tel: 739-139; twin $127 weekdays, $75 weekends.

Terrace Regency Hotels, 345 The Terrace; tel: 859-829; twin $150, 10 minutes walk to downtown.

The Quality Inn, Oriental Parade, 73 Roxburgh Street; tel: 850-279; $159.50 weekdays, $100 weekends, convenient and central location.

Bay Plaza Hotel, 40-44 Oriental Parade; tel: 851-304; twin $145 weekdays, $98 weekends.

Harbour City Motor Inn, corner of Victoria and Webb Streets; tel: 849-809; twin $121.

Port Nicholson Hotel, corner of Cambridge Terrace and Wakefield Street; tel: 845-903; standard room $110, suite $125. Central location.

MOTELS

Adelaide Motel, 209 Adelaide Road; tel: 898-138; kitchen and serviced units, twin $80.

Apollo Motel, 49 Majoribanks Street; tel: 848-888; motel flats and serviced units, twin $88.

Capital Hill Apartments, 54 Hill Street; tel: 723-716; twin $98.

Iona Towers, 140 Abel Smith Street; tel: 850-404; twin $104.50.

Oakleys Motel, 331 Willis Street; tel: 846-173; twin $66.

747 Motel, 80 Kilbirnie Crescent; tel: 873-184; twin $75.

Wallace Court Motel, 88 Wallace Street; tel: 853-935; kitchen and serviced units, twin $88.

PRIVATE HOTELS & GUEST HOUSES

Ambassador Travel Hotel, 287 The Terrace; tel: 845-696; twin $66 without facilities, $77 with facilities.

Hampshire House, 155 Ghuznee Street; tel: 843-051; twin $52

Rowena Guest House, 115 Brougham Street; tel: 857-862; twin $49.50 (bed and breakfast) or twin budget $35.

Victoria Bed and Breakfast, 5 Pirie Street; tel: 858-512; twin $60.

MOTOR CAMPS

Besides the hotels, motor-inns and motels listed, there are numerous small motels dotting the country. Many offer kitchen facilities and often full kitchens and dining tables to make it possible for families to take many of their meals in the units. At some motels a cooked breakfast is available, and the units are serviced daily.

Most "Motor Camps," as they are called, offer communal washing, cooking and toilet facilities. The camper is required to supply his own caravan (trailer) or tent, but camps in the larger towns and in the cities have cabins available.

Motor Camps are licensed under the Camping Ground Regulation (1936) and they are all graded by the Automobile Association. It is important for travellers to check on the standards with the Automobile Association and to check camp site availability and, if necessary, make bookings over the summer months because New Zealanders are inveterate campers.

FARMHOUSE & HOME STAYS

Accommodation is available now on farms throughout the country. Visitors may share the homestead with the farmer and his family, or, in many cases may have the use of a cottage on the farm. This is one of the fastest growing forms of holiday in New Zealand over the past decade and it is an excellent way for visitors to see the real New Zealand which has been dependent on pastoral farming for its economic well being since the earliest colonial days. Farming families are usually excellent hosts at the friendliest personal level.

Many New Zealand families, both on farm and in the towns, will be pleased to host both local and overseas visitors. These hospitable places may be contacted through the following organisations:

Farmhouse and Country Home Holidays Ltd., 2 Aberdeen Road, Castor Bay, Auckland 9; tel: 4108-280

New Zealand Travel Hosts, 279 Williams Street, Kaiapoi, Christchurch; tel: 276-340

New Zealand Farm Holidays, P O Box 256, Silverdale, Auckland; tel: 372-024, fax: 68-474

Rural Holidays New Zealand Ltd, P O Box 2155, Christchurch; tel: 661-919, fax: 793-087

Rural Tours, P O Box 228 Cambridge; tel: 8055-2872, fax: 277-154

Hospitality Haere Mai, 243 Symonds Street, Auckland; tel: 391-560, fax: 393-869

Town and Country Home Hostings, 23 Queen Street, Cambridge; tel: 273-686, fax: 273-466

The **Youth Hostel Association** offers an extensive chain of hostels to members throughout New Zealand. Details of their location and membership of the organisation can be obtained from: Youth Hostel Association of New Zealand, P O Box 436, Christchurch, New Zealand.

FOOD DIGEST

WHAT TO EAT

The abundance, variety and quality of fresh meat and garden produce fill the New Zealand larder with riches on which an authentic tradition of cuisine has been built, New Zealand's market gardens are perhaps only equalled by those in California. The surrounding seas are the source of at least 50 commercially viable varieties of fish and shellfish.

The proliferation of imaginative restaurants and the multitude of excellent home cooks has only come about in the last 20 years. During this time cuisine went from the monotonous roast meat and boiled vegetable followed by stodgy puddings, to the gastronomic delights evolved by following and adapting the cuisine of other countries. New Zealand cuisine has created dishes using foods readily available locally. In the past it was thought that the only style of food was the cooking of the country's English forefathers and the English French cooking taught to budding professional chefs. Where once no leeway was allowed, chefs have now shrugged off these shackles and realise that cooking is imagination and flair not just rigid adherence to the basics. With many New Zealanders travelling extensively overseas, insular attitudes towards food have long disappeared.

So what are the riches of New Zealand's food? Vegetables such as asparagus, globe artichokes and avocados—luxuries in some countries—are abundant. Silver beef, or Swiss chard, which is treasured elsewhere, is virtually taken for granted in New Zealand. Kumara is the waxiest and most succulent of the world's sweet potatoes and pumpkin, put to good use in the country's cooking, is often shunned in other countries. New Zealand's kiwifruit, apples, tamarillos, passion-fruit, boysenberries, strawberries and pears are among the fruits shipped all over the globe. Other fruits include pepinos, babacos and prince melons.

New Zealand lamb is perfection; a crown roast or lamb spare ribs are well worth a try, as is the beef. Fish is abundant and of superior quality as well as the shellfish—crayfish, lobster, paua (abalone), tua tua and toheroa. Game is also plentiful.

Wine has vastly improved. Until 20 years ago only hybrid grapes were grown to produce sherries, ports and mediocre table wines. It is now generally accepted that the country has some of the best white wines. New Zealand's cool maritime climate and its summer rains produce light, elegant fruity wines. More attention is being given to the production of red wines which have consequently begun to emerge in the past few years.

While tacos, kebabs and pizzas are happily offered alongside the more traditional meat pies and fish and chips, so too is wine, by the glass or carafe, served alongside the traditional glass or jug of beer. New Zealanders, with Australians, are among the biggest beer drinkers in the world. It has been claimed that many of New Zealand's export beers, also available locally, rank equal with the great beers of Denmark and Germany. Beer has regained respectability as the drink to have with meals.

WHERE TO EAT

There are hundreds of good restaurants in Auckland, Wellington, Christchurch and Dunedin and many places in between.

All the resort towns have good quality restaurants and an increasing number of them specialise in ethnic meals, most notably Chinese, Indian and Italian. Some of the better-known and well-established restaurants are listed below. BYO, of course, means "Bring Your Own" and indicates a restaurant licensed for the consumption, though not the sale, of alcohol.

AUCKLAND

Achilles, corner of St. Heliers Bay Road and Tamaki Drive. Tel: 557-590

Antoines, 333 Parnell Road. Tel: 798-757

Ariake, Quay Towers. Tel: 792-377

Bonaparte's, corner of Victoria and High Streets. Tel: 797-896

Cafe Niche, 102 College Hill, Ponsonby, (BYO). Tel: 788-548

Denvonport Cafe, 18 Victoria Road, (BYO). Tel: 458-351

Fisherman's Wharf, Northcote Point. Tel: 418-3955

Flutes, 407 Mt. Edeen Road, (BYO). Tel: 601-143

Green Elephant Cage, 590 Dominion Road, Balmoral, (BYO). Tel: 689-516

Harbourside, 1st floor, Ferry Building, Quay Street. Tel: 370-486

Java Jive, Ponsonby, (BYO). Tel: 765-870

Kismat, 507 Mt. Albert Road, Three Kings, (BYO). Tel: 653-687

La Bussola, 421 Parnell Road. Tel: 733-328

Le Brie, St. Patrick's Square. Tel: 733-935

Marina, Half Moon Bay. Tel: 537-0905

New Orient, Strand Arcade, Queen Street. Tel: 797-793

Number Five, 5 City Road. Tel: 770-909

Ponsonby Brasserie, 282 Ponsonby Road. Tel: 763-330

Porterhouse Blue, 58 Calliope Road, Devonport. Tel: 450-309

Prego, 226 Ponsonby Road. Tel: 763-095

Rick's Cage American, Victoria Park Market. Tel: 399-074

The Replete Vegetarian, 555 Dominion Road, (BYO). Tel: 606-090

Rosinis, 20 High street. Tel: 735-326

Tony's 27, Wellesley Street. Tel: 734-196

Tony's 32, Lorne Street. Tel: 732-138

Tony's 71, Tamaki Drive, Mission Bay. Tel: 585-419

Wheeler's, 43 Ponsonby Road. Tel: 763-185

CHRISTCHURCH

Bahn Thai, 319b Stanmore Road, Richmond, (BYO). Tel: 811-611

Budapest, 107 Manchester Street, (BYO). Tel: 660-778

Chung Wah II, 61-63 Worcester Street. Tel: 793-894

Coachman Inn, 144 Gloucester Street. Tel: 793-476

Fisherman's Table, 1060 Ferry Road, Ferrymead. Tel: 844-123

Golden Triangle Malaysian, Triangle Centre, (BYO). Tel: 663-951

Grimsby's, corner of Kilmore and Montreal Streets. Tel: 799-040

Henry Africa's, 325 Stanmore Road. Tel: 893-619

Il Felice, 150 Armagh Street, (BYO). Tel: 667-535

Kanniga's Thai, Sapphire Room, 663A Colombo Street, (BYO). Tel: 668-524

Kanniga's Thai, Carlton Courts, Papanui Road, (BYO). Tel: 556-228

Kurashiki, MFL Building, corner of Gloucester/Colombo Streets. Tel: 667-092.

La Dolce Vita, 2 Latimer Square (corner of Hereford Street). Tel: 663-561

Mykonos Taverna, 112a Lichfield Street, (BYO). Tel: 797-452.

Oscars of Merivale, 190 Papanui Road, Merivale. Tel: 557-382

Saigon Vietnamese, 71 Kilmore Street. Tel: 795-721

Scarborough Fare, Scarborough Road, Sumner. Tel: 266-987

Shangri-La, 321 Durham Street. Tel: 795-720

Tiffany's, corner of Durham and Lichfield Streets. Tel: 791-350

DUNEDIN

Blades, 450 George Street. Tel: 776 548

95 Filleul, 95 Filleul Street. Tel: 777 233

Savoy, 50 Princes Street. Tel: 778 977

Thyme Out, 5 Stafford Street. Tel: 740 467

WELLINGTON

Angkor Cambodian Restaurant, 43 Dixon Street. Tel: 849-423

Armidillo Cafe, 129 Willis Street. Tel: 858-221

The Beefeater, Marac House, 105 The Terrace. Tel: 738-195

Brer Fox, 10 Murphy Street, (BYO). Tel: 712-477

Cheminee, 70 Rongotai Road, Kilburnie, (BYO). Tel: 872-412

Genghis Khan Mongolian BBQ, 25 Majoribanks Street. Tel: 843-592

The Grain of Salt, 232 Oriental Parade. Tel: 848-642

Great Expectations, 60 Ghuznee Street, (BYO). Tel: 849-596

Il casino, 108 Tory street. Tel: 857-496

La Spaghettata, 15 Edward Street. Tel: 842-812

Le Normandie, 116 Cuba street. Tel: 845-000

Le Routier, 92 Upland Road, (BYO). Tel: 758-981

Marbles, 89 Upland Road, (BYO). Tel: 758-490

Nicholsons Brasserie, 245 Oriental Parade. Tel: 843-835

Pierres, 342 Tinakori Road, (BYO). Tel: 726-238

Shorebird Seafood Restaurant, 301 Evans Bay Parade. Tel: 862-017

Thorndon Cafe, 328 Tinakori Road, (BYO). Tel: 735-805

Wellington settlement, 155 Willis Street, (BYO). Tel: 858-920

CULTURE PLUS

New Zealand has a relatively short recorded history but all the main centres, most of the provincial cities and many quite small towns have museums. There has also been an explosion of interest in the visual arts since World War II and art galleries with fine collections have been established.

MUSEUMS

National Museum of New Zealand, Buckle Street, Wellington.

This fine 50-year-old building, features, displays of Maori traditional art and culture including wood carvings and decorated houses, canoes, weapons and other artefacts. The displays amount to one of the best collections of Polynesian art and artefacts in the world, and there are also Micronesian and Melanesian collections and many exhibits from Southeast Asia. Other exhibits are: European discovery and settlement from New Zealand, geological history of the region; collections of flora and fauna, including the remains of the large flightless bird which once inhabited New Zealand, the Moa. Open 10 a.m. to 4:45 p.m. daily (The National Art Gallery is in the same building.)

Far North Regional Museum, Centennial Buildings, South Road, Kaitaia.

Collections include a "colonial" room, Maori artefacts, and a reconstructed Moa display, also a large room which houses the de Surville anchor and associated display, and the Northwood photographic collection. Open 10 a.m. to 5 p.m. (Mon. to Fri.), 1 p.m. to 5 p.m. (Sat and Sun.), and 10 a.m. to 7 p.m. Christmas to February (everyday).

Captain Cook Memorial Museum, York Street, Russell.

Named after Captain James Cook, the museum houses mainly local relics of early

European settlement. These include specimens of Maori culture, war exhibits, whaling gear, and relics of the early traders and missionaries. Open 10 a.m. to 4 p.m. (Mon. to Sat.), 2 p.m. to 4 p.m. (Sun.), 8 a.m. to 5 p.m. daily during school holidays.

Auckland Institute and Museum, Auckland Domain.

Set in beautiful parklands in Auckland's best-known park, the War Memorial Museum's exhibitions include a wonderful selection of Maori and Pacific artefacts and carvings. Other sections include material devoted to: New Zealand natural history; Asian, and other, applied arts; maritime and war history; the history of Auckland; and a planetarium. The Institute administers the Institute Library, Auckland Astronomical Society, an anthropology and Maori Studies section, the Auckland Maritime Society, a conchology section, and the Ornithological Society of New Zealand. Open: 10 a.m. to 5 p.m daily.

The Bath House—Rotorua's Art and History Museum

The gallery houses a number of collections tracing the development of painting and print making in New Zealand. Included are major works by Christopher Perkins, Rita Angus, Colins McCahon, Toss Woollaston, W.G. Baker and a host of other contemporary New Zealand painters. Also, an impressive collection of images of the Maori in paintings and portraits.

The museum boasts a collection 6,000 prints of the volcanic Plateau area, and a colonial cottage reflecting the period 1870-1900 when Rotorua was settled by Europeans. There is a Kauri gum collection and a wildlife display which relates to the timber industry which dominates the region. A new wing has also been dedicated to the local Te Arawa Maori people and portrays a wide variety of their artefacts.

Canterbury Museum, Rolleston Avenue, Christchurch.

Opened in 1870, the museum is the world's largest display hall on Antarctica. Exhibits include an 87-foot (27-metre) skeleton of an Antarctic blue whale and equipment used in various expeditions. There is an associated reference library and theatre where films are shown. Other features include a hall of oriental art, an ornithological display, a costume gallery, a street of shops, and a Maori cultural section including artefacts from the moa-hunting era. Open 10 a.m. to 4:30 p.m. daily.

Lakes District Museum, Buckingham Street, Arrowtown.

The collection is housed in a two-storey, renovated, former bank building built in 1875 and contains mining and geological items such as gold and mineral specimens, gold-miners' tools, and relics of the Chinese miners. Domestic and agricultural items, old implements and machinery, and a collection of horse-drawn vehicles are also on display. A collection of 3,000 early photographs, books and documents, relates to local history from 1862 to the 1920s. Open: 9 a.m. to 5 p.m., daily.

Otago Museum, Great King Street, Dunedin.

It houses excellent collections and displays including Pacific collections, halls of Melanesia and Polynesia, a Maori hall, halls of maritime history and marine life, ceramics including Greek pottery and sculpture, New Zealand birdlife and an Otago historical collection. Open: 10 a.m. to 5 p.m. (weekdays), 1 p.m. to 5 p.m. (weekends).

Otago Early Settlers Museum, 220 Cumberland Street, Dunedin.

First opened in 1908, collections include records and documents of emigration and early settlement in the Otago area. A wide range of pioneer relics, including folk crafts, costumes, whaling relics, gold relics and household devices. Paintings and photographs depicting early settlers and settlements can also be seen. Open: 8:30 a.m. to 4:30 a.m. (Mon. to Fri.), 10:30 a.m. to 4:30 p.m. (Sat.), 1:30 p.m. to 4:30 p.m. (Sun.).

Museum of Transport and Technology (Motat), Great North Road, Western Springs, 5 km from downtown Auckland.

Displays include aircraft, working tramway and railway, the development of printing and photography, calculating machines from the abacus to the computer, vintage cards, carriages, and a colonial village where buildings are preserved and restored.

Among the many exciting exhibits can be found are the remains of Richard Pearse's aircraft which twice flew successfully in March 1903, three months after the Wright Brothers and "Meg Merrilees," an F class saddle-tank locomotive built by the Yorkshire Engine Co. of Leeds, England, in 1874. Open: 9 a.m. to 5 p.m. (weekdays), 10 a.m. to 5 p.m. (weekends and public holidays).

The Steam Traction Society Museum, Lethbridge Road 4 km north of Feilding.

Unique in New Zealand in that it specialises in British traction engines, steamrollers, and portable engines. Twenty exhibits, in various states from running, being restored, to awaiting restoration, can be seen there. Open: Sunday afternoons, the third Sunday of each month being a Steam Day. Also open at any time by arrangement with the Secretary.

The Ferrymead Trust, situated on a 40-hectare site alongside the Heathcote River, Christchurch.

The trust's historic park includes many historical exhibits: vintage machinery, cars, bicycles, gigs, fire engines, tramcars, railway engines, aeroplanes, home appliances, and agricultural and printing equipment. Special features include rides on a 1.5 km tramway and 1-km railway. The last Kitson steam tram locomotive with trailers built in Leeds, England, in 1881, may be seen. Open: 10 a.m. to 4:30 p.m. daily.

Queenstown Motor Museum, Brecon Street, Queenstown.

This museum complex contains more than 60 exhibits which, though periodically changed, always include veteran and vintage cars and motor cycles, as well as post vintage and post World War II models and aero engines. some of the many makes on display are Rolls Royce, Bentley, Aston Martin, Maserati, Mercedes, and many other European specialist cars, as well as a range of American cars including the Model T Fords. Open: 9 a.m. to 5:30 p.m. daily.

Army Memorial Museum, State Highway No. 1, south of Waiouru.

The museum houses many artefacts from New Zealand's military history including weapons, uniforms, photographs, paintings, medals, equipment, diaries, personal effects, and other memorabilia from the Maori Wars to the present day. Open: 9 a.m. to 4:30 p.m. daily.

Waikato Museum of Art and History, corner of Victoria and Grantham Streets, Hamilton.

This handsome, five-level building takes full advantage of its riverbank location. The restored Maori war canoe, Te Winika, and contemporary Tainui carving and tukutuku weaving are on permanent display. A changing programme of exhibitions draws on the museum's large collection of New Zealand fine art, Tainui and Waikato history. National and international touring exhibitions also feature regularly.

ART GALLERIES

New Zealand has 21 public art galleries. The largest ones are listed below.

The Auckland City Art Gallery, Wellesley/Kitchener Street, Auckland.

First opened in 1888 its collection include New Zealand paintings, sculpture, drawings, prints and photographs from the 1800s to the present day. Also an extensive Frances Hodgkins collection. There are European Old Master paintings and drawings, a small Gothic collection, and a collection of 19th and 20th-century Japanese prints. Also international sculptures and prints. Open: 10 a.m. to 4:30 p.m. daily. Free guided tours at 12 p.m. (Mon. to Fri.), 2 p.m. (Sun.).

Govett-Brewster Art Gallery, Queen Street, New Plymouth.

This is one of the best collections of contemporary art in New Zealand. Most New Zealand artists of note are represented, with works by Patrick Hanly, Michael Illingworth, Colin McCahon and Brent Wong. Also an important collection of Len Lye kinetic sculptures, painting and film. Open: 10:30 a.m. to 5 p.m. (Mon. to Fri.), 1 p.m. to 5 p.m. (Sat. and Sun.).

Sargeant Gallery, Queen's Park, Wanganui.

This has a permanently exhibited New Zealand collection, which includes oils, watercolours, and prints from the 19th and 20th centuries. Also included is 19th and 20th century Western art, with British oils, watercolours and prints, as well as European works including drawings by Poccetti, The Denton Collection of 19th and 20th century photography, and an exhibition of World War I cartoons and posters. Open: 10:30 a.m. to 4 p.m. (Mon. to Fri.), 10:30 a.m. to 12 p.m. (Sat.), 1:30 p.m. to 4 p.m. (Sun.).

Manawatu Art Gallery, 398 Main Street, Palmerston North.

The gallery collection concentrates on New Zealand works, from as early as 1880 and including also works by all major contemporary painters. It houses two large collections of drawings by James Cook, and oils, watercolours and drawings by H. Linley Richardson. Open: 10 a.m. to 4:30 p.m. (Tue. to Fri.), 1 p.m. to 5 p.m. (Sat., Sun. and public holidays).

Dowse Art Gallery, Civic Centre, Lower Hutt.

This gallery concentrates on New Zealand art, mainly contemporary works, with some earlier works. Open: 10 a.m to 4 p.m. (Mon. to Fri.), 1 p.m. to 5 p.m. (Sat. and Sun.).

National Art Gallery, Buckle Street, Wellington.

The National Gallery's collections include New Zealand, Australian, British and foreign 19th and 20th century paintings, drawings, graphic art and sculpture. Accent is on New Zealand art from 1840, with a wide selection of early watercolours, oil paintings and drawings. Also a wide range of etchings and engravings of old and modern Masters. Open: 10 a.m. to 4:45 p.m. daily.

Wellington City Art Gallery, 50-52 Victoria Street.

This gallery concentrates less on collecting work, than on mounting temporary New Zealand art and design. Open: 10 a.m. to 6 p.m. daily, and 10 a.m. to 8 p.m. (Wed.).

Bishop Suter Art Gallery, Bridge Street, Nelson.

The main collections are water colours, which include works by John Gully, J.C. Richmond, C.Y. Fell, Frances Hodgkins and James Nairn. Open: 10 a.m. to 4 p.m. (Tues. to Sun.).

Robert McDougall Art Gallery, Botanic Gardens, Rolleston Avenue, Christchurch.

The Robert McDougall Art Gallery houses representative works of Dutch, French, Italian and especially British painting, drawing, and graphics from about 1600. The gallery aims to provide a chronological survey of the development of painting, drawing, printmaking and sculpture as European art forms. The New Zealand collection is one of the most comprehensive in the works, especially of the Canterbury region. Open: 10 a.m. to 4:30 p.m daily.

Dunedin Public Art Gallery, Logan Park, Dunedin.

First established in the 1880s, it houses a large collection of 18th and 19th century English watercolours, as well as major oil portrait and landscape artists from between the 16th and 19th centuries. The New Zealand collection of oils and watercolours ranges from the mid-19th century, and includes a retrospective collection of Frances Hodgkins. Open: 10 a.m. to 4:30 p.m. (Mon. to Fri.), 2 p.m. to 5 p.m. (Sat., Sun. and public holidays).

Other provincial public art galleries are:
Forum North Arts Centre, Whangarei.
Waikato Art Museum, Hamilton.
Hawke's Bay Exhibition Centre, Hastings.
Aigantighe Art Gallery, Timaru.
Forrester Art Gallery, Oamaru.
Hocken Library, University of Otago, Dunedin.

THINGS TO DO

This section lists New Zealand's popular attractions such as amusement parks, adventure and wildlife parks in Auckland, Christchurch and Wellington.

AUCKLAND

Auckland Safariland, 69 Redhills Road, Massey. Tel: 377-728

Rainbows End Adventure Park, corner of Great South and Wiri Station Roads. Tel: 277-9870

Footrot Flats, Te Atatu Road. Tel: 834-7017

Victoria Park Market, opposite Victoria Park, city. Tel: 396-140

Kelly Tarltons Underwater World, Orakei Wharf, 23 Tamaki Drive. Tel: 589-318

Microworld, corner of Halsey and Madden Streets. Tel: 370-227

New Zealand Heritage Park, Ellerslie Panmure Highway, Mt. Wellington. Tel: 590-424

CHRISTCHURCH

Orana Park Wildlife Park, Willows Road.

WELLINGTON

The cable car, Lambton Quay/Kelburn. Tel: 856-579

Parliament Buildings and the Beehive, Bolton Street. Tel: 749-199. Daily tours

Wellington Zoo, Manchester Street, Newtown. Tel: 898-130

Botanic Gardens and Rose Garden. Tel: 757-084

SHOPPING

Sheepskin

With more than 60 million sheep it comes as no surprise that New Zealand's major shopping attraction is its sheepskin and woollen products. You are unlikely to find cheaper sheepskin clothing anywhere in the world and the colour and variety of sheepskins and sheepskin products make an ideal gift or souvenir. Most shops stock a huge range of coats and jackets made from sheepskin, slinkskin, opossum, deerskin, leather and suede. Car seat covers are popular as are the sheepskin floor rugs. The bigger retailers pack and post any items overseas.

Woodcarvings

Maori carve wood for the tourist trade and woodcarvings are widely available. The most traditional Maori area of New Zealand is the East Cape and you should use your initiative and hunt in this area if your looking for more authentic woodcarvings.

Greenstone

New Zealand jade, more commonly referred to as greenstone, cannot match the quality of Chinese or Burmese jade but nevertheless is a distinctive Kiwi product. Widely available, the jade is worked into jewellery, figurines, ornaments and Maori *tikis*. The West Coast (South Island) is the major area where greenstone continues to be mined. Factories in the West Coast town of Greymouth and Hokitika allow visitors to see the jade being worked.

Handicrafts

There has been an explosion of crafts in recent years, the products of which are sold by local craftsmen and craftswomen *in situ* and by shops catering specifically to tourists. Pottery is perhaps the most widely available craft product though patchwork, quilting, padded boxes, canework, handspun knitwear and weaving, woodcarving, Kauri woodware, wooden toys, bark pictures, paintings, glassware and leatherware are among the enormous range of crafts.

WHERE TO SHOP

Most shopping needs can be catered for in Auckland, Wellington and Christchurch. Auckland's Queen Street is an obvious place in which to part company with one's money; while Karangahape Road, one of Auckland's busiest and oldest established central commercial streets, offers a wealth of interesting shopping. Located at the "top" of Queen Street, "Karangahape" translates as "winding ridge of human activity" and aptly describes the bustle. It is the variety of stores, together with an ethnic cross-section comprising Auckland's Polynesian and European community that gives the street its character. Small second-hand-clothing and furniture shops compete for business with spacious department stores. Another centre for shopping in Auckland is the harbourside Downtown complex. Open from 9 a.m. to 5:30 p.m. (Mon. to Thurs.), 9 a.m. to 9 p.m. (Fri.) and 9:30 a.m. to 12:30 p.m. (Sat.), the centre caters to just about every shopping whim. A glass-walled walkway connects with the Downtown Airline (Bus) Terminal, itself a shopping centre, making it an excellent location for tourists wanting a last-minute browse through the shops.

In Wellington the main shopping streets are in Willis Street and Customhouse Quay; while in Christchurch, the Cathedral Square vicinity offers the best bargains. Anybody intending to pass through Queenstown can rest assure that the street bristle with souvenir shops. Prices are always fixed and bargaining is definitely the exception. Queenstown is an exception to the usual retailing hours. It caters for visitors with seven-day-a-week shopping and many stores also stay open in the evening.

USEFUL ADDRESSES

EMBASSIES & CONSULATES

Argentina
Argentine Consulate-General, Harbour View Building, 52 Quay Street, Auckland. Tel: 391-757.

Australia
Australian High Commission, 72-78 Hobson Street, Thorndon, Wellington. Tel: 736-420; fax: 736 420; telex: NZ 3375.

Australian Consulate-General, Union House, 32-38 Quay Street, CPO Auckland. Tel: 32-429, 795-725; fax: 770-798; telex: NZ 2516

Austria
Consulate of Austria, 1 McColl Street, Auckland. Tel: 545-457; fax: 504-941

Belgium
Embassy of Belgium, Robert Jones House, 1-3 Willeston Street, Wellington. Tel: 729-58/9; fax: 712-764; telex: NZ 31452.

Consulate of Belgium, Penthouse, Fisher International Building, 18 Waterloo Quadrant, Auckland. Tel: 799-960; fax: 399-570.

Brazil
Consulate of the Federative Republic of Brazil, 8 Commerce Street, Auckland. Tel: 735-728.

Britain
British High Commission, Reserve Bank Building, 2 The Terrace, Wellington. Tel: 726-049; fax: 711-974; telex: 3325.

British Consulate-General, Fay Richwhite Building, 151 Queen Street, Auckland. Tel: 303-2973 (Information); fax: 303-1836.

Canada
Canadian High Commission, ICI House, 67 Molesworth Street, Wellington. Tel: 739-577; fax: 712-082; telex: NZ 3577.

Canadian Consulate, Princes Court, 2 Princes Street, Auckland. Tel: 398-516/7/8; fax: 373-111; telex: NZ 21645 CANAD.

Chile
Embassy of the Republic of Chile, Robert Jones House, 1-3 Willeston Street, Wellington. Tel: 735-180/1; telex: 31034.

Consulate of the Republic of Chile, 21-39 Jellicoe Road, Panmure, Auckland. Tel: 5278-068.

China
Embassy of the People's Republic of China, 2-6 Glenmore Street, Wellington. Tel: 721-382 (Embassy), 721-384 (Consular Office); fax: 499-0419; telex: 3843.

Cook Islands
Office of the Cook Islands Representative, 61 Kanpur Road, Broadmeadows, Wellington. Tel: 780-945.

Consular Office of the Cook Islands, Cook House, 330 Parnell Road, Parnell, Auckland. Tel: 794-140; telex: NZ 21013 COOKCOM.

Costa Rica
Consulate-General of Costa Rica, 50 Lunn Avenue, Mt. Wellington, Auckland. Tel: 527-1523; telex: NZ 21535 SINTON.

Czechoslovakia
Embassy of the Czechoslovak Socialist Republic, 12 Anne Street, Wadestown, Wellington. Tel: 723-142; telex: 31437.

Denmark
Royal Danish Consulate, 10 Venessa Crescent, Glendowie, Auckland. Tel: 556-025; fax: 554-200; telex: 61223 DANISH.

Ecuador
Consulate of the Republic of Ecuador, Wool House, 2nd floor, 10 Brandon Street. Tel: 738-366; telex: 3547 MACSHIP.

El Salvador
Consulate of El Salvador, 24 Seccombes Road, Epsom, Auckland. Tel: 549-376

Fiji

Embassy of the Republic of Fiji, Robert Jones House, 1-3 Willeston Street, Wellington. Tel: 735-401/2; fax: 499-1011; telex: NZ 31406 FIJIREP.

Finland

Consulate of Finland, 42 Bassett Road, Remuera, Auckland. Tel: 548-341; telex: NZ 21261 HEPOL.

France

Embassy of France, Robert Jones House, 1-3 Willeston Street, Wellington. Tel: 7200-200/1 (Chancery and Consulate); telex: 3580.

Consulate of France, c/o Christchurch Teachers College, Christchurch. Tel: 482-059.

Germany (West)

Embassy of the Federal Republic of Germany, 90-92 Hobson Street, Thorndon, Wellington. Tel: 736-063/4; telex: NZ 30131 AA WEL

Hon. Consulate of the Federal Republic of Germany, 12 Albert Street, Auckland. Tel: 773-460; fax: 393-003; telex: NZ 2455 COLMAR.

Greece

Consulate-General of Greece, 8th floor, Cumberland House, 237 Willis Street. Tel: 847-556; fax: 854-608; telex: NZ 31656 GRECONS.

Holy See

Apostolic Nunciature, 112 Queen's Drive, Lyall Bay, Wellington., Tel: 873-470.

Iceland

Consulate-General of Iceland, 88 Oriental Parade, Wellington. Tel: 857-934.

India

High Commission of India, 10th floor, Princess Tower, 180 Molesworth Street, Wellington. Tel: 736-390/1; telex: NZ 31676 (HICOIND).

Indonesia

Embassy of the Republic of Indonesia, 70 Glen Road, Kelburn, Wellington. Tel: 758-695; telex: 3892.

Iran

Embassy of the Islamic Republic of Iran, The Terrace, Wellington. Tel: 850-093; telex: NZ 30687.

Ireland

Consulate-General of Ireland, 2nd floor, Dingwall Building, 87 Queen Street, Auckland. Tel: 793-708; fax: 390-725; telex: NZ 21437.

Israel

Embassy of Israel, Plimmer City Centre, Plimmer Steps, Wellington. Tel: 722-362, 722-368; fax: 499-0632; telex: 31221.

Italy

Embassy of Italy, 34 Grant Road, Thorndon, Wellington. Tel: 735-339, 728-302; telex: NZ 31571 ITALDIPL.

Consular Agency of Italy, Dingwall Building, 87-93 Queen Street, Auckland. Tel: 395 749.

Japan

Embassy of Japan, Norwich Insurance House, 3-11 Hunter Street, Wellington. Tel: 731-540; fax: 712-951; telex: NZ 3544.

Consulate-General of Japan, National Mutual Centre, 37-45 Shortland Street, Auckland. Tel: 34-106; telex: NZ 2665 RYOJIAK.

Kiribati

Consulate of the Kiribati Republic, 33 Great South Road, Otahuhu, Auckland. Tel: 276-3789; fax: 276-3342; telex: NZ 2572.

Korea

Embassy of the Republic of Korea, Level 6, Elders House, 86-96 Victoria Street, Wellington. Tel: 739-073; telex: NZ 3352 GONGKWAN

Consulate of the Republic of Korea, The Allan McLean Building, corner of Colombo Street and Oxford Terrace, Christchurch. Tel: 790-040.

Malaysia

High Commission for Malaysia, 10 Washington Avenue, Brooklyn, Wellington. Tel: 852-439, 852-019.

Consulate of Malaysia, 14 Hazeldean Road, Christchurch. Tel: 389-059; telex: NZ 4365.

Malta

Consulate of the Republic of Malta, 18 Barlow Place, Birkenhead, Auckland. Tel: 799-860; fax: 391-4181; telex: NZ 2541.

Mexico

Consulate of Mexico, 1-3 Arawa Street, Grafton, Auckland. Tel: 394-109, 398-712; fax: 777-675; telex: NZ 69806.

Nauru

Consulate-General of Nauru, Samoa House, 283 Karangahape Road, Auckland. Tel: 799-348; telex: NZ 21506 NAURCON.

Netherlands

Royal Netherlands Embassy, Investment Centre, corner of Ballance and Featherston Streets, Wellington. Tel: 738-652; telex: NZ 3987.

Consulate of the Netherlands, 6th floor, Aetna House, 57 Symonds Street, Auckland. Tel: 795-399.

Niue

Consular Office of Niue, Samoa House, 283 Karangahape Road, Auckland. Tel: 774-081, 389-720; telex: NZ 60175.

Norway

Royal Norwegian Consulate, 7th floor, Westpac Securities Building, 120, Albert Street, Auckland. Tel: 771-944; fax: 777-638; telex: NZ 60694

Pakistan

Consulate of Pakistan, 12 Burwood Crescent, Remuera, Auckland 1. Tel: 544-099; telex: NZ 2553.

Papua New Guinea

Papua New Guinea High Commission, Princess Towers, 180 Molesworth Street, Wellington. Tel: 731-560/1/2; telex: NZ 31353.

Peru

Embassy of the Republic of Peru, 35-37 Victoria Street, Wellington. Tel: 725-171/2; telex: NZ 30148 LEPRU.

Consulate of Peru, 45 Neilson Street, Onehunga, Auckland 6. Tel: 543-341; fax: 501-761.

Philippines

Embassy of the Philippines, 50 Hobson Street, Thorndon, Wellington. Tel: 729--848, 729–921.

Consulate-General of the Philippines, NZ Dairy Board Building, 93-97 Dominion Road, Mt. Eden, Auckland. Tel: 689-986; fax: 600-029; telex: NZ 2358.

Poland

Embassy of the Polish People's Republic, Apartment D, 196 The Terrace, Wellington. Tel: 712-455/6; telex: NZ 30147 POLAMB.

Portugal

Consulate of Portugal, 117 Arney Road, Remuera, Auckland 5. Tel: 548-266; telex: NZ 2553 CPOAK.

Singapore

Singapore High Commission, 17 Kabul Street, Khandallah, Wellington. Tel: 2792-076/7; telex: NZ 3593 SINWAKIL.

Spain

Consulate of Spain, Papakura, Auckland. Tel: 298-5176; fax: 299-8057.

Sri Lanka

Consulate of the Democratic Socialist Republic of Sri Lanka, 16 Cosy Place, Howick, Auckland. Tel: 534-5646.

Sweden

Embassy of Sweden, Greenock House, 39 The Terrace, Wellington. Tel: 720-909/10; fax: 712-097; telex: NZ 3660 SVENSK.

Consulate of Sweden, Emcom House, 75 Queen Street, Auckland 1. Tel: 735-332; fax: 735-702; telex: NZ 63107 SWEDTRA.

Switzerland

Embassy of Switzerland, Panama House, 22-24 Panama Street, Wellington. Tel: 721-593/4; telex: NZ 31539 AMSUIS

Swiss Consular Agency, 48 Carr Road. Mount Roskill, Auckland. Tel: 658-866; telex: MUL. AK/NZ 21057 INTCOM

Thailand

Royal Thai Embassy, 2 Cook Street, Karori, Wellington. Tel: 768-618/9; telex: NZ 30162.

Turkey

Consulate-General of the Republic of Turkey, 201 Symonds Street, Auckland. Tel: 771-844; fax: 771-844.

Tuvalu

Consulate-General of Tuvalu, 33 Great South Road, Otahuhu, Auckland. Tel: 276-3789; fax: 276-3342; telex: NZ 2572.

USSR

Embassy of the Union of Soviet Socialist Republics, 57 Messines Road, Karori, Wellington. Tel: 766-113 (Embassy), 766-742 (Consular Office), 847-190 (Information Section); telex: NZ 3213.

United States of America

Embassy of the United States of America, 29 Fitzherbert Terrace, Wellington. Tel: 772-068; fax: 781-701; telex: NZ 3305

Consulate-General of the United States of America, General Building, corner of Shortland and O'Connell Streets, Auckland. Tel: 32-724; fax: 336-0870; telex: NZ 3305

Uruguay

Consulate of Uruguay, 178 Cashel Street, Christchurch. Tel: 798-600 ext: 8885; fax: 793-771; telex: NZ 4460 PGGCH

Western Samoa

Western Samoa High Commission, 1A Wesley Road, Kelburn, Wellington. Tel: 720-953/4; telex: NZ 31043 PALOLO

Consulate-General of Western Samoa, Samoa House, 283 Karangahape Road, Newton, Auckland. Tel: 31-012; telex: NZ 21477 KONSULA

Yugoslavia

Embassy of the Socialist Federal Republic of Yugoslavia, 24 Hatton Street, Karori, Wellington. Tel: 764-200

Hon. Consul of the Socialist Federal Republic of Yugoslavia, AMP Building, corner of Queen and Victoria Streets, Auckland. Tel: 774-630, 378-581

FURTHER READING

Bearing in mind that New Zealand boasts the highest per capita readership of books and periodicals anywhere in the world it is well worth paying a visit to some of New Zealand's fine bookshops. Whitcoull's is the nation's major bookstore chain (and stationer) and offers a good selection of quality titles. There is a wealth of reading related to New Zealand and some of the smaller and private bookstores are only too pleased to guide you to a choice.

COLLECTIONS & ANTHOLOGIES

A Book of New Zealand, ed. by J.C. Reid and Peter Cape, Collins, 1979. An anthology of New Zealand writing, embracing fiction and non-fiction. Most of the passages included are brief excerpts from well-known works.

Anthology of Twentieth Century New Zealand Poetry, selected with an introduction by Vincent O'Sulliva. Oxford University Press, 1976.

Automobile Association Road Atlas of New Zealand, Hamlyn, 1978:

Automobile Association Book of New Zealand Countryside, Hamlyn, 1978:

Automobile Association Book of New Zealand Walkways, Landsdowne Press, 1982.

Encyclopaedia of New Zealand, ed. by A.H. McLintock, 3 vols. NZ Government Printer, 1966. A complete and detailed reference work on New Zealand.

Heinemann New Zealand Dictionary, ed. by H.W. Orsman, Heinemann Educational, 1979.

Into the World of Light: An Anthology of Maori Writing, ed. by Witi Ihimaera and D.S. Long. Heinemann, 1982

New Zealand Atlas, ed. by Ian Wards, Government Printer, 1976.

New Zealand Encyclopaedia, ed. by Gordon McLauchlan, David Batemsan Ltd., 1984. A one-volume, family A-to-Z book covering all aspects of New Zealand life.

New Zealand in Maps. ed. by A.G. Anderson, Hodder and Stoughton (London), 1977.

New Zealand Love Poems, chosen by James Bertram, McIndoe, 1977.

New Zealand Short Stories, chosen by Lydia Wevers, Oxford University Press, 1984.

Oxford Book of Contemporary New Zealand Poetry, chosen by Fleur Adcock, Oxford University Press, in association with Auckland University Press, 1982.

Penguin Book of New Zealand Verse, ed. by Allen Curnow, Penguin, 1966.

Wise's New Zealand Guide, a gazetteer of New Zealand, Wise Publications, 1979 (7th edition).

GENERAL

Alexander, L., *Adventure Holidays in New Zealand*. Independent Newspapers Ltd., 1982.

Archey, Sir Gilbert, *Maori Art and its Artists*, Collins, 1977.

Braithwaite, Erroll, *New Zealand and its People*, Government Printer, 1974.

Blumhardt, D., and Brake, B., *Craft in New Zealand*, Reed, 1981.

Buck, Sir P., *The Coming of the Maori*, Whitcombe and Tombs, 1974. An account of the migration to New Zealand by the first Polynesians, written by a distinguished Maori and Pacific scholar.

Buller, Sir W.L., *Birds of New Zealand* (new edition ed. by E.G. Turbott). Whitcombe and Tombs, 1967.

Burnett, A.A. and R., *The Australia and New Zealand Nexus*, Australian Institute of International Affairs, Canberra, 1978.

Burton, D., *Two Hundred Years of New Zealand Food and Cookery*, Reed, 1982.

Cameron, Don. *Memorable Moments in New Zealand Sport*, Moa Publications, 1979.

Chester, R.H. and McMillan, N.A.C., *Men in Black*, Moa Publications, 1979. A biographical dictionary of all those who have played Rugby for New Zealand and a history of international marches involving New Zealand's All Blacks.

Cobb, L., and Duncan, J., *New Zealand's National Parks*, Hamlyn, 1980.

Costello, J. B., *New Zealand Galloping Greats*, Moa Publications, 1977. A history of New Zealand's greatest racehorses.

Cross, Ian, *The God Boy*, Whitcombe and Tombs, 1972. One of the most successful novels published since World War II by a New Zealand writer.

Docking, G.C., *Two Hundred Years of New Zealand Painting*, A.H. and A.W. Reed, 1971.

Dollimore, H.N., *The Parliament of New Zealand and Parliament House*, Government Printer, 1973.

Downes, P.E., *Shadows on the Stage: The first Seventy Years of Theatre in New Zealand*, McIndoe, 1975.

Easton, B., *Social Policy and the Welfare State in New Zealand*, Allen &Unwin, 1980.

Fleming, Sir C.A., *The Geological History of New Zealand and its Life*, Auckland University Press, 1979.

Forster, R.R., and L.M., *Small Land Animals of New Zealand*, McIndoe, 1970.

Forrester, Rex. and Illingworth, N., *Hunting in New Zealand*, A.H. and A.W. Reed, 1979.

Frame, Janet, *Owls Do Cry*, W.H. Allen, 1961; *A State of Siege*, Pegasus Press, 1967; *Living in the Maniototo*, Braziller (New York), 1979. A selection of three novels by New Zealand's best known living writer of fiction.

Franklin, S.H., *Trade Growth and Anxiety—New Zealand Beyond the Welfare State*, Methuen, 1978. An account of social and political developments in New Zealand since World War II.

Gee, Maurice, *Plumb*, Faber and Faber (London), 1979; *Meg*, Faber and Faber (London), 1981; *Sole Survivor*, Faber and Faber (London), 1983. *Plumb* is one of the best known and critically praised novels of recent years in New Zealand. *Meg* and *Sole Survivor* are the later works in this trilogy.

Grimshaw, P., *Women's Suffrage in New Zealand*, Oxford University Press, 1972.

Guthrie-Smith, W.H., *Tutira: The Story of a New Zealand Sheep Station*. A.H. and A.W. Reed, 1969 (4th edition). This is a New Zealand classic, the work of a sheep farmer and amateur naturalist in the late 19th and early 20th centuries.

Henderson, J. Jackson, K. and Kennaway, R., *Beyond New Zealand, the Foreign Policy of a Small State*, Methuen, 1980.

Hilliard, Noel, *Maori Girl*, Heinemann (London), 1971. This novel is one of the biggest sellers written by a New Zealander in the past 20 years.

Houghton, B.F., *Geyserland; A Guide to the Volcanoes and Geothermal Areas of Rotorua*, The Geological Society of New Zealand.

Hunt, Sam, *Collected Poems*, Penguins Books, 1980. A collections of the work of a contemporary folk poet.

Hyde, Robin, *The Godwits Fly*, Hurst and Blackett (London), 1938. The best known novel by a New Zealand woman.

Ihimaera, Witi, *Tangi*, Heinemann, 1974; *Whanau*, Heinemann, 1974; T*he New Net Goes Fishing*. Heinemann, 1977. Three works by the best known Maori fiction writer.

King, Michael, and Barriball, Martin, *New Zealand in Colour*, A.H. and A.W. Reed, 1982.

Laing, R.M. and Blackwell, E.W., *Plants of New Zealand*, Whitcombe and Tombs, 1964.

Lousley, D.P., *Guide to the Ski Fields of the South Island*, McIndoe, 1976.

McCormick, E.H., *New Zealand Literature; A Survey*, Oxford University Press (London), 1959; *Portrait of Frances Hodgkins*, Oxford University Press, in association with Auckland University Press, 1981, *Omai, Pacific Envoy*, Auckland University Press, 1977.

McDowall, R.M., *New Zealand Freshwater Fishes: A guide and Natural History*, Heinemann Educational, 1978.

McLauchlan, Gordon, *The Farming of New Zealand*, Australia and New Zealand Book company, 1981. A popular history of New Zealand farming.

McLean, M.E. and Orbell, M., *Traditional Songs of the Maori*, Oxford University Press and Auckland University Press, 1979.

Metge, J., *The Maoris of New Zealand*, Routledge (London), 1976. A full account of Maori life before and after European settlement. The best introductory book on the subject.

Mitcalfe, B., *Maori Poetry: The Singing Word*, Price Milburn, 1974.

Moore, L.B., and Irwin, J.B., *The Oxford Book of New Zealand Plants*, Oxford University Press, 1978.

Morrieson, Ronald Hugh, *Scarecrow*, Angus and Robertson (Sydney), 1963; *Came a Hot Friday*, Angus and Robertson (Sydney), 1964. Two of four black comedy novels written by a small town New Zealander unknown in his lifetime, which have become remarkably successful since the end of the 1970s, and have been reissued by Heinemann, Dunmore Press and Penguin several times since the first barely noticed publication in Sydney in the 1960s.

Morton, J.E. and Miller, M., *The New Zealand Sea Shore*, Collins (London), 1973.

Salmon, J.T., *The Native Trees of New Zealand*, Reed, 1980.

Sargeson, Frank, *Collected Stories*, Penguin, 1982. A full collection of the stories of a man who for many years was the best known short story writer and who had an international reputation during the 1940s and 1950s.

Simmons, D.R., *The Great New Zealand Myth; A Study of the Discovery and Origin Traditions of the Maori*, A.H. and A.W. Reed, 1976. A recent commentary by an ethnologist on the meanings of the Maori traditions relating to the discovery of New Zealand by Polynesian seafares.

Simpson, T.E., *Kauri and Radiata: Origin and Expansion of the Timber Industry of New Zealand*, Hodder and Stoughton, 1973.

Sinclair, Keith, *History of New Zealand*, Allen Lane (London), 1980 (also in paperback by Penguin). This is the most popular history of the country ever published, written by the Professor of History at the University of Auckland. It is a standard work.

Stirling, E., *Eruera, The Teaching of a Maori Elder*, Oxford University Press, 1980.

Thomson, K.W., *Art Galleries and Museums of New Zealand*, A.H. and A.W. Reed, 1981.

Tuwhare, Hone, *No Ordinary Sun*, McIndoe, 1977. A best-selling collection of the work of New Zealand's leading Maori poet.

Yerex, David, *The Farming of Deer, World Trends and Modern Techniques*. Agricultural Promotion Associates, 1982. A world authority writes on New Zealand's development of unique pastoral farming of deer.

CREDITS

INDEX

333

G

H

N

Pearse, Richard, 111
Pelorus Sound, 178
Penguin Bay, 228
penguins, 227
Peninsula Wars, *see* wars
Penryhn, 251
Performing Arts School (Auckland), 273
Permian period, 19
Perryer, Peter (photographer), 271
petrochemical industry, 63
Photoforum, 271
Picton (town), 177, 178
Picton Bay, 177
Piercy Island, 121
Piha, 111
Pilgrims, The, 188
Pink and White Terraces, *95, 142,* 143, 144
Pipiriki, 159
Pitcairn Island, 54
Pleistocene glacial, 24, 25
Plimmer, John, 166
Pliocene period, 24
Pohangina Reserve, 157
Pohangina River, 157
Pohara Beach, 181
Poho-o-Rawiri, 153-154
Pohutu, 140
pohutukawa tree, 117, 123, 153
Pohutukawa Tree, The (play), 274
Police Station, Dunedin, 231
politics, 52, 54, 55, 56, 59, 60, 62-63, 73-74, 85-86
Polynesian Airlines, 108, 249
Polynesian Pools, 138
Polynesians, 22, 25, 29, 32, 35, 36, 80, 109, 117, 219, 249, 251, 259
Pompalier, Bishop, 227
Pompallier House, 121
Pompolona Hut, 242
Poor Knights Islands, 283
Porirua, 169
Port Chalmers, 55
Port Charles, 126
Port Hills, 187, 192
Port Jackson, 43, 44, 126
Port Levy, 193
Port William, 245
Porter Heights, 202
Porter's Pass, 202
Portobello, 227, 228
Post Office, Central, (Auckland) 105
potteries, *266–267,* 275
pou whenua (totem pole), 156
Poukai Wildlife Reserves, 135
Pouakai Mountains, 135
pounamu (nephritic jade), 218, 264
Poverty Bay, 37, 149, 154, 296
power boats, 283
power station, 146, *200*
Press, The (newspaper), 189-190
Priest Pool, 138
primary production, 60, 63
Prix de l'Arc de Triomphe (horse-race), 292
Protestantism, 250
Protestants, 208
Provincial Council, Christchurch, 191
pubs, 85, 112, 230
Puhirake, Rawhiri, 128
Puhoi pub, *112,* 113

Pukapuka, 251
Pukeiti Rhododendron Trust, 135
Pukekura Park, 135
Pukiti Church, 159
Punakaiki, *212,* 213
Putaruru, 133

Q

Queen Charlotte Sound, 177
Queen Elizabeth Hospital, Rotorua, 139
Queen Elizabeth II, *58* 110, 163, 276
Queen Elizabeth II Park, 192
Queen Elizabeth Square, 105
Queen Mary Hospital, 200
Queen Street, Auckland, *55,* 56
Queen Victoria, 119
Queens Park, 2366
Queenstown, 200, 203, 217, *218,* 220, 221, 223, 224, 242
Quintin Hut, 242

R

race courses, 157, 158, 291
Rachel Springs, 138
racial strife, 62
radio stations, 253, 247, 272
Rahu Saddle, 200
rahui (prohibition), 32
Rai Valley, 179
railway, 156, 232
railway station, 201
Rainbow Mountain, 141
Rainbow Springs, 141
Rainbow Station, 200
rainfall, 60, 202, 210, 250
Rakahanga, 251
Rakaia, 195
Rakaia River, *201,* 203
Rakino, 113
rangatira (chiefs), 261
rangatira (noble families), 31
Rangi, 15
Rangitaiki Plains, 129
Rangitane, *see* tribes
Rangitata River, 203
Rangitikei River, 146, 159
Rangitoto, 102, 113
Rarotonga, *83,* 250-251, 252, 253
Rarotonga Sailing Club, 252
Rarotongan, (The), 253
Ratana, 158
Rattlesnake, HMS (ship), 49, 108
Read, Gabriel (gold miner), 219, 221
reclamation projects, 165, 167, 170
Redcliffs, 192
Redwood, Henry, 291
reefs, 213, 250, 251
Reefton, 200, 213
Reeves, William Pember, 54
Reform Party, 55
refugees, 69, 87
Remarkables, The, 223
reservations, 77
Resolution (ship), 177

S

Y–Z

B
C
D
E
F
G
H
I
J
a
b
c
d
e
f
g
h

j
k
l